McGill Legal Studies

General Editors

Professors John E.C. Brierley and Paul-A. Crépeau

© Centre de recherche en droit privé & comparé du Québec

Quebec Research Centre of Private & Comparative Law

McGill University
3647 Peel
Montreal, Quebec, Canada H3A 1X1
Tel.: (514) 392-8024 / 6772

All rights reserved. No portion of this book may be reproduced in any form or by any means, mechanical or electronic, without the prior written permission of McGill University.

Tous droits réservés. Toute reproduction par procédé mécanique ou électronique est interdite, sans l'autorisation écrite de l'Université McGill.

ISBN: 0-7717-0128-4

Dépot légal : Bibliothèque nationale du Québec, quatrième trimestre 1984

37694

McGill Legal Studies
No. 5

THE UNBORN CHILD'S RIGHT TO PRENATAL CARE

A COMPARATIVE LAW PERSPECTIVE

By

Edward W. Keyserlingk. B.A., L.Th., L.S.S., LL.M.

Project Director, Law Reform Commission of Canada,
Lecturer, Dept. of Law, Carleton University

CENTRE DE RECHERCHE EN DROIT PRIVÉ & COMPARÉ DU QUÉBEC

QUEBEC RESEARCH CENTRE OF PRIVATE & COMPARATIVE LAW

Montreal
1984

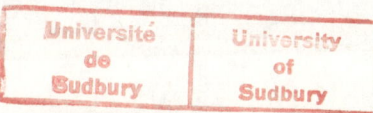

McGill Legal Studies

NO. 1 - George V.V. Nicholls, *The Responsibility for Offences and Quasi-Offences under the Law of Quebec*, Toronto, Carswell, 1938, pp. 164

NO. 2 - George S. Challies, *The Doctrine of Unjustified Enrichment in the Law of the Province of Quebec*, Toronto, Carswell, 1940, pp. 139

NO. 3 - Francisco Cuevas Cancino, *La nullité des actes juridiques*, Montréal, Wilson et Lafleur, 1950, pp. 224

NO. 4 - Madeleine Cantin Cumyn, *Les droits des bénéficiaires d'un usufruit, d'une substitution et d'une fiducie*, Montréal, Wilson et Lafleur, 1980, pp.134

FOREWORD

The Law of Persons has emerged over the past decade as one of the most important fields of private law. Advances in medical technology, changes in social mores and a worldwide concern with individual human rights have generated enormous challenges for our existing legal order. Problems only dimly perceived as recently as twenty years ago are today among those most pressing for resolution. Whatever one's private law tradition, appropriate legal responses to these challenges must be developed.

Mr. Keyserlingk's study constitutes a significant doctrinal contribution to one branch of the Law of Persons: that touching the status of the unborn child. The monograph surveys a vast legal panorama in both common law and civil law jurisdictions. After an exhaustive analysis of the present law in Canada, the author carefully reviews current judicial developments as well as the law reform proposals set out in Quebec's Draft Civil Code. These are then compared with Quebec's recently proposed reform to the Law of Persons, which comparison, it must be observed, reveals serious defects in the actual proposal to the legislature.

From a detailed examination of available medical and sociological data, the author justifies a shift in legal emphasis from postnatal compensation to prenatal protection. Existing civil law and common law rules are subjected to searching evaluation and criticism. Of special concern to the author is the problem of reconciling the notion of prenatal rights with the claim of pregnant women to seek abortions. As is to be expected in a study of a rapidly evolving legal domain, the monograph concludes with several specific recommendations for legislative and judicial law reform.

This is the fifth work in the *McGill Legal Studies* series, and the first to have had its origins in our Institute of Comparative Law. The Faculty is especially pleased that it is now able to develop the series through the publication of the best theses submitted to the Institute of Comparative Law. Increasingly, private law doctrine in Quebec is enriched by the scholarly contributions from its graduate faculties.

The preparation of the monograph for publication has been made possible in part through funding obtained from the Fonds F.C.A.C. and awarded by the Publications Grants Committee of the Faculty of Graduate Studies and Research of McGill. We are indebted to these two bodies for this tangible expression of support.

Publication was also assisted by grants from two special funds of the Faculty of Law. One of these, the Wurtele Fund, originates in the proceeds of a legacy of the Honourable Mr. Justice Wurtele. Established in 1928 as a publishing fund upon the initiative of the late Percy E. Corbett, then Dean of the Faculty, this Fund is employed to subsidize the publication of English language civil law treatises and monographs. In a memorandum to the Board of Governors of McGill University, Dean Corbett outlined the objectives for the fund in the following terms:

> The general plan of the Faculty is to set to work on a series of treatises on the Civil Law of this province. There is no such general treatise in English, with the consequence that lawyers in other parts of Canada and in the United States have no means, unless they possess a good knowledge of French, of acquainting themselves with the law and jurisprudence of Quebec. The study of comparative law is receiving increasing attention, and it is a study of great value not only in the solution of problems arising in the conflict of laws but for the thorough understanding of fundamental legal principles. It is thought, therefore, that anything which would render the legal system of this province, which is unique on this continent, more available for comparative study, would be a worthy contribution by this Faculty to the advancement of legal learning.

A contribution was also secured from the Wainwright Trust, established by the Faculty in furtherance of the testamentary wishes of Arnold Wainwright, Q.C. The donor, a prominent member of the Quebec Bar and lecturer at McGill, was committed to the development of the civil law of Quebec and to the encouragement of its greater understanding throughout Canada. In view of the objectives of these two funds, the comparative focus of Mr. Keyserlingk's study is to be considered a significant attribute. Promoting the civilian tradition and publicizing its genius in the North American legal milieu through comparative study are most worthy projects for both the Wurtele Fund and Wainwright Trust.

Finally I would note that editorial work for this study was co-ordinated by the Quebec Research Centre of Private and Comparative Law under the general editorship of Professors John E.C. Brierley and Paul-André Crépeau. To these especially we are grateful for encouraging and nurturing this important study.

Roderick A. Macdonald
Dean, Faculty of Law
McGill University

Montreal
July 11, 1984

PREFACE

This book, written in 1983, could not have survived its preconception and prenatal stages without the assistance of a large number of people. All of them deserve and have my sincere gratitude. First on this list is of course my wife, Rachelle, who contributed her enduring patience and support as wife and "house grammarian". The book is dedicated to her with love.

I am also indebted to a number of colleagues and friends in the field of medical law. First on this list are Jean-Louis Baudouin of the Faculté de droit, Université de Montréal, and Margaret Somerville of the Faculty of Law, McGill University. Their encouragement, and enthusiasm regarding this and other ventures is greatly appreciated. Robert Kouri of the Faculté de droit, Université de Sherbrooke and Bartha Knoppers of the Faculty of Law, McGill University, will hopefully find echoes in this book of many stimulating discussions we had on these and related issues.

A very special acknowledgement is due to Professor Paul-André Crépeau, Director of the Institute of Comparative Law at McGill University, who shared his impressive knowledge with me both in the courses he taught and while directing the LL.M. thesis on which this book is based.

Those with whom and for whom I worked and continue to work at the Law Reform Commission of Canada indirectly contributed greatly to this law reform study. They helped to make my work a constant challenge and pleasure, and encouraged such contributions to legal research outside the confines and mandate of the Commission alone. In this group I include especially: Mr. Justice Antonio Lamer, Mr. Justice Francis Muldoon, Commissioner Louise Lemelin and Mr. Justice Allen Linden. I have also learned much from the various members of the Commission's Protection of Life Project which I have been directing for the past eight years.

The analyses and proposals of this book have benefited greatly from discussion and correspondence with a number of physicians. Among them were especially Dr. Stanley Mercer of the Children's Hospital of Eastern Ontario, and Doctors May Cohen and Wendell Watters of McMaster University. While they did not agree with all my proposals, they were unfailingly generous with their time and comments.

My students in the medical law course I teach at Carleton University can also take some credit for this book. Their challenging questions and lively reactions about these and related issues greatly helped me to articulate my premises and clarify my positions.

A number of people contributed much time and effort by way of typing and proof-reading. First on this list is Heather Kelly. Others were Betty Rosenberg, Barbara Main and Monique Boivin-Déziel.

Finally, my thanks to Professor Paul-André Crépeau and to Dean John Brierley for encouraging me to publish this study in the McGill Legal Studies Series and for making helpful editorial suggestions.

         E.W.K.
         June, 1984

TABLE OF CONTENTS

FOREWORD · i
PREFACE v
ABBREVIATIONS xi
INTRODUCTION 1

CHAPTER. 1: PRESENT RIGHTS AND STATUS
OF THE FETUS 5

1. Criminal law - homicide, abortion and the unborn child 6

2. The impact of new medical knowledge on "unborn law" 10

3. From property rights to the right of action for prenatal injury 12

   i) The Civil law perspective 12

      a) Patrimonial rights 12
      b) The right of action for prenatal injury 16
      c) The unborn as person in Draft Code and Bill 106 20

   ii) The Common law perspective 28

      a) Property rights 29
      b) The right of action for prenatal injury . 31

4. Wrongful death, wrongful birth and wrongful life 41

   i) The Common law perspective 41

      a) Wrongful death 41
      b) Wrongful birth 45
      c) Wrongful life 47
      d) Preconception injury to parents 51

ii) The Civil law perspective ... 53
    a) Wrongful death ... 53
    b) Wrongful birth and wrongful life ... 56
    c) Preconception injury to parents ... 58

CHAPTER II: JUSTIFYING AND DEFINING AN EXPANDED RIGHT TO PRENATAL CARE - THE MEDICAL EVIDENCE AND LEGAL PARAMETERS ... 61

1. The fetus at risk - the medical data ... 62

  i) Defects and deformities ... 62

  ii) Drugs ... 66

  iii) Alcohol ... 68

  iv) Cigarettes, exposure to infectious diseases, inadequate maternal diet ... 70

  v) Workplace hazards ... 72

    a) Chemical hazards ... 74
    b) Physical hazards ... 75
    c) Biological hazards ... 76

2. The right to prenatal care defined and delimited ... 77

  i) From interests to (legal) rights ... 77

  ii) Narrowing the "right to be born healthy" ... 80

  iii) Expanding the "right to non-negligent acts" ... 86

  iv) Expanding the circle of those with duties - the liability of the pregnant mother-to-be ... 91

CHAPTER III: FROM POSTNATAL COMPENSATION TO PRENATAL PROTECTION — 101

1. Viable birth - from suspensive to resolutory condition — 101

2. The unborn as child - the Common law perspective — 103

   i) Parental duties and childrens' rights — 103

   ii) The unborn child as "child in need of protection" in statute and case law — 106

   iii) Court-ordered medical intervention on pregnant women for the sake of the unborn child - from transfusions to fetal surgery — 116

       a) Maternal transfusions — 118
       b) Caesarean sections — 121
       c) Fetal surgery — 123
       d) The candidates for court-ordered interventions — 126
       e) Weighing benefits, risk and prognosis — 129
       f) A formula for decision making — 137

3. The unborn as child - the Civil law perspective — 139

   i) Rights of the child as rights of the unborn — 140

   ii) The unborn as child whose "safety and development" is compromised — 144

   iii) Court-ordered medical intervention for the sake of the unborn child — 148

4.	Protection of the unborn child in the workplace	157
	i) Exclusionary employment policies	158
	ii) The woman's right to refuse work and be reassigned	166
	iii) Single exposure standards to protect all workers of both sexes and the fetus	172

CHAPTER IV: BALANCING PRENATAL CARE AND ABORTION   177

1. Interpreting abortion in the Criminal Code   177
2. Resolving the conflicting rights   181

CHAPTER V: CONCLUSION - WHETHER AND WHAT TO LEGISLATE   185

BIBLIOGRAPHY	193
TABLE OF CASES	201
TABLE OF STATUTES	203
INDEX OF SUBJECTS	205

ABBREVIATIONS

A.2d	Atlantic Reporter, Second Series
A.C.	Appeal Cases
A.L.R.	American Law Reports
Adv. Ped.	Advances in Pediatrics
All E.R.	The All England Law Reports
Alta. L.R. (2d)	Alberta Law Reports, Second Series
Am. J. Epidemiol	American Journal of Epidemiology
Am. J.L. Med.	American Journal of Law and Medicine
Am. J. Obstet. Gynec.	American Journal of Obstetrics and Gynecology
Am. Pharm.	American Pharmacy
Am. R.	American Reports
Ann. Hum. Gen.	Annals of Human Genetics
B.R.	Cour du Banc du Roi (de la Reine)
C.A.	Cour d'appel (Québec)
Can. Bar Rev.	Canadian Bar Review
C.C.	Civil Code (Quebec)
C.C.P.	Code of Civil Procedure (Quebec)
C. de B.	Cahiers de Bioéthique
C. de D.	Cahiers de droit
C.H.R.R.	Canadian Human Rights Reporter
C.L.L.C.	Canadian Labour Law Cases
C.R.N.S.	Criminal Reports New Series
C.S.	Cour supérieure (Québec)
Cal. Rptr.	West's California Reporter
Can. L.R.B. Rep.	Canadian Labour Relations Board Reports
Cr. C.	Criminal Code
D.L.R.	Dominion Law Reports
Eng.	English Reports
F. 2d	Federal Reporter, Second Series
F. Supp.	Federal Supplement
Fam. L.Q.	Family Law Quarterly
H.C.R.	Hastings Center Report
H.C.S.	Hastings Center Studies
Hof. L.R.	Hofstra Law Review

Hous. L. Rev.	Houston Law Review
Is. L.R.	Israel Law Review
J.A.M.A.	Journal of the American Medical Association
J. L. Med.	Journal of Legal Medicine
J. Med. E.	Journal of Medical Ethics
J. Fam. L.	Journal of Family Law
J. Ped.	Journal of Pediatrics
J. Ped. Surg.	Journal of Pediatric Surgery
L.A.C.	Labour Arbitration Cases
L. Med. Q.	Legal Medical Quarterly
L.R. Ir.	Law Reports Irish
Mass.	Massachusetts Reports
McGill L.J.	McGill Law Journal
Notre Dame Law.	Notre Dame Lawyer
N.E.	North Eastern Reporter
N.E.J.M.	New England Journal of Medicine
N.W.	North Western Reporter
N.Y.S.	New York Supplement
Nutr. Rev.	Nutrition Reviews
O.W.N.	Ontario Weekly Notes
Obstet. Gynec.	Obstetrics and Gynecology
Osgoode Hall L.J.	Osgoode Hall Law Journal
P.	Pacific Reporter
Ped. Clin. N. Am.	Pediatrics Clinics of North America
R.D.U.S.	Revue de droit de l'Université de Sherbrooke
R. du B.	Revue du Barreau
R.F.L. (Ont.)	Reports of Family Law (Ontario)
R.J.T.	Revue Juridique Thémis
R.P.	Rapports de pratique
R.S.C.	Revised Statutes of Canada
R.S.O.	Revised Statutes of Ontario
R.S.Q.	Revised Statutes of Quebec
S.C.	Session Cases
S.C.R.	Supreme Court Reports
S.E.	South Eastern Reporter
S.W.	South Western Reporter
U. Toronto L.J.	University of Toronto Law Journal

U. Penn. L.R.	University of Pennsylvania Law Review
U.S.	United States Supreme Court Reports
V.R.	Victorian Reports
Ves.	Vesey's English Chancery Reports
W.W.R.	Western Weekly Reports
Wis.	Wisconsin Reports

INTRODUCTION

Both Civil law and Common law systems are increasingly concerned with devising effective legal protections for the weaker and more defenceless members of society. In many respects the prenatal period represents the time of greatest vulnerability in the life of the child. Yet neither legal system has so far provided adequate legal protections against prenatal abuse and neglect.

Three obstacles can be identified. One is the continuing ambiguity in both Civil law and Common law about the legal status and rights of the unborn child. A second is the inevitable conflicts which would result between the rights and interests of the fetus and those of others if the unborn child is acknowledged to have prenatal rights. A third is the need to devise protective legal mechanisms adapted to the unique fact of the unborn child's total dependence on its mother-to-be.

This study attempts to respond to each of those problems by arguing the following: the ambiguity about the legal status and rights of the unborn child can no longer be tolerated – the unborn child should be clearly acknowledged to have legal personality, and (therefore) the right to prenatal care and protection; criteria can be devised by which to balance and resolve resulting conflicts with other parties, including the pregnant woman; some specific protective legal mechanisms to apply in the prenatal stage could be adapted from those already available to children in need of protection.

This study will defend the proposition that the proposed right to prenatal care and protection is largely only a logical extension of traditional legal positions in both Civil law and Common law systems. The justification and urgency for now going further is the need to respond legally to new medical findings about the unborn child's needs and vulnerability, and to the availability of new and evolving medical interventions for treating the unborn child *in utero*.

A comprehensive treatment of this issue in Canada could hardly do otherwise than consider the subject from a comparative law perspective. There is of course the obvious and practical reality that the Canadian legal mosaic consists of two legal systems, Civil law and Common law. A legal analysis of a subject as important as this one would be seriously flawed from the outset if only one of them were to be considered. But a still more fundamental justification is the fact that on the particular subject of the unborn child each system provides important sources and insights.

In many respects the Civil law system of Quebec and the Common law system of the other provinces are remarkably similar and complementary in their present positions and future possibilities regarding the unborn child. Much of the time in this paper, the issues raised and proposals considered will be sufficiently general and policy-oriented that they will apply more or less equally to both systems, requiring no separate and explicit reference to each system. But in other instances attention will be drawn to some important differences in concepts and legal mechanisms.

An obvious difference with much significance for the subject of this study is the existence and role in Quebec of the Civil Code. An important part of that significance lies in the fact that the Civil Code is presently being comprehensively revised to enable it to respond more adequately to present day priorities and challenges. It is earnestly hoped that this study will contribute in some manner to that reform.

It is of course assumed in this study that law reform and legal mechanisms cannot be the only means of promoting and protecting prenatal health. Given the sensitive and unique nature of the relationship between unborn children and pregnant women, not to mention the complex nature of the family itself, a too hasty recourse to legal solutions could do more harm than good. Clearly, the provision of training programs in prenatal care, combined with the best and most widely available prenatal services prossible, will be the most appropriate contributions by society to prenatal care and protection. But that said, law does nevertheless have an important role to play in this matter. It must be played with restraint and sensitivity, but at the moment it is hardly a player at all. The result is that of all the stages in life, only the prenatal stage is generally unprotected by law.

Chapter I

**PRESENT RIGHTS AND
STATUS OF THE FETUS**

The unborn child's right to prenatal care is being proposed and defended in this study as a further and needed stage in a long line of legal responses concerning the rights, needs and legal status of the unborn child. It is advanced by this writer as a right with a history and a context, not at all one emerging *tabula rasa*, or existing in isolation from other fetal rights or the rights of other parties.

But as defined in this study a right of the unborn child to prenatal care would also in several essential respects be new. It would fill gaps in rights already available to the unborn, and bring more coherence, consistency and clarity to an area of law notorious for incoherence, inconsistency and lack of clarity. It would allow a more adequate legal response to expanding medical evidence about the unborn child's needs and vulnerabilities and the essential continuity between unborn and born child.

It is appropriate and even necessary to begin this inquiry and proposal by considering the history and "state of the question" of the unborn child's right to prenatal care. Only by first tracing that history and context are we able to identify and then build upon the roots and precedents of this right.

The aim of this chapter is not to provide detailed criticism of each stage and position, but simply to offer an historical and contextual outline of the state of the question, thereby identifying some of the achievements to date and some remaining anomalies and gaps. Later sections of this study devoted to amplifying and defending a right to prenatal care will draw upon some of these positions either to note their limitations in greater detail, or to build upon their positive elements and (especially) to suggest solutions and reforms.

1. *Criminal law - homicide, abortion and the unborn child*

Brief reference to the position of the Criminal Code is in order at the outset. The reference at this point can be brief for three reasons. The first is that the focus in this chapter, as in the book generally, will largely exclude criminal law considerations. The second is that more analysis will be provided of criminal law and the Criminal Code in Chapter IV dealing with the need to balance the unborn child's right to prenatal care and protection with the pregnant woman's right to abortion, as allowed by s.251 Cr.C.

A third and more general reason for brevity as regards criminal law is one sometimes overlooked or left unstated in analyses and proposals on subjects such as abortion or fetal status. Whatever the position of the Criminal Code on the juridical status of the conceived but unborn child for purposes of criminal responsibility, it need not necessarily bind or limit the viewpoints of provincial law and statutes on the issue of fetal status and rights for purposes within the jurisdiction of the provinces and provincial law.[1]

---

[1] Given the differences between the Civil law system of Quebec and the Common law system of which the Criminal Code is an expression, this freedom to legislate in Quebec on this issue otherwise than does the Criminal Code, would appear evident. But the same freedom would seem to be equally available to the other provinces.

In this regard the following observation by Mayrand is relevant:

"Lorsqu'il constitue un crime, l'avortement est aussi un délit civil; mais, dans les circonstances où le Code criminel n'en fait pas un crime, l'avortement est-il contraire à l'inviolabilité de la personne proclamée par le Code civil?

Le Code civil peut-il défendre ce que le Code criminel permet? Plus précisément, l'avortement thérapeutique prévu à l'article 251, (par. 4) du Code criminel pourrait-il être contraire à l'article 19 du Code civil?

Le droit civil peut considérer comme un délit ou un quasi-délit un acte que le Code criminel ne considère pas comme un crime. Pour que le principe de l'inviolabilité de la personne, énoncé à l'article 19 du Code civil, ne vienne pas en conflit avec les diverses dispositions du Code criminel sur les infractions contre la personne, il faut cependant que les deux lois diffèrent dans leur but et dans leur effet pratique.

Trancher cette difficulté de droit constitutionnel permettrait de dire si une province peut prohiber l'avortement thérapeutique dans les circonstances où le Code criminel ne le prohibe pas lui-même. (A. MAYRAND, *L'inviolabilité de la personne humaine*, Wilson & Lafleur, Montréal, 1975, at p.75).

Nevertheless, the Criminal Code does in fact opt for a general stand regarding fetal status which is similar to (though considerably less nuanced than) provincial law and statutes in Quebec and the common law provinces. As well, it is arguable that the Criminal Code betrays a degree of incoherence quite similar to that of private law and provincial statutes in both legal systems. As such, for the sake of presenting as complete a picture as possible it is appropriate to briefly indicate at this point what that Criminal Code position is.

Criminal law relates to the status and rights of the unborn child in two areas - homicide and abortion. Regarding homicide the two operative sections of the Criminal Code are 205 and 206. Section 205(1) Cr.C. states in part, "A person commits homicide when, directly or indirectly, by any means, he causes the death of a human being". Section 206 Cr.C. indicates when one becomes a human being for Criminal Code purposes:

> 206(1) A child becomes a human being within the meaning of this Act when it has completely proceeded, in a living state, from the body of its mother whether or not it has breathed, it has an independent circulation, or the navel string is severed.

On the basis of these sections it is clear that killing an unborn child *in utero* is not homicide because it is not yet (for Criminal Code purposes) a human being.

There are however four qualifications to be noted, all of them somewhat paradoxical, especially the first, since the unborn child is not considered a human being. The first is that abortion ("procuring a miscarriage") is nevertheless a criminal act according to s.251 Cr.C. unless the abortion has been approved by the therapeutic abortion committee of an accredited hospital because the pregnant woman's life or health is in danger.

It is worth noting that though the protection to the unborn afforded by s.251 Cr.C. is qualified and limited by the exceptional conditions just indicated, it is a protection available at every stage of gestation, and not just from the time of viability. As Kouri has noted:

Ainsi, sont considérés comme égaux devant la loi, l'embryon rudimentaire et le foetus dans un état très avancé de développement. La viabilité de *l'infans conceptus* est donc absolument étrangère à la discussion.[2]

A second qualification is that of s.206(2) Cr.C. which states that if a child is born alive and then dies as a result of an (intentional) injury before or during its birth, that constitutes homicide.[3]

A recent application of this principle and section involved an assailant who inflicted knife wounds on a pregnant woman, penetrating her amniotic sac and causing her to give premature birth five days later. The fetus died nineteen minutes after birth because its lungs were not sufficiently developed. The assailant was tried and sentenced for wounding the pregnant woman. After serving six months of her sentence for that charge, a Manitoba County Court judge (Gordon Barkman) ruled that the assailant could be tried for manslaughter in the death of the six month old fetus. The assailant's lawyer argued that his client could not be so charged because it would be trying her twice for the same act of stabbing. To which Judge Barkman replied, "It is only the one act, but apparently two persons were affected by the same act".[4]

A third qualification is found in s.221(1) Cr.C. which states that killing an unborn child in the act of birth, even though not yet actually born, is an indictable offence. But this

---

[2] R. KOURI, "Réflexions sur le statut juridique du foetus", (1980-81) 15 R.J.T. 193, at p.199

[3] In effect this subsection, combined with s.206 (1), is a modified enactment of the historical common law position found for example in Coke's *Third Institute*:

"If a woman be quick with childe, and by a potion or otherwise killeth it in her wombe, or if a man beat her, whereby the childe dyeth in her body, and she is delivered of a dead childe, this is a great misprison (misdemeanour) and no murder; but if the childe be born alive and dyeth of the potion, battery or other cause, this is murder; for in law it is accounted a reasonable creature, in rerum natura, when it is born alive".
(3 Coke, *Institutes* 58 (1648)

[4] *Globe and Mail*, May 3, 1983, at p.7.

in turn is qualified by s.221(2) which states that s.221 does not apply to one who in good faith causes the death of the child in an effort to save the mother's life. Clearly in this case (as in s.251 Cr.C.) when there is a conflict between allowing the child to be born alive and saving the mother's life, the policy choice favours preserving the mother's life.

A fourth modification is supplied by s.226 Cr.C. This section states that a pregnant woman about to give birth who fails to obtain the necessary assistance because she intends that her child shall die, is guilty of an indictable offence even though the child dies immediately before or during birth. Strictly speaking then, the child could die without having been born alive, and therefore not yet a human being for criminal law purposes, yet the pregnant woman could be criminally responsible.

A number of conclusions follow from what precedes. First of all, from the criminal law standpoint the unborn child is not a human being until born alive.[5] Yet that unborn child nevertheless enjoys some protections even before birth. But those protections give way when in conflict with the rights to life and health of those the (criminal) law considers human beings. As Deleury expresses it,

> C'est dire qu'en droit criminel, sans pour autant être considéré comme une personne, l'enfant conçu mais non encore né jouit d'une certaine protection, mais cette protection s'arrête lorsqu'elle entre en conflit avec la vie ou la santé de celles qu'on considère légalement comme des êtres humains.[6]

---

[5] This despite the fact that the crime of abortion is found under the heading of, "Offences Against the Person" (Sections 196-281.3 Criminal Code). Mayrand makes that observation, but rightly adds: "Cependant, cette personne ne serait pas un être humain s'il faut en croire la définition de l'article 206 du Code criminel ... ". A. MAYRAND, *op. cit.,supra*, n.1, at p.71.

[6] E. DELEURY, "Naissance et mort de la personne humaine, ou les confrontations de la médecine et du droit", (1976) 17 *C. de D.* 265, at p.275. MAYRAND concludes in a similar fashion: "Il résulte tout de même de ces textes que le Code criminel attache moins d'importance à la vie embryonnaire qu'à celle d'une personne déjà née". *Op. cit., supra*, n.1, at pp.71,72.

Regarding the abortion prohibition specifically, Weiler and Catton make essentially the same point regarding conflicts between unborn children and those who are already born, in this case the pregnant woman:

> A possible explanation of the abortion provisions is that the law is extending its protection to the potentiality of human life, but that when the potentiality of life conflicts with the rights of those actually living, the rights of the latter will prevail.[7]

We will turn next to a survey of the legal positions other than in criminal law regarding the status, rights and protections of the fetus up to the present time. Both systems of law will be considered, the Civil law (of Quebec) and the Common law system. The latter will include the views and decisions in the common law provinces of Canada, the United States the United Kingdom and Australia. It will be concluded that the still largely missing element in the legal protections available to the unborn child is that of anticipatory and preventive interventions while still unborn. It will also be concluded that the unborn child's juridical status and basic rights (to life and inviolability) remain uncertain and incoherent. Given that uncertainty and incoherence there is as yet no firm basis for a right to prenatal care and protection.

2. *The impact of new medical knowledge on "unborn law"*

In tracing the evolution and expansion of the legal response to the unborn child through the stages which follow, it is possible and instructive to relate aspects of the legal evolution to the expansion of medical and biological knowledge about the needs and development of the unborn child. Medicine and biology have increasingly focused directly on the unborn child as an entity in many essential respects distinct from (though dependent upon) its pregnant mother. At the same time, despite remaining gaps, uncertainties, questions and incoherence, the legal attitudes towards the same unborn child have moved all the way from merely

---

[7] K. WEILER and K. CATTON, "The Unborn Child in Canadian Law", (1976) 14 *Osgoode Hall L.J.*

defending their property rights, then to allowing actions for prenatal injury, then to moving away from the "viable when injured" rule (in the United States) and even (quite recently) to the occasional brush with court-ordered surgery on a pregnant woman for the sake of the fetus. That there has been this evolution in both medicine and law is more than just coincidental, as we shall indicate in the sections which follow.

It should not of course be supposed that evolving and reformulating legal attitudes towards the unborn child is a simple matter of responding only to new medical data isolated from other societal considerations, social trends and the competing rights of other parties. Clearly this has not been so, and should not be so. Partly in the light of medical findings establishing the needs and distinctiveness of the unborn child, the corresponding expansion of its appropriate rights and protections will involve in some respects the shrinking or adjustment of existing and competing rights of other parties who have an impact upon that unborn child (parents, physicians and employers for example). But even armed with the most comprehensive medical data possible, the expansion of unborn rights and protections will itself be limited by the justifiable claims and status of others.

A concrete example is of course the evident fact that at some point rights of the unborn child to inviolability and prenatal care and protection must be balanced by the pregnant woman's rights to inviolability and (by present law) to abortion. Medical data can be helpful but not always decisive in resolving such conflicts as we shall indicate in a later section of this study.

A further limitation on the impact of medical data has to do with problems of causality and proof in establishing responsibility for example for prenatal injury. It is one thing to establish with reasonable probability that certain actions, omissions or subtances can have particular effects on the health and integrity of the unborn. But in concrete instances of prenatal injury it is difficult and sometimes impossible to determine to the satisfaction of a court whether the injury was caused by environmental influences attributable to an identifiable party's negligence, or genetic predispositions neither predictable nor culpable.

As we shall indicate later, it may be time to devise tests of prenatal negligence which are fairer to the defendant in an action for damages. Fair tests and results are particularly called for if, as we shall later argue, pregnant women should be included among those with a duty to provide adequate prenatal care and protection.

3. *From property rights to the right of action for prenatal injury*

Though there are some basic similarities in the civilian and common law positions regarding the unborn child's property rights and the right of action for prenatal injury, there are some differences which suggest the appropriateness of treating the Civil law and Common law perspectives separately. As well, though there is substantial agreement with regard to conclusions, each system has different emphases and builds its positions regarding the unborn on somewhat different traditions or a different mix of doctrines and principles. That too is a reason for the separate treatment that follows.

i) *The Civil law perspective*

a) *Patrimonial rights*

It is often affirmed that in Quebec Civil law (as in French Civil law) and in contrast to criminal law, juridical personality may be assigned to the unborn child even before birth. Deleury for example has stated:

> ... si l'existence civile commence en principe à la naissance pour se terminer avec la mort, la naissance n'apparaît pas toujours comme la condition nécessaire de l'acquisition de la personnalité. L'enfant simplement conçu, en effet, est déjà à être sujet de droit.[8]

---

8 DELEURY, *op. cit., supra*, n.6, at pp. 276, 277

A. Mayrand has written to the same effect:

> La personnalité de l'enfant avant sa naissance est plus aisément reconnue en droit civil qu'en droit pénal. Le législateur québécois n'a probablement pas tenu compte de la distinction que fait le Code criminel entre l'enfant encore dans le sein de sa mère et un être humain.[9]

However, at least prior to the decision in *Montreal Tramways Co.* v. *Léveillé*[10] in 1933 and its recognition of the unborn's right to sue for prenatal injury, the recognition of the unborn's legal personality was in practice based largely on his possession of patrimonial rights. Generally speaking, "patrimonial" rights in civil law are the totality of a person's assets and liabilities which have a monetary value. The patrimony does not include those rights not having a monetary value such as political rights. The patrimony does not cease with the death of its owner - it is transmissible to his heirs. Extra-patrimonial rights in civil law are the totality of rights of a person which are *not* appreciable in monetary terms and are not transmissible. Among these rights are for example those to life, reputation and physical integrity. But consideration of the Civil Code articles relevant to those patrimonial rights makes it very clear that there is an indispensable condition, a suspensive condition, attached to the unborn child's juridical personality. The suspensive condition is that he must be born alive and viable.[11] In effect

---

9   MAYRAND, *op. cit.*, *supra*, n.1, at pp. 73, 74

10 *Montreal Tramways Co.* v. *Léveillé*, [1933] S.C.R. 456.

11 As KOURI has noted (*op. cit.*, *supra*, n.2, at pp. 195, 196), the meaning of the words "alive" and "viable" are not as evident as it may appear. Modern medicine forces one to be considerably more nuanced than the traditional formula defining being alive, "having proceeded from its mother's womb and breathing". There are, after all, other signs of life which can now be readily observed beyond just breathing. As for the meaning of "viable", Kouri notes, "L'autre condition de la personnalité, celle de la viabilité, dissimule derrière sa simplicité apparente, de véritables difficultés d'appréciation. Grâce à sa connotation médicale, la notion de viabilité possède un dynamisme propre car elle évolue avec le progrès de la périnatalité". As he notes, it is not unusual today to save children born prématurely after only 24 weeks of gestation and sometimes less. Two criteria for viability in the legal context appear operative - the adequate maturity of the fetus and its proper formation. A newborn would therefore not be viable if born for example without organs necessary for existence, or with its vital organs too under-developed to survive.

that condition is an expression of the traditional Civil law maxim, *infans conceptus habetur pro nato quoties de commodo ejus agitur* (the unborn child shall be deemed to be born whenever its interests require it).

Apart from the single disposition of a possibly general nature with respect to the rights of the unborn (a.345 C.C., examined below), the Civil Code itself is primarily and explicitly concerned with the patrimonial rights of the unborn. The relevant articles are: 338, 345, 608, 771, 838 and 945.

Article 338 C.C. provides the "persons" to whom curators may be given, among them children conceived but not yet born. Article 608 C.C. acknowledges that the conceived but unborn at the moment a succession devolves is "civilly in existence", but only for purposes of inheritance, and viable birth is a suspensive condition to actual inheritance. As for a. 777 C.C., it deals with the capacity to give or receive *inter vivos*, and once again the unborn child may receive gifts only upon viable birth. Article 838 C.C. stipulates that the capacity to receive by will also applies to the conceived but unborn, again on the suspensive condition of viable birth.

Bill 107, introduced in 1982 as *An Act to add the reformed law of successions to the Civil Code of Quebec*,[12] proposes essentially the same right of the conceived but unborn child to inherit, subject to the traditional suspensive condition. Article 664 of Bill 107 states in part,

> Human persons who exist at the time the succession devolves may inherit, as may absentees and children conceived but yet unborn, if they are born alive and viable.

This analysis was confirmed in the Quebec decision of *Allard* v. *Monette*, (1928) 66 C.S. 291, in which it was held (at p. 294) that:

"L'impossibilité de vie peut résulter de deux causes, soit de la faiblesse et de l'extrême débilité de la constitution, soit de la difformité totale ou d'imperfections dans l'un des organes nécessaires à l'existence. Dans ces conditions l'enfant doit être déclaré non viable parce qu'il est reconnu que la nature, par ses propres forces, et la science, par ses procédés, n'ont pu empêcher la mort à laquelle il a succombé."

[12] *An Act to Add the Reformed Law of Successions to the Civil Code of Quebec* (Bill 107), introduced December 17, 1982.

Article 345 of the Civil Code merits careful attention at this point. It states:

> The curator to a child conceived but not yet born is bound to act for such a child whenever its interests require it; he has until its birth the administration of the property which is to belong to it and afterwards he is bound to render an account of such administration.

Our question is whether this article and the role of the "curator to the womb" is limited to protecting the unborn child's patrimonial rights (as suggested by the second part of the article), or is the phrase "whenever its interests require it" to be taken generally, as an expression of the traditional Civil law maxim referred to earlier that an unborn child shall be deemed to be born whenever its interests require it? More specifically, does this article support a case for the protection of the unborn child's extra-patrimonial rights (such as inviolability and health) whenever its interests require it?

Judge Lamont in the *Léveillé* decision held that a.345 C.C. need not apply only to patrimonial matters. In his view the property and inheritance matters which are the subject of various Code articles are only ". . . illustrative instances of the rule that an unborn child shall be deemed to be born whenever its interests require it, but that they in no way limit the meaning of article 345 C.C. which is general in its terms".[13] But while Judge Lamont and the various sources cited in that decision are undoubtedly correct from the standpoint of legal theory, in actual practice article 345 C.C. appears to have been applied only to the administration of property referred to in the second part of the article itself. This writer could find no examples of its actual use for matters other than patrimonial. The following is probably an accurate description of the limited practical application of article 345 C.C.:

> Étant donné que l'enfant conçu mais non encore né n'est pas encore une personne son curateur ne peut avoir de pouvoirs que sur ses biens. Il joue un rôle strictement administratif... que les auteurs interprètent de façon très restrictive.[14]

---

13 *Montreal Tramways Co.* v. *Léveillé, loc. cit. supra* n.10, at p. 462.

14 L. PATENAUDE, *Capacité (tutelle et curatelle)* La Librairie de l'Université de Montréal, 1975, at p.128

As such, at least prior to the decision in *Léveillé*, this article and the *nasciturus* rule it expresses would seem to offer little practical support for the existence of a protective stance in Québec Civil law towards extra-patrimonial rights of the unborn child. The emphasis of the Civil Code on patrimonial rights of the unborn and the suspensive condition of viable birth do not manifest an effective or explicit concern for the person and well-being of the unborn child as such and while still unborn. The available anticipatory mechanism of curatorship to the womb, and the acknowledged patrimonial rights, for all practical purposes only constitute protections of the unborn child's property in anticipation of birth.

b) *The right of action for prenatal injury*

Of interest at this stage in the study are instances of prenatal injuries to unborn children *in utero* who are subsequently born alive and viable. Instances of prenatal injury resulting in the death of the child will be considered later in the "wrongful death, wrongful life" section.

On the one hand the decision in *Léveillé* (awarding damages to a child for prenatal negligence) obviously constituted a landmark decision. It established a number of points about unborn rights more clearly and emphatically than any previous Civil law (or common law) decision. Mainly of course it established that negligent injuries to an unborn child while *in utero* justified the unborn child's right of action (if born alive and viable) for damages. Secondly, and contrary to the 1884 dictum by Holmes in *Dietrich* v. *Northampton*,[15] it held that the conceived but unborn child is not only a separate biological entity but also has a legal personality not identifiable in all respects with that of its mother.

---

[15] *DIETRICH* v. *NORTHAMPTON*, 52 Am. R. 242 (1884). Holmes held that an unborn child has no existence as a human being separate from its mother; therefore it may not recover for the wrongful conduct of another.

The most frequently quoted and most eloquent part of the judgment is this:

> If a child after birth has no right of action for prenatal injuries, we have a wrong inflicted for which there is no remedy, for, although the father may be entitled to compensation for the loss he has incurred and the mother for what she has suffered, yet there is a *residuum* of injury for which compensation cannot be had save at the suit of the child. If a right of action be denied to the child it will be compelled, without any fault on its part, to go through life carrying the seal of another's fault and bearing a very heavy burden of infirmity and inconvenience without any compensation therefor. To my mind it is but natural justice that a child, if born alive and viable, should be allowed to maintain an action in the courts for injuries wrongfully committed upon its person while in the womb of its mother.[16]

The central legal consideration was whether the unborn child could come within the term "another" in article 1053 C.C., and Judge Lamont decided this in the affirmative:

> ... I am of the opinion that the fiction of the civil law must be held to be of general application. The child will, therefore be deemed to have been born at the time of the accident to the mother. Being an existing person in the eyes of the law it comes within the meaning of "another" in article 1053 C.C. and is, therefore, entitled through its tutor to maintain the action.[17]

Despite its landmark quality in that it expanded the unborn child's rights beyond exclusively patrimonial matters, it is arguable that it did not in reality clarify or evolve the fundamental question of the legal status of the unborn child. The basis for the decision was the traditional "fiction" of the Civil law involving the "deeming of birth" at the time of the accident and the bestowal of legal personality and rights to inviolability and legal action only on the suspensive condition of live and viable birth.

As such the assertion in the previous quotation that the unborn child is "an existing person in the eyes of the law" at the time of the injury is of little practical consequence as an anchor for preventive legal protections *before* birth. As long as

---

16 *Montreal Tramways* v. *Léveillé, loc. cit. supra,* n.10 at p. 464.

17 *Id.,* at p. 465

the suspensive condition of live and viable birth remains, the legal concern can only be exclusively *post factum* (because post viable birth) and compensatory (because the damage will have been done), but not anticipatory and preventive.

The manner of applying the suspensive condition of live and viable birth and its implications for the legal protection of the unborn child while still unborn are still clearer in this further quote from the statement of Judge Lamont:

> ... although the child was not actually born at the time the Company by its fault created the conditions which brought about the deformity of its feet, yet, under the civil law, it is deemed to be so for its advantage. Therefore *when it was subsequently born alive and viable* it was clothed with all the rights of action which *it would have had* if actually in existence at the date of the accident. The wrongful act of the Company produced its damage on the birth of the child and the right of action was then complete.[18] [Emphasis added]

Judge Cannon's statement in the same *Léveillé* decision leaves little doubt that in his view prenatal injuries are not in reality injuries at all in the eyes of the law as long as the child remains unborn, and that for all practical purposes the right to action for compensation is only born if and when the child is born. He stated in part,

> ... aussi longtemps qu'elle était dans le sein de sa mère, il est évident *qu'elle ne souffrait aucun dommage, aucun inconvénient et aucun préjudice.* Aucune action en responsabilité n'était ouverte. Ce n'est que lorsque le préjudice certain a été souffert que ses droits ont été lésés, qu'elle est devenue une victime ayant des droits à réparation. C'est de ce moment, après sa naissance, *que son droit a commencé.*[19] [Emphasis added]

Given that the case for a right to prenatal care and protection must be based upon the need to protect the unborn child from actual or threatened injuries or abuse *while still unborn,* the statement and principle just quoted does little or nothing to strengthen that case. After all, it was maintained that what is subsequently (on birth) shown to have been a real

---

18   *Id.*, at p. 463.

19   *Id.*, at p. 477.

prenatal *physical* injury, was not in the intervening months prior to birth or in the event of non-viable birth, an injury in the eyes of the *law*.

In conclusion, it is tempting to reconsider the assertions quoted earlier by Deleury and Mayrand (pp. 12-13) to the effect that birth is not always a necessary condition for the acquisition of personality (Deleury), or that the personality of the child before birth is more easily recognized by Civil law than criminal law (Mayrand). While theoretically correct once qualified as they both do, the assertions nevertheless may claim too much in the light of the above considerations. The qualification of live and viable birth for all practical purposes would seem almost to deny and not just qualify the assertions of legal personality before viable birth.

Kouri has noted that by applying this suspensive condition a result is that both stillbirths and children born alive but not viable must in effect be considered never to have existed. He went on to make the following observation:

> Pendant la gestion et jusqu'au moment de sa naissance vivante et viable, les droits de l'enfant ne sont que potentiels. "... *et son seul intérêt né et actual est de voir se réaliser la condition suspensive*..." L'enfant conçu ne possède aucun droit de la personnalité et ne bénéficie donc pas d'un droit à l'inviolabilité. Or, ce vide juridique est inacceptable car il demeure une réalité scientifique que la naissance n'est qu'une étape parmi plusieurs dans le processus de vie... Comment est-il possible de ne pas accorder un droit à l'inviolabilité à un enfant **in utero** quelques moments avant sa naissance, lorsque ce même enfant une fois né profitera pleinement de tous les avantages inhérents à la personnalité?[20]

---

20 KOURI,*op. cit.*, *supra*, n.2, at pp. 196, 197. Words italicized are attributed by Kouri to M. - T. MEULDERS-KLEIN, "Rapport sur le corps humain, personnalité juridique et famille en droit belge", 26 *Travaux de l'Association Henri Capitant* (1975) 28. As will be discussed later in this paper, Kouri's proposed solution is that the unborn child be acknowledged to be a legal person on the *resolutory* (rather than suspensive) condition of *not* being born alive and viable. As such the unborn child would be considered inviolable while still *in utero*. (Kouri, p.197).

c) *The unborn as person in Draft Code and Bill 106*

Does the Draft Civil Code (of Quebec) acknowledge the juridical personality and inviolability of the conceived but unborn child, and thus provide a more effective basis for a right to prenatal care? It would seem that (at least potentially) provisions of the Draft Civil Code could provide that more secure foundation.

Several provisions of the present Civil Code and the Quebec Charter of Rights and Freedoms are quite explicit about the juridical personality and inviolability of human beings. For example, a.18. C.C. affirms (in part):

Every human being possesses juridical personality.

Article 19 C.C. affirms that:

The human person is inviolable. No one may cause harm to the person of another without his consent, or without being authorized by law to do so.

In a.1 of the Quebec Charter of Rights and Freedoms both the juridical personality and the basic rights of human beings are affirmed:

Every human being has a right to life and security, to physical integrity and the liberty of his person. He also possesses juridical personality.

But none of the above (or other) articles of the Civil Code or Charter provide a list or definition as to who are to be included within the class of human being, who are entitled to possess juridical personality, be inviolable and enjoy the basic rights attached to that status. There is no indication that these articles were intended to apply to the conceived but unborn child.[21] It is even arguable that the wording of a.18 (para.2) C.C. implies that the real interest of the legislator in

---

21 On the other hand of course these articles do not *exclude* the unborn child from inclusion in the status of human being or from possession of the basic rights indicated. It could be argued that determinations as to who should be included within the meaning of "human being" in these articles

a.18 was to affirm that aliens as well as citizens have juridical personality, rather than to state a general principle which would include all (de facto) "human beings", including the unborn.[22]

For its part, the Draft Civil Code appears to go much further in this matter. First of all, article 1.1 Draft Code, based upon a.18 C.C., omits paragraph 2 of the latter article thus generalizing the principle and making it potentially more applicable to the unborn child as well. Article 1.1 Draft Code states simply: "Every human being possesses juridical personality".

Both articles, 608 C.C. and 345 C.C. were omitted from the Draft Civil Code. Article 1.28 Draft Code states:

> A child conceived is deemed born provided he is born live and viable.

The Commentary on the Draft Code tells us that this article is based upon a.608 C.C. It is obviously a legislative expression of the *infans conceptus* maxim referred to earlier.

While one cannot see in this proposed article an explicit acknowledgement of the unborn child's juridical personality, if read in conjunction with 1.1 and 1.15 Draft Code, it could more readily accomodate the status and rights of the unborn child than its antecedents in the present Code. It is no longer focused primarily and explicitly on patrimonial rights as are both articles 608 C.C. and 345 C.C. The more general nature of a.1.28 Draft Code appears to support the conclusion that there need no longer be any limitation to the rights or interests for which the unborn child may be "deemed born".

---

are not primarily questions of law as such, but rather questions for evolving medical knowledge, social policy choices and so forth, and that the generality and open-endedness of these provisions is therefore preferable. However, in a later section of this paper it will be argued that the *explicit* legislative inclusion of the unborn child within the meaning of human being (or child) is in fact justifiable and preferable.

22 Article 18 (para. 2) of the Civil Code reads:

> "Whether citizen or alien, he has the full enjoyment of civil rights, except as otherwise expressly provided by law".

On the other hand however, the application of the wider principle embodied in a.1.28 Draft Code is still conditional on the traditional suspensive condition of viable birth. As such and in that respect it is subject to the same observations made earlier with regard to that condition.

The recently introduced Bill 106,[23] comprising the long awaited reform of the Civil Code's Book One (the Law of Persons) was the focus of much discussion and debate. A number of submissions were made to the National Assembly's Standing Committee on Justice, making it possible to identify some common trends in those criticisms. Much of that criticism is focused on that Bill's position on the status and rights of the unborn child.

A first and general regret is that this Bill is in many essential respects quite different from and inferior to the Law of Persons as proposed by the Civil Code Revision Office in its Draft Code completed in 1977. Given the time, effort and expertise devoted to that effort for more than ten years it is to say the least puzzling that Bill 106 emerged more or less *tabula rasa* and with an unknown or at least un-acknowledged parentage.[24] Obviously if Bill 106 had been a marked improvement upon Book One of the Draft Code, then one could applaud this quite new effort, but by general consensus it was a regression, not an improvement.

---

[23] *An Act to Add the Reformed Law of Persons to the Civil code of Quebec* (Bill 106), introduced December 17, 1982.

[24] This observation was also expressed in the recent submission on Bill 106 by a group of Professors of the Faculty of Law, University of Sherbrooke, Professors BERNARDOT, KOURI and NOOTENS, "Mémoire portant sur le Projet de Loi No. 106". They state in this regard,

> "Depuis plusieurs années, dans les milieux juridiques et surtout dans les facultés de droit, nous avons entrepris l'étude du droit des personnes en prenant pour acquis que, sauf quelques modifications, le projet présenté devant l'Assemblée Nationale serait celui préparé par l'Office de Révision du Code civil. Pourquoi a-t-on voulu mettre de côté un travail de plus d'une dizaine d'années et si bien réussi par cet organisme subventionné par l'État à coup de millions de dollars? (pp. 18-19).

A second preliminary criticism has to do with the matter of organic unity and coherence. The piecemeal manner and puzzling order in which the Books of the reformed Code are being introduced invites incoherence and disunity, both within each Book and between them. One of the great merits and goals of codification is after all the opportunity to have a body of codified law which is coherent and logical, and in which the various parts flow from some clearly articulated first principles. Instead of the expected order, Book Two (The Family - Bill 89) was introduced first (in 1980), and only recently Book One (Persons - Bill 106) and Book Three (Succession - Bill 107).[25]

A degree of incoherence and an absence of organic unity in the reform process has been the inevitable and predictable result. This result was regretted and predicted several years ago by P.-A. Crépeau who noted:

> Au stade de l'implementation de la réforme, on peut légitimement s'interroger sur l'opportunité de procéder à la mise en place de la réforme, si l'on peut dire, par pièces et morceaux successifs... Ainsi, on a récemment procédé à la réforme de la famille à partir du Livre deuxième du Projet de Code civil. Mais présenter à l'Assemblée nationale le Livre deuxième sans présenter le Livre premier sur le droit des personnes et le Livre troisième sur le droit des successions, n'est-ce pas opérer une coupure artificielle dans ce qui à été conçu et présenté comme un ensemble, dont les parties sont organiquement reliées et interdépendantes?[26]

A third general criticism of Bill 106 is that there is a total absence of commentaries and explanations as to the exact intent of its articles and the reasons for the formulations proposed. As a result one is often forced to speculate as to the meanings and implications of certain articles. This too is in marked contrast with the texts and methodology of the Draft Civil Code produced by the Civil Code Revision Office.

---

25 Bill 107 *op.cit. supra*, n.12.

26 P.-A. CRÉPEAU, "Les lendemains de la réforme du Code Civil", (1981) 59 *Can. Bar. Rev.* 625, at p. 628.

We will now consider briefly several aspects of Bill 106 itself as it concerns the unborn child. The article of most interest is article 1:

> Every human being possesses juridical personality. He is the subject of rights from birth till death.[27]

Whereas the first sentence of the article is essentially the same as a.18 C.C., of crucial importance to our issue is obviously the second sentence of the article asserting that one has juridical personality only from birth to death. Clearly that assertion would exclude from juridical personality and consequent rights the conceived but unborn.

That position is in marked contrast with the trend and evolution identified above regarding the status and rights of the unborn. Admittedly, as already noted, there remains a degree of ambiguity, hesitation and incoherence in jurisprudence and doctrine regarding the unborn child, particularly on the subject of its legal status. But all that notwithstanding, gains have been made, some rights acknowledged, and new questions and challenges are pushing the issue in the direction of expanding and clarifying the status and rights of the unborn child, not narrowing and further muddying them.

As it now stands this article is out of step with present law, with another article in Bill 106 itself (a.123), with Bill 107, and by implication it ignores a number of urgent new issues and challenges.

While neither the present Civil Code nor the Draft Civil Code consider the unborn child as a person, they do at least acknowledge a "conditional" personality, the condition being viable birth. Neither that conditional personality, nor the fact

---

[27] It is worth noting that this official english version of article 1 of Bill 106 appears to differ from the French version in the first part of the second sentence. The French version reads: "Il est *sujet de droit* depuis sa naissance jusqu'à sa mort". To be the "subject of rights" is not the same as to be "sujet de droit". Space limitations do not permit a further discussion of the differences in meaning between the two language versions.

that legal personality can be extended to the unborn when its interests demand it, can be accommodated by the proposed article 1. The formulation is regressive in that it would seem to rule out even the two sorts of conditional rights already explicitly extended to the unborn, patrimonial rights and the right of action for prenatal injury.

Article 1 of the Bill, in explicitly denying (even conditional) legal personality and rights to those not yet born is necessarily excluding by implication even patrimonial rights. But in this the article appears to contradict another article of the same Bill, namely article 123, which states:

> The father and mother of a minor child, if they are of full age or emancipated, are tutors to their child *plene juro*.
>
> The father and mother are also tutors *to a child conceived but yet unborn* and are responsible for acting on his behalf in all cases where his pecuniary interests require it. [Emphasis added]

But if (according to a.1) the unborn child has not even conditional juridical personality and is not the subject of rights, how can he have a tutor named to protect his patrimonial rights?

Article 1 appears to be equally in contradiction with a.664 of Bill 107 on the subject of successions. That article as well acknowledges the patrimonial rights of the unborn child. It states:

> Human persons who exist at the time the succession devolves may inherit, as may absentees and *children conceived yet unborn*, if they are born alive and viable. [Emphasis added]

Lastly, article 1 and Bill 106 generally do not reflect a number of new problems and challenges encouraging a more explicit and protective legal stance as regards the status and rights of the unborn. In its submission to the Standing Committee, the Quebec Human Rights Commission had this to say on that point:

> En posant comme règle que l'être humain n'est sujet de droit qu'à partir de sa naissance, le Projet évite les problèmes nouveaux que posent l'expérimentation, la fertilisation et la recombinaison générique...[28]

Another submission, presented by a group of jurists of the Centre of Private and Comparative Law of McGill University, made a similar point and concluded that ideally what is required is legislative recognition of juridical personality from the time of conception in order to provide adequate protection. That submission stated in part:

> Dans le contexte biomédical actual qui permet la conception d'êtres humains en dehors de l'organisme humain maternel et qui, de plus, permet d'intervenir sur le foetus humain... il nous apparaît nécessaire, raisonnable et opportun, à défaut de la part du législateur québécois de lui conférer, de plein droit, dès sa conception, la personnalité juridique, d'établir... des normes spécifiques en regard d'une atteinte à son intégrité.[29]

In the absence of any explanation or commentary by those who drafted this article, one is tempted to conclude that they were simply unaware of the "state of the question" of present doctrine and jurisprudence concerning the unborn, and equally uninformed about the new biomedical challenges referred to above. It has also been speculated that article 1 of Bill 106 was formulated as it is in order to preserve the woman's right to abortion.[30] But until and unless the veil of silence on the part of its drafters is lifted, one can do little more than speculate as to the real motives.

---

[28] Commission des droits de la personne du Québec, "Commentaires de la Commission des droits de la personne du Québec sur le Projet de la loi no. 106", April 26, 1983.

[29] Centre de droit privé et comparé du Québec, Université McGill, "Mémoire relatif au Projet de loi 106", March, 1983, at p.9.

[30] This is a suggestion proposed in the submission from the Quebec Human Rights Commission. The relevant text is the following:

> A-t-on vulu par l'article 1 préserver les droits de la femme à l'avortement? Si tel est le cas, plutôt que d'enlever des droits au foetus, peut-être vaudrait mieux reconnaitre ce droit aux femmes de façon positive. De plus, il serait étonnant par ailleurs que les femmes voulant porter à terme une grossesse et mettre au monde un enfant sain se réjouissent qu'on veuille priver leur enfant conçu mais non encore né de tous droits extrapatrimoniaux.
> (*Op. cit., supra*, n.28 at p.5)

Various revisions to Bill 106 were proposed in order to bring article 1 into line with present law and new biomedical threats. The Quebec Human Rights Commission for example recommended that the second sentence of a.1 be omitted.[31] In effect that would leave a.1 equivalent to a.18 C.C. and a.1.1 Draft Code.

The submission by a group of professors of the Faculty of Law, University of Sherbrooke, proposed omitting the second sentence of a.1, Bill 106, and the dropping of the single word "pecuniary" in a.123, Bill 106. The latter change would adapt a.123 to the spirit of the (revised) general principle of a.1, not limiting to patrimonial matters the interests of the unborn for which its parents could be appointed tutors.[32]

The submisson of a group of jurists from the Centre of Private and Comparative Law of McGill University, like the other two submissions, also proposed that the second sentence of article 1 be omitted. But it proposed as well an addition to a.11, Bill 106. The subject of a.11, Bill 106 is that of inviolability and it states the following:

Every person is inviolable and is entitled to his physical integrity.

No harm may be done to the physical integrity of a person without his free and enlightened consent given according to law nor unless it is authorized by law.

The McGill submission recommended adding the following paragraph:

On ne peut porter atteinte à l'intégrité d'un être humain avant sa naissance que dans la mesure prévue par la loi.[33]

---

31   Id., at p.6. The Commission also recommended that there be organized within the Civil Code a special juridical regime specific to the prenatal condition.

32   Op. cit., supra, n.24, at p.2.

33   Op. cit., supra, n.29, at p.9.

The Quebec Chamber of Notaries was another group which proposed omitting the second sentence from a.1 of Bill 107.[34] It argued in its submission that not to do so would seriously compromise the rights of the fetus.

As for the Human Rights Commission of the Assembly of Roman Catholic Bishops of Quebec, it submitted that the phrase, "the conceived child is held to be born provided it is born alive and viable" should be added to a.1 of Bill 106.[35] In proposing the retention of 1.28 Draft Code, that Commission argued that the rights of the child from conception would be protected.

What all these submissions have in common then are at least two points. One is that from the standpoint of the unborn child, the enactment of Bill 106 would be a regressive step because it would be to categorically deny even the conditional juridical personality and rights already available. Secondly, they therefore agree that the second sentence of article 1 must be omitted, or at the very least qualified by the addition of what was proposed in 1.28 Draft Code.

ii) *The Common law perspective*

From the Civil Law perspective we turn now to the state of the question as to the juridical status and rights of the fetus in Common law. The two sorts of fetal rights of interest at this point in the study are the two just considered in the Civil Law context - property rights and the right of action for prenatal injury. As with the previous section this one too must of necessity be somewhat summary in nature.

---

34 La Chambre des notaires du Québec, "Mémoire relatif au Projet de loi 106", March, 1983, at p.2.

35 "L'Épiscopat et la Commission des droits demandent de protéger les droits du foetus", *Le Devoir*, April 14, 1983, at p.2.

a) *Property rights*

As in the Civil Law tradition so in the Common law, the earliest affirmations of the rights of the unborn child were made in the context of property law. In fact these rights have been claimed to be as ancient as the common law itself.[36] Both the age of these rights in this tradition and the similarity in this respect to the Civil Law tradition are evident in these words from Blackstone in 1762:

> An infant... in the mother's womb, is supposed in law to be born for many purposes. It is capable of having a legacy... made to it. It may have a guardian assigned to it; and it is enabled to have an estate... as if it were then actually born.[37]

As in Civil Law, the earliest records and cases indicate that the same suspensive condition of live birth has always applied. A very early statement to that effect is in *The Earl of Bedford's case,* which held:

> Although *filius in utero matris est pars viscerum matris*... yet the law in many cases hath consideration of him in respect of the apparent expectation of his birth.[38]

In still another early English case, in reply to the allegation that a child was a "non-entity", the following was held:

> Let us see what this non-entity can do. He may be vouched in a recovery... He may be an executor. He may take under the Statute of Distributions. He may take by devise. He may be entitled under a charge for raising portions. He may have an injunction; and he may have a guardian.[39]

---

36 See for example W.J. MALEDON, "The Law and the Unborn Child: The Legal and Logical Inconsistencies", 46 *Notre Dame Law.* 349, at p.351.

37 W. BLACKSTONE, *Commentaries* (1762), at p.130.

38 *The Earl of Bedford's Case,* Michaelmas Term, 28 & 29 Eliz., 77 Eng. 421.

39 *Thellusson* v. *Woodford,* (1798) 4 Ves. 227 at 322; 31 Eng. 117, at p. 163. This case was cited by Lamont J. in *Montreal Tramways Company* v. *Léveillé, loc.cit., supra,* n.10 at p.460.

A number of other English cases affirmed these property rights. One was *Marsh* v. *Kirby,* (1634), 21 Eng. Rep. 512. In this case, at the time of a testator's death his wife was pregnant. The child once born inherited the

In Canada as in Anglo-American Common law generally, the same principles regarding property and the unborn apply now. A 1973 British Columbia decision, for example, *Re Sloan Estate*, affirmed that if a testator makes a bequest to his "surviving children" or "all living children", a conceived but unborn child was allowed to inherit provided it is to his benefit to do so and provided he is subsequently born alive.[40]

But on closer examination of the decision and reasons offered in support of the property rights of the unborn, one is led to conclude that in reality the interest and right being protected by the law is not so much the unborn child's right to inherit, but the testator's right to dispose of his property. As such, allowing an unborn child to inherit may in reality be something less than a recognition of even a *conditional* juridical personality. The recurring issue for the courts in these cases is the intent of the testator. Shaw and Damme observe the following:

> It is important to note that the testator's intent was the primary concern of the courts, not the personhood of the fetus. To deny the fetus property rights would frustrate that intent.[41]

---

estate in preference to collateral relatives. Another was *Hale* v. *Hale*, (1692), 24 Eng. Rep. 25. In this instance it was held that a trust must be interpreted to allow a child born after the death of the testator to be considered "living" at the time of the testator's death and allowed to take under the trust. *Burdett* v. *Hopegood*, (1718), 24 Eng. Rep. 485, was still another such early decision in the same line. In this case a child born after the testator's death was able to take under the will of his father.

40 *Re Sloan Estate*, [1937] 3 W.W.R. 455 (B.C.S.C.) at pp. 463-465. In fact this decision went still further and held that even when a testator leaves property to specifically named chldren, an as yet unborn and un-named child once subsequently born is also entitled to inherit.

41 M.W. SHAW and C. DAMME, "Legal Status of the Fetus", in A. Milunsky and G. Annas (editors), *Genetics and the Law*, Plenum Press, N.Y., 1975, 3 at p.4. B. DICKENS made a similar point when he wrote, "A child *en ventre sa mère* may contingently acquire property, the contingency again being live birth. The purpose of the rule is not to protect the personal rights of the unborn child, however, but to give effect to the intentions of the donor of the property, particularly a testator". *Medico-Legal Aspects of Family Law*, Butterworths, Toronto, 1979 at p.74.

Weiler and Catton come to essentially the same conclusion:

> In construing a will in such cases, the court is entitled to put itself in the position of the testator and to consider the intention evidenced by the words used. Thus, if the court finds that the potential existence of such child placed plainly within "the reason and motive of such gift" the court will resort to a legal fiction and construe the will so as to include the child by finding him alive at the relevant date. This fiction is not applicable when the result would be detrimental to the infant.[42]

In conclusion then, the Common law position is similar to that of the Civil Law tradition with regard to the two conditions under which an unborn child may inherit, namely that such inheritance is to the benefit of that child, and on the suspensive condition that he is subsequently born alive. But in Common law this may not in reality be an affirmation of the personhood or even rights of the unborn child so much as it is a matter of protecting the rights of testators to dispose of their property.

As stated earlier, one of the hypotheses of this study is that ultimately a secure right of the unborn child to prenatal care and protection should be built upon the firm foundation of the explicit and unambiguous legal recognition of the juridical personality and basic rights of the unborn child in his own right. At least in the area of property law we do not find that sort of recognition. We will turn next to the right of action for prenatal injuries in the Common law tradition in order to pinpoint the content and scope of that right.

b) *The right of action for prenatal injury*

As earlier in this study when considering this right of action in the context of the Civil Law, here too we will examine at this point only instances of prenatal injuries to unborn children *in utero* who are subsequently born alive. Instances of prenatal injury resulting in the death of the child will be considered below in the "wrongful death, wrongful life" section. Although there is essential agreement in all Common

---

[42] WEILER and CATTON, *op. cit., supra*, n.7, at p. 643.

law jurisdictions about the content and scope of the unborn child's right of action for prenatal injury, there are some differences as well.

The earliest common law case to deal in an explicit manner with the issue of negligently inflicting prenatal injuries on a fetus was the 1884 American case of *Dietrich* v. *Northampton*.[43] In that instance a pregnant woman fell on the defendant's road, premature labour and birth were precipitated, and the child died fifteen minutes after birth. Mr. Justice Holmes held however that a cause of action did not lie because at the time of the injury the child was a part of the mother. In the United States this precedent survived until the 1946 decision in *Bonbrest* v. *Kotz*,[44] a decision we will consider below.

Another early decision was the 1891 British case of *Walker* v. *Great No. Ry. of Ireland*.[45] This case involved a claim by the plaintiff child against the defendant railroad that while her pregnant mother was a passenger on a train, she had been injured and the plaintiff child was born crippled as a result. In this instance relief was denied in large part because it was held that there was no duty owed to the plaintiff child because there was no contractual relationship. A further consideration in the denial of relief was the matter of proof. In this regard the statement of Judge O'Brien is of interest:

> The pity of it is as novel as the case - that an innocent infant comes into the world with the cruel seal upon it of another's fault, and has to bear a burden of infirmity and ignominy throughout the whole passage of life... But there are instances in the law where rules of right are founded upon the inherent and inevitable difficulty or impossibility of proof. And it is easy to see on what a boundless sea of speculation in evidence this new idea would launch us. What a field would be opened to extravagance of testimony, already great enough - if Science could carry her lamp... into the unseen laboratory of nature... There may be a question of evidence

---

[43] *Dietrich* v. *Northampton, loc. cit. supra,* n.15.

[44] *Bonbrest* v. *kotz,* 65 F. Supp. 138 (D.C.D.C. 1946).

[45] *Walker* v. *Great No. Ry. of Ireland,* (1891), 28 L.R. Ir. 69 (Q.B.)

[plaintiff's counsel] modestly put it; but the law may see such danger in that evidence, may have such a suspicion of human ignorance and presumption, that it will not allow any question of evidence to be entered into at all.[46]

Subsequent American cases for many years after this and largely on the basis of the *Walker* decision, added the "problem of proof" reason to other reasons (especially those of no duty and lack of precedent) to deny relief to prenatally injured unborn children.

In common law Canada the earliest case to consider the extra-patrimonial rights of the unborn child was the 1923 Ontario decision of *Smith v. Fox*.[47] A pregnant woman was injured in an automobile accident. An action was brought by the woman and her husband as next friend of the unborn child, but while the child was still unborn. Riddell J. held that an action at the suit of the child could lie only if two conditions were fulfilled, that the child be born alive and that the injury be capable of being estimated pecuniarily. Since in this case the child was not yet born, there could be no assessment of damages, "... unless and until the birth and separate existence of the child – that is still hypothetical... I think the action premature".[48]

Though in *Smith v. Fox* damages were not actually awarded, the right itself of the unborn child to sue for prenatal injury was affirmed, if the specified conditions had been met. They were in fact met in the subsequent 1972 Ontario decision of *Duval v. Séguin*, which did award damages to a prenatally injured child.[49] Like *Smith v. Fox*, this case involved a pregnant woman injured in an automobile accident. The pregnant woman's child was born prematurely and with serious physical and mental handicaps.

---

46 *Id.*, at pp. 81-82.

47 *Smith v. Fox*, [1923], 3 D.L.R. 785 (Ont. S.C.).

48 *Id.*, at p.787.

49 *Duval v. Séguin*, (1972), 26 D.L.R. (3d) 418 (Ont. H.C.). An Australian decision in the same year also awarded damaged for prenatal injuries, *Watt v. Rama*, [1972] V.R. 353 (S.C.).

In awarding damages to the child (Ann), Judge Fraser based his decision in large part on the *Léveillé* decision discussed earlier in this paper, at least concerning the legitimacy of such an action and the suspensive condition of live birth. But whereas in *Léveillé*, the at least conditional personality of the unborn child at the time of the accident was affirmed,[50] here in *Duval* that legal fiction and the whole question of juridical personality is more or less side-stepped. In *Duval* damages were awarded essentially on grounds of foreseeable risk and duty. In the words of Judge Fraser:

> Ann's mother was plainly one of a class within the area of foreseeable risk and one to whom the defendants therefore owed a duty. Was Ann any the less so? I think not. Procreation is normal and necessary for the preservation of the race. If a driver drives on a highway without due care for other users it is foreseeable that some of the other users of the highway will be pregnant women and that a child *en ventre sa mère* may be injured. Such a child therefore falls well within the area of potential danger which the driver is required to foresee and take reasonable care to avoid.[51]

Having established that duty and foreseeability constitutes sufficient grounds for awarding damages, Judge Fraser concludes:

> In my opinion it is not necessary in the present case to consider whether the unborn child was a person in law or at what stage she became a person. For negligence to be a tort there must be damages. While it was the foetus *en ventre sa mère* who was injured, the damages sued for are the *damages suffered by the plaintiff Ann since birth* and which she will continue to suffer as a result of that injury.[52] [Emphasis added]

As already observed above in discussing the *Léveillé* decision, here too in *Duval*, the intervening months between the accident and the birth do not in the eyes of the law qualify

---

50 *Montreal Tramways Co.* v. *Léveillé, loc. cit. supra*, n.10 at p. 465.

51 *Duval* v. *Séguin, loc. cit. supra*, n.49 at p.433

52 *Ibid.* B. Knoppers observes that the *Duval* approach would avoid conflict with abortion. That may be so, but that conflict would be avoided at the expense of coherence and fairness. Also, it would preclude any foundation on which to base a right of the fetus to care and protection in the prenatal period. See B. KNOPPERS, "Le Statut juridique du foetus: du droit comparé au droit en devenir," (1980) 2 *C. de B.* 205, at p.219.

as a period meriting even compensation, and much less, presumably, protection. It could hardly be otherwise given the legal fiction of being "deemed born" at the time of the accident only if and when actually born alive. In this regard there is much similarity between the last sentence of the above quote from *Duval*, and this already quoted excerpt from Cannon J. in *Léveillé*:

> ...aussi longtemps qu'elle était dans le sein de sa mère, il est évident qu'elle ne souffrait aucun dommage, aucun inconvénient et aucun préjudice.[53]

Clearly therefore, though there were important differences in accent in the reasons for judgment between the Civil Law case of *Léveillé* and the Common law case of *Duval*, there is an essential similarity in the manner in which both legal systems describe the legal interest concerning the period between the accident and birth.

In the United States, it was only in 1946 that a United States District Court, much influenced by the *Léveillé* decision, finally held that *Dietrich* was not the last word on the subject and decided that injuries to an unborn child are after all compensable in a tort action brought by the child once born. This was the case of *Bonbrest v. Kotz*.[54]

However, even before that decision it had long been argued in articles and some dissenting judgments that such actions should be allowed. An example was the dissent by Chief Justice Brogan in 1942 in *Stemmer v. Kline*.[55] He argued that the courts should not flinch from breaking with the earlier position that the unborn child has no separate existence, when in all other areas of law a child is acknowledged to have separate being when it is to its benefit.

---

53 *Montreal Tramways Co. v. Léveillé, loc. cit. supra*, n.10 at p. 477.

54 *Bonbrest v. Kotz, loc. cit., supra*, n.44.

55 *Stemmer v. Kline*, 26 A. 2d 684, at p. 685 et Seg. (N.J.C.A. 1942). See particularly p. 687. For a similar and earlier dissent see that of Judge Boggs in *Allaire v. St. Luke's Hospital*, 56 NE 638 at p. 640 (I ll. S.C. 1900)

As for *Bonbrest* itself, the court made a clean break with earlier American decisions by holding a physician liable for injuries to the fetus during delivery. *Bonbrest* itself became the precedent on the basis of which a new trend developed, a trend in which earlier decisions not acknowledging such an action were overruled, and in new actions courts consistently began to allow such suits. As with (Quebec) Civil Law decisions and decisions in Common law Canada already considered, the same suspensive condition applied and applies in the United States - subsequent birth. And it is now accepted that the right to recover damages for prenatal injuries suffered by the unborn child belongs to the child itself and not to the parents or others.[56]

However, at first a significant restriction was applied by American courts. These actions could not be brought unless the injury occurred when the unborn child was in a viable state, capable of being born and living independently from the mother. *Bonbrest* itself was an example, in that it made the issue of viability at the time of the accident the crucial factor in allowing the recovery.

That limitation and restriction has long been recognized in legal and medical writing to be artificial and unjust, quite incompatible with medical knowledge and the vulnerability of the fetus. As Roland Chase, for example, observed:

> ... there is no valid medical basis for a distinction based on viability, since the fetus is just as much an independent being prior to viability as it is afterward... Of course the proof necessary to support a claim for prenatal injuries may be more difficult where it is alleged that the injuries occurred early in gestation, but this is not a valid reason to deprive a prenatally injured child of his right to attempt to produce such proof.[57]

A similar observation was the following:

---

56 See R.F. CHASE, "Liability for Prenatal Injuries", 40 ALR 3d 1222 (1971), at p. 1228.

57 CHASE, *ibid*, refers to *Puhl* v. *Milwaukee Auto Inc. Co.* 99 N.W. 2d 163 (Wis. 1959), in support.

> The difficulty of proving causation bears no relationship to the viability or non-viability of the fetus at the time of the accident; rather, the magnitude of the proof problem varies according to the particular facts of each case. Indeed - and this is a fact of utmost importance - there is substantial medical authority which indicates that congenital structural defects occasioned by environmental factors can be sustained *only* within the earliest stages of the *previable* period. Judicial disallowance of actions for injuries to non-viable fetuses may well be a denial of the most meritorious claims.[58]

These arguments were obviously persuasive to American courts, because the "viable when injured" rule is very definitely on the decline. Courts in many states have now expressly dropped the "viable when injured" rule and have acknowledged the separate nature of the unborn child from conception onwards for the purpose of actions for prenatal injuries, always of course on the condition of live birth.[59]

In the United Kingdom the legal position regarding prenatal injuries is as original as it is indefensible. It is out of step with the evolution of case law and doctrine in other Common law jurisdictions, and equally out of step with recent medical and biological knowledge about the development and vulnerability of the unborn child.

Given the almost total absence of case law consideration of the extra-patrimonial rights of the unborn child in the United Kingdom until very recently, the law in the United Kingdom was taken by surprise and quite unprepared to respond adequately to the thalidomide tragedy when it struck. Partly as a result of that tragedy, the U.K. Law Commission was given the task of studying the issue of injuries to unborn children and proposing an appropriate statute to provide for civil liability in the event of prenatal injuries to unborn children. The Law Commission issued a Working Paper in

---

[58] C.A. Lintgen, "Note: The Impact of Medical Knowledge on the Law Relating to Prenatal Injuries", (1962) 110 *U. Penn. L.R.*, 554 at p. 563.

[59] See on this point, CHASE, *op. cit., supra*, n.56 at pp. 1227-1228; LINTGEN, *op. cit., supra*, n.58 at pp. 563-564. Among the decisions which have discarded the "viable when injured" rule are the following: *Bennet* v. *Hymers*, 147 A. 2d 108 (N.H. S.C. 1958); *Smith* v. *Brennan*, 157 A. 2d 497 (N.J.S.C. 1960).

1973,[60] a Report to Parliament in 1974 containing a Draft Congenital Disabilities (Civil Liability) Bill,[61] and in 1976 the Bill proposed by the Commission was enacted as the *Congenital Disabilities (Civil Liability) Act*.[62]

The Law Commission's Report and the Congenital Disabilities Act make it evident that their goal was the two-fold one of assigning civil liability to those who negligently injure unborn children while *in utero* provided such children are born alive, but to provide for such liability without granting any actual rights to the unborn child while unborn. This double aim is stated for example in the first two of the summarized recommendations in the Commission's Report:[63]

(1) Legislation should deal with the rights of a living person and no rights should be given to the foetus.

(2) The general principle should be that wherever pre-natal injury is caused intentionally, negligently or by a breach of statutory duty there should be liability for that injury.

This two-fold goal is accomplished by the introduction of the notion of derivative responsibility. Regarding liability at common law, the Commission concluded that:

> ...as a general rule, whenever there is liability at common law *to a mother* for an act or omission which causes pre-natal injury, the child should be entitled to recover damages.[64]

---

[60] U.K. Law Commission, *Injuries to Unborn Children*, Working Paper No.47, Her Majesty's Stationary Office, London, 1973.

[61] U.K. Law Commission, *Report on Injuries to Unborn Children*, No.60, Her Majesty's Stationary Office, London, 1974.

[62] *Congenital Disabilities (Civil Liability) Act 1976*, 46 Halsbury's Statutes of England, 1837 (3rd edition), 1976.

[63] *Report, op. cit., supra*, n.61 at p. 42.

[64] *Id.*, at p.15.

Regarding breach of statutory duty, the Commission comes to a similar conclusion regarding "derivative" liability:

> ... the general rule should be that where a breach of statutory duty owed *to a pregnant woman* causes pre-natal injury to her child, that child should be entitled to recover damages for his disability.[65]
> [Emphasis added]

In the explanatory notes accompanying subsections (1) to (3) of the Draft Bill (the wording of which was unchanged in the Act of the same name), we read the following:

> The liability of the defendant is a derivative one, in that the combined effect of subsections (1) to (3) is to make liability to the child depend on a pre-existent liability to one or other of the parents in respect of the matters giving rise to the disabled birth. Thus... there is no nexus of legal duty, whether at common law or under statutes, as between the defendant and the child *in utero*.[66]

---

[65] *Id.*, at p. 21. For a critique of this principle and the Report generally, see I. KENNEDY and R.G. EDWARDS, "A Critique of the Law Commission Report on Injuries to Unborn Children and the Proposed Congenital Disabilities (Civil Liability) Bill", (1975) 1 *J. Med. E.* 116, at p.121.

[66] *Report, op. cit., supra*, n.61 at pp.46-48. The relevant subsections (1) to (3) of the *Congenital Disabilities (Civil Liability) Act* 1976 are the following:

1. (1) If a child is born disabled as the result of such an occurrence before its birth as is mentioned in subsection (2) below, and a person (other than the child's own mother) is under this section answerable to the child in respect of the occurrence, the child's disabilities are to be regarded as damage resulting from the wrongful act of that person and actionable accordingly at the suit of the child.
   (2) An occurrence to which this section applies is one which -
      (a) affected either parent of the child in his or her ability to have a normal, healthy child; or
      (b) affected the mother during her pregnancy, or affected her or the child in the course of its birth, so that the child is born with disabilities which would not otherwise have been present.
   (3) Subject to the following subsections, a person (here referred to as "the defendant") is answerable to the child if he was liable in tort to the parent or would, if sued in due time, have been so; and it is no answer that there could not have been such liability because the parent suffered no actionable injury, if there was a breach of legal duty which, accompanied by injury, would have given rise to the liability.

That the United Kingdom position assigns a juridical status to the unborn child considerably less even than that of the Civil Law or other Common law jurisdictions is particularly evident in the following unequivocal assertion:

> The plaintiff (unborn child) has no legal existence at the time of the injury nor has he, prior to birth, an existence separate from his mother.[67]

On the basis of that principle the Law Commission concludes that the unborn child is in the same class as a drowning man or a stranger. In addressing the issue of liability by omission for example, the Commission stated:

> One is under no duty at common law to save a drowning man or to shout a warning to a stranger who is about to be run over. If however, some special relationship exists or has been assumed, the duty to act arises... But as we have seen, no such relationship can be present when one party to it is not in existence... (Therefore) whether a failure to act which causes prenatal injury ought to ground liability to the child should depend upon whether a special relationship exists between the tortfeasor and mother...[68]

That conclusion is perhaps the clearest indication available of what results if the unborn child is not acknowledged to have legal existence and is granted rights only derivatively rather than in his own right. In the absence of liability in tort to the mother-to-be, the unborn child would have no more right to compensation for injury than would a drowning man or a stranger about to be run over.

There are at least three serious problems with that position. One is that many acts and omissions injurious to the child are not necessarily harmful to the mother-to-be and thus need not involve any violation of a duty to her. That point will stand out more clearly after the discussion in Chapter II on the

---

[67] *Id.*, at p.11. The U.K. decision in *Paton* v. *Trustees of BPAS*, [1978] 2 All E.R. 987 (Q.B.), largely on the basis of the Law Commission's Report, emphasized the same point in concluding, (at p. 989), "The foetus cannot, in English law... have any right of its own at least until it is born and has a separate existence from the mother".

[68] *Report, op. cit., supra,* n.61 at p. 15.

health effects on the unborn child of various acts, omissions and substances.

A second problem with the Law Commission's position is that the mother-to-be herself is the one positioned by nature to do potentially the most good and the most harm for her unborn child. This too will emerge from the survey and analysis in Chapter II. Therefore, if liability to the child can arise only in the event of liability to a parent, then a wide range of otherwise negligent and harmful acts or omissions would go un-compensated. The Law Commission and the *Congenital Disabilities Act*, in denying to a child a right of action against its mother for prenatal injury,[69] are of course prepared to allow that gap to exist. We are not, and will so argue in a later section dealing with parental liability.

A third problem is that if the unborn child's right of action for compensation were to be restricted in the manner enacted in the *Congenital Disabilities Act*, then it seems logical to conclude that the sort of anticipatory (to birth) and protective legal interventions of interest in this paper would be even more restricted if allowed at all. In the first place, the unborn child is not granted legal existence prior to birth, and secondly, it would usually be actual or threatened *parental* abuse or neglect which might invite the anticipatory and protective intervention of legal mechanisms.

4. *Wrongful death, wrongful birth and wrongful life*

i) *The Common law perspective*

a) *Wrongful death*

Both actions for prenatal injury and actions for "wrongful death" have a similar goal, that of compensation rather than prenatal care or protection. But whereas in actions for prenatal injury, the action is brought by the child and the compensation sought is for that injured child, actions for the

---

[69] *Id.*, at pp. 21-28, and *Congenital Disabilities (Civil Liability) Act 1976*, *loc. cit., supra*, n.62, section 1 (2)

wrongful death of an unborn child are brought by the child's survivors and the compensation is for them. Their purpose is to provide compensation to the parents for the loss of their "potential child". For this reason it has been argued that sucessful actions for wrongful death (as opposed to actions for prenatal injury) in the United States do not constitute recognition by courts of the legal rights or personality of the unborn child.

Crockett and Hyman for example claim that:

> ... permitting recovery for the wrongful death of an unborn does not indicate a court's recognition of a fetus' legal rights. Rather, recovery for the wrongful death of the unborn should be seen as a desire on the part of the judiciary to fulfill the purpose of tort law by providing compensation for the parents' loss of a potential child.[70]

Support for that position is to be found in *Roe* v. *Wade*, in which the (U.S.) Supreme Court stated:

> Such an action [wrongful death], however, would appear to be one to vindicate the parents' interest and is thus consistent with the view that the fetus, at most, represents only the potentiality of life.[71]

But a study of the use made by American courts of the various wrongful death statutes[72] suggests that courts faced with wrongful death actions involving prenatal injuries may not in fact be loathe to ascribe juridical personality to unborn children who die as a result of injuries *in utero*, whether they die after live and viable birth, or *in utero*. Parents have been awarded compensation in both sorts of cases.[73]

---

[70] K. CROCKETT and M. HYMAN, "Live Birth: A Condition Precedent to Recognition of Rights", (1976) 4 *Hof. L.R.* 805, at p. 824.

[71] *Roe* v. *Wade*, 410 U.S. 113 (1973), at p. 162.

[72] Actions for wrongful death are generally felt (in the United States at least) to require statutory support, unlike actions for prenatal injury which are based on common law principles. See, S.E. SEGAL, "Wrongful Death and the Stillborn Fetus - A Current Analysis", (1970) 7 *Hous. Law Review*, 449.

[73] For more specifics concerning wrongful death decisions in the United States see, R.E. KRUGER, "Wrongful Death and the Unborn Child: An Examination of Recovery after *Roe* v. *Wade*", (1973-74) 13 *J. Fam. L.* 99; CHASE, *op. cit., supra*, n.56, at pp. 1255-1261.

In permitting actions for prenatal injuries involving a child *born alive who subsequently dies*, those courts would appear to be granting essentially the same degree of "retroactive" juridical personality to that child while he was still unborn as acknowledged in actions for prenatal injury. In the first place, the child was born alive, and thus has met the suspensive condition of live birth. Secondly, though it is the survivors who bring the action for their own compensation, the wrongful death statutes being applied generally require that the wrongful act which causes death be such that *the decedent* could have brought an action against the wrongdoer if death had not resulted.[74] It is therefore not difficult to bring a child born alive who subsequently dies, within the meaning of "person" in wrongful death statutes.

As for children who are both injured *in utero* and who die *in utero* as a result of the injury, it is even more obviously the case that when courts award compensation to the survivors for their wrongful death, they are implicitly and inescapably acknowledging the juridical personality of those unborn children. Once again, the issue for the courts is whether or not the deceased unborn child comes within the meaning of "person" in the relevant wrongful death statute. A number of American courts have answered in the affirmative whether the child was born or not. In doing so they have in effect waived for these actions (alone) the traditional suspensive condition for juridical personality, namely live and viable birth. In cases in which the injured and deceased unborn child *can* be brought within the meaning of person, the survivors are able to claim "moral" damages for the loss of a person.

---

[74] A typical statutory provision of this type is that of Minnesota, which states: "When death is caused by the wrongful act or omission of any person or corporation, the personal representative of the decedent may maintain an action therefor if he might have maintained an action, had he lived,, for an injury caused by the same act or omission". Minn. Stat. Ann. 573.02.

A recent example of such a decision is that of *M.E. Mone* v. *Greyhound Line*[75] which stated:

> We agree with the majority of jurisdictions that conditioning a right of action on whether a fatally injured child is born dead or alive is not only an artificial and unreasonable demarcation, but unjust as well.[76]

On the basis of that principle the same court rendered its decision in these words:

> ...We hold that, where, as here, an eight and one-half month unborn viable fetus is killed, the fetus is a person for purposes of our wrongful death statute,...[77]

The state of the question in common law Canada concerning these actions for wrongful death is as yet unclear.[78] One such action was initiated in 1973 in the North

---

[75] *M.E. Mone* v. *Greyhound Line*, 331 N.E. 2d, 916 (Mass. S.J.C. 1975).

[76] *Id.*, at pp. 919, 920.

[77] *Id.*, at p. 920. The precedent case in the United States regarding an action for the wrongful death of an unborn child is the 1949 decision in *Verkennes* v. *Corniea*, 229 Minn. 365 (1949) 38 N.W. 2d 838. That decision refers to and is largely based upon the principles and rulings established by *Montreal Tramways Co.* v. *Léveillé* and *Bonbrest* v. *Kotz* referred to earlier in this paper (at n.10 and n.44 respectively). As such, *Verkennes* provides one indication of many that actions for the wrongful death of an unborn child grew out of and are closely related to actions for prenatal injury.

A further indication of the relationship between the two types of action in the United States has to do with the issue of viability. Courts in jurisdictions which have to date only granted a right of action for prenatal injuries to a viable fetus, have applied the same condition to wrongful death actions. In these States, a right to bring this action is allowed only when the deceased child was viable at the time of the injury which caused his death. For details see, CHASE, *op. cit.*, *supra*, n.56, at p. 1257.

Yet there is also a basic difference between actions for prenatal injury and actions for wrongful life in the matter of the unborn as person. Though *Verkennes* relies heavily on *Léveillé* and *Bonbrest* in concluding that a fetus which dies *in utero* may be considered "person" for the sake of wrongful death statutes though not born alive, *Léveillé* and *Bonbrest*, as already indicated earlier, come to quite a different conclusion. Both insist on the suspensive condition of live birth. Little wonder then that Deleury observes, "Le droit privé américain présente donc, lui aussi, un certain nombre de contradictions,... ", *op. cit. supra*, n.6 at p. 286.

[78] WEILER and CATTON, *op. cit.*, *supra*, n.7, at pp. 655, 656.

West Territories involving a suit by a father of an unborn child against an airline.[79]

Weiler and Catton have persuasively stated the case for allowing such actions in Canada:

> If there be no recovery for the unborn's wrongful death, either directly through its parents' loss of expectation, then it would be cheaper for a defendant to inflict injury sufficient to cause the death of the unborn rather than simply to damage him. In this way the defendant could escape a claim for damages. Such an anomaly in the law is offensive. The fundamental basis of tort law is compensation for loss suffered . . . the parents of the unborn have suffered a real loss of expectation and potential services. Although it would be difficult to assess the quantum of such damages, it has been suggested that one could subtract the potential expenses of bringing up a child from his potential earning power, bearing in mind that a child has an obligation to support his parents in old age.[80]

b) *Wrongful birth*

Wrongful birth has been a recognized cause of action in common law for at least fifty years. It may be defined as, " . . . an action in damages brought by the parent or parents of a child who is alleged to have been born as a result of negligence of, or breach of contract by the defendant."[81] Courts have also, and perhaps more precisely, labelled such actions "wrongful pregnancy" or "wrongful conception".[82]

---

79 In a recent conversation with the then counsel for the plaintiff, Judge J. Karswick (now an Ontario Family Court Judge) this writer learned that that case did not proceed to trial.

80 WEILER and CATTON, *op. cit., supra*, n.7, at pp. 656, 657.

81 G.B. ROBERTSON, "Civil Liability Arising from 'Wrongful Birth' Following an Unsuccessful Sterilization Operation", (1978) 4 *Am. J.L. Med.* 131, at p. 132. The expression "wrongful birth" may also denote in some cases actions brought by the siblings of a child allegedly born due to defendant's negligence, the claim being that the wrongful birth reduces the share of the family income and parental attention available to the other children. To date no such claims have been successful. See ROBERTSON, at p.132, n.2.

82 See M.W. SHAW, "The Potential Plaintiff, Preconception and Prenatal Torts", in Milunsky and Annas, editors, *Genetics and the Law II*, Plenum Press, N.Y., 1980, 225, at p.226 and notes 11 and 12.

Robertson has identified five factual contexts in which the question of civil liability for wrongful birth arises:

> In the first, and by far the most common, a child is born allegedly as a result of an unsuccessful sterilization operation. In the second, a child is born allegedly as a result of the negligent dispensing, by a pharmacist or physician, of oral contraceptives. In the third fact situation, a birth occurs allegedly as a consequence of the denial of a pregnant woman's right to choose to have an abortion, and in the fourth, the birth allegedly follows upon an unsuccessful abortion operation. Finally, one case has been reported in which the plaintiffs claimed that their defective child had been born because of the negligent preconception advice of a genetic counsellor...[83]

In view of the fact that what is generally claimed to be the "wrong" in wrongful birth actions, is the birth itself of a healthy, normal child (not that it was born defective), the fifth example referred to by Robertson is best classified as an action for "wrongful life" and will be discussed in our next section.[84]

These actions would not appear to constitute any direct or indirect legal recognition of the juridical personality of the unborn child, nor offer legal protection to the unborn child while unborn or even compensation to the child after birth. First of all the wrong usually complained of is the birth itself, not a birth with defects and not a prenatal injury to the child. Secondly it is the parents who bring the action on their own behalf, not the child. That being so, it will not be necessary to attempt an evaluation of the pros and cons of this controversial action, and the various complications associated with it such as identifying the injury to the parents and assessing damages.[85]

---

[83] ROBERTSON, op. cit., supra, n.81 at pp. 134, 135 and n.7.

[84] For more unsuccessful sterilizations, see GREEN, "Law, Sex And the Population Explosion", (1977) 1 L. Med Q., 82, at p.87.

[85] A comprehensive discussion of these complications and difficulties is provided by ROBERTSON, op. cit., supra, n.82, at p.226.

c) *Wrongful life*

The action for what is generally called "wrongful life" is fundamentally different from a "wrongful birth" action in that the former is brought by a child itself (not the parents) as a result of its own (often though not necessarily defective) birth. Kouri notes that in the United States wrongful life litigation has generally arisen in two contexts, that of children born out of wedlock and that of children born with birth defects.[86]

An example of a decision arising out of the child born out of wedlock context is the 1964 decision of *Zepeda* v. *Zepeda*,[87] and an example involving birth defects is the 1967 decision in *Glietman* v. *Cosgrove*.[88] Until relatively recently actions for wrongful life have not been successful. Courts had consistently held (as did the court in *Gleitman* v. *Cosgrove* for example) that these actions must fail because it is impossible to assess damages given what is involved in the complained of injury. That assessment would involve a comparison between "non-existence" and the plaintiff child's present existence. Another reason for this refusal to grant damages is that advanced in *Zepeda*, until recently the precedent decision for wrongful life actions, which held that:

> The legal implications of such a tort are vast, the social impact could be staggering.... Encouragement [by allowing this action] would extend to all others born into the world under conditions they might regard as adverse. One might seek damages for being born a certain color, another because of race; one for being born with a hereditary disease, another for inheriting unfortunate family characteristics....We have decided to affirm the dismissal of the

---

[86] See R. KOURI, "Non-therapeutic Sterilization - Malpractice, and the Issues of 'Wrongful Birth' and 'Wrongful Life' in Quebec Law", (1979) 57 *Can. Bar. Rev.* 89, at p. 96. For a detailed list of American cases involving wrongful life claims, see ROBERTSON, *op. cit., supra*, n.81, at p. 133, n.3.

[87] *Zepeda* v. *Zepeda*, 190 N.E. 2d 849, (Ill. App. Ct. 1964). In this case the plaintiff, an illegitimate child, sued his father, who had had an adulterous relationship with the child's mother. The injury claimed for was the burden of illegitimacy.

[88] *Gleitman* v. *Cosgrove*, 227 A 2d 689 (N.J.S.C. 1967).

complaint. We do this, despite our designation of the wrong committed herein as a tort, because of our belief that law making [sic] ... should not be indulged in where the result could be as sweeping as here.[89]

Some legal writers, however, maintained that arguments against allowing actions for wrongful life were not convincing, and that the actions should be allowed. Capron for example insisted that it was not in reality impossible to calculate damages in such cases since judges and juries make similar distinctions and measurements all the time in wrongful death cases.[90] Capron also argued that it was not illogical for the plaintiff child to claim that, 'I'd rather not be here suffering as I am, but since your wrongful conduct preserved my life I am going to take advantage of my regrettable existence to sue you'.[91]

A chink in the armour of the precedent established by *Zepeda* against recognition of this action was made in 1977 in two decisions delivered in New York by the same court, namely *Becker v. Schwartz*[92] and *Park v. Chessin*.[93] In *Becker* the claim was that if the physicians had performed an amniocentesis on 37 year-old Mrs. Becker as they should have, they would have learned that the child had trisomy 21. The issue in *Park* was that parents who had already had a child fatally afflicted with polycystic kidney disease relied upon the defendant doctors' advice that the disease was not hereditary and there was no real chance of having other children with this disease. But they did have another child with the same disease. In this case the court permitted the child's claim for pain and suffering to stand. The basis proposed for this break

---

[89] *Zepeda v. Zepeda*, loc. cit. supra, n.87 at pp. 858-859.

[90] A. CAPRON, "The Wrong of 'Wrongful Life' ", in Milunsky and Annas, (editors), *Genetics and the Law II, op. cit., supra*, n.82, 81.

[91] *Id.*, at p. 89.

[92] *Becker v. Schwartz*, 400 N.Y.S. 2d 119 (App. Div. 1977).

[93] *Park v. Chessin*, 400 N.Y.S. 2d 110 (App. Div. 1977).

with precedent was the twofold one of the parents' right to abortion and the child's right to be born whole. The court held that:

> Inherent in the abolition of the statutory ban on abortion ... is a public policy consideration which gives potential parents the right... not to have a child. This right extends to instances in which it can be determined with reasonable medical certainty that the child would be born deformed. The breach of this right may also be said to be tortious to the fundamental right of a child to be born as a whole, functional human being.[94]

It should, however, be noted that these two lower court decisions granting the children standing to sue for wrongful life were not upheld by New York's Court of Appeals. The highest court in New York did uphold the actions by the parents, but not that of the children. In so deciding, the court based itself on the traditional position referred to above, the "impossibility" of assessing damages.[95]

More recently however, a California decision did permit recovery on the part of the child despite the opposite position just noted on the part of the Court of Appeals of New York. This 1980 California decision was that of *Curlender v. Bio-Science Laboratories*.[96] The plaintiff child was born with Tay-

---

94   *Id.*, at p. 114

95   *Park v. Chessin*, No. 560, Dec. 27, 1978 (N.Y. Ct. of Appeals). In the Court's words:

> "Whether it is better never to have been born at all than to have been born with even gross deficiencies is a mystery more properly left to the philosophers and the theologians ... Simply put, a cause of action brought on behalf of an infant seeking recovery for wrongful life demands a calculation of damages dependent upon a comparison between the Hobson's choice of life in an impaired state and non-existence. This comparison the law is not equipped to make."

But CAPRON observes with reason, "... once the right of *parents* to collect for their economic losses is accepted, as it was in the *Becker-Park* decision [sic] it becomes difficult not to allow the child to recover for its own injuries directly. The underlying theory of the child's case is the same as that of the parents". *Op. cit., supra*, n.90, at p. 90.

96   *Curlender v. Bio-Science Laboratories*, 165 Cal. Rptr. 477 (C.A. 1980).

Sachs disease. The laboratory had been retained by her parents to determine whether or not they were carriers of recessive Tay-Sachs genes. The tests as reported were negative. Yet their daughter was born defective, suffering greatly and with a life expectancy of only four years. The damages sought were for emotional distress, the loss of 72.6 years of life and punitive damages on the grounds that the laboratory disregarded the health, safety and well-being of the plaintiff. The court awarded damages to the child, though only on the basis of the child's actual life expectancy of four years. In so deciding, the court stated: "The reality of the 'wrongful life' concept is that such a plaintif both *exists* and *suffers*, due to the negligence of others".[97]

The judgment itself and much learned comment on it subsequently, provided an important clarification as to what is (or should be) involved in successful actions for wrongful life, not claims to recover simply because one was born, but born deformed. Capron had already observed before this particular decision, that:

> The wrong actually being complained of is the failure to give accurate advice on which a child's parents can make a decision whether not being born would be preferable to being born deformed.[98]

Annas concludes about this decision:

> There is a major difference between a child who is unwanted or illegitimate, but healthy (the type of children involved in the original cases in which the courts first coined the term "wrongful life"), and a child who is born with a severe deformity or disease. Unlike a severe deformity, illegitimacy is simply not an *injury*.[99]

From the perspective of the concerns addressed in this study, one may conclude about actions for wrongful life in a similar vein to what was concluded above regarding actions for wrongful birth. Though in the case of these actions it is the child itself who brings the action, nothing more is implied

---

[97] *Id.*, at p. 488.

[98] CAPRON, *op. cit., supra,* n.90, at p. 89.

[99] G. ANNAS, "Righting the Wrong of Wrongful Life", (1981) 11 *H.C.R. 8.*

regarding the unborn child's juridical status, rights and protections than was already established earlier in our consideration of actions for prenatal injury. In both these actions there is a prenatal wrong complained of, but the action by the child is only brought after live birth. As such, the traditional suspensive condition of live birth applies in both actions. As well, in all three actions the goal is not prenatal protection, but postnatal compensation.

d) *Preconception injury to parents*

A last cause of action worthy of mention is what could be termed an action for a child damaged by preconception injury to its parents. It has been known for some time that injury to either parent before conception can cause the child subsequently conceived to be born with one or more serious disabilities. One example is the exposure of the mother or father to radiation sufficient to cause gene mutations. Another would be a woman's preconception pelvis injury which later causes injury to a child subsequently conceived, either during gestation or during the birth. A third example would be that of ineffective or dangerous contraceptives taken prior to conception.

In common law Canada there has not yet been a decision establishing liability for such preconception torts.[100] In the United States, however, at least two such claims have been allowed. Both claims were similar to actions for wrongful life generally in that the children would have had a normal and healthy childhood were it not for the defendant's wrong. But their unique and novel aspect was that the injury or wrong complained of happened before conception.

The first case, *Jorgensen* v. *Meade Laboratories*[101] involved an action by the father who sued a pharmaceutical company and claimed that the oral contraceptives taken by his

---

[100] See DICKENS, *Medico-Legal Aspects of Family Law, op. cit., supra,* n.41, at p. 88.

[101] *Jorgensen* v. *Meade Johnson Laboratories Inc.*, 483 F. 2d 237 (U.S.C.A. 10th Cir. 1973).

wife before conception damaged the mother's chromosomal structure and caused the mongolism afflicting his twin daughters. The claim was allowed. In the second case, *Renslow* v. *Mennonite Hospital*,[102] eight years after receiving the wrong RH-type blood transfusion at the age of 13, a woman gave birth to a child with erythoblastosis fetalis, and the child suffered irreversible brain damage. In this case it was the child who sued (successfully) the physician and the hospital for preconception negligence. The action was allowed because in the first place a minor may recover for prenatal injuries if born alive. Secondly, even though the negligence occurred years before the plaintiff was conceived and injured, once duty and causation are established, tort liability has not been barred only because the wrongful conduct occurred before the resultant injury. The *Renslow* court concluded that, "When analyzed in this manner *Jorgensen* and the present case are simply cases involving actions for prenatal personal injuries."[103]

In the United Kingdom the issue was addressed at some length by the U.K. Law Commission in its *Report on Injuries to Unborn Children* already referred to earlier.[104] The Law Commission recommended that actions for preconception negligence should in fact be allowed when such negligence results in the birth of a disabled child.[105] This recommendation was enacted in the *Congenital Disabilities (Civil Liability) Act*,[106] which provides for such actions in section 1.(2) (a) of that Act.

---

[102] *Renslow* v. *Mennonite Hospital*, 351 N.E. 2d 870 (Ill. C.A. 1976).

[103] *Id.*, at p. 874.

[104] U.K. Law Commission, *Report op. cit.*, *supra*, n.61, at pp. 11, 29-31.

[105] *Id.*, at pp. 30, 43. The test and limitation proposed is, "... whether the parents or either of them know or ought to know at the time of the conception that, because of something which has happened to one of them previously, there is a risk that a child born of the intercourse will be disabled". In the Commission's view this knowledge would be an intervening circumstance breaking the chain of causality between the act or omission and the injury.

[106] *Congenital Disabilities (Civil Liability) Act*, 1976, *loc, cit.*, *supra*, n.62.

Once again, we may conclude about these actions for preconception injury to parents, that their allowance by case law and statutes does not in reality say more about the unborn child's legal personality, rights or protections than is already affirmed in the allowance of actions for prenatal injury generally. As the *Renslow* decision indicated, they are essentially only cases involving actions for prenatal injury.

ii) *The Civil Law perspective*

a) *Wrongful death*

In considering actions for wrongful death in the Common law context, it was concluded that (at least in the United States) when damages are awarded to the survivors for an injured unborn child who dies *in utero*, there is an implicit and inescapable acknowledgement of the unborn child's juridical personality.[107] That is so because in jurisdictions with wrongful death statutes the only way to award damages to survivors is to bring the deceased within the meaning of "person" as used in those Acts. If accomplished, then the survivors are able to claim moral damages for the loss of a "person". Our present question addressed to the Civil Law is whether the same conclusion may be drawn in the Civil Law context. In effect the issue in the Quebec context is whether the wrongfully killed unborn child can be brought within the meaning of "person" in a.1056 of the Civil Code.

That article reads in part as follows:

> In all cases where the person injured by the commission of an offence or quasi-offence dies in consequence ... his consort and his ascendant and descendant relations have a right ... to recover from the person who committed the offence, or his representatives, all damages occasioned by such death. The same right of action belongs to ... the father and mother following the death of their natural child ....

In both Common law and Civil Law systems the damages claimed in suits for wrongful death are for the losses to the survivors. The deceased unborn child cannot claim damages

---

107 See, *supra*, p. 42.

for his own loss of life or the violation of his integrity. But whereas in French Civil Law the parents may seek to be compensated for their economic losses, the loss of benefits normally resulting from the birth of a child and for moral damages, it is somewhat different in Quebec Civil Law which for example does not normally compensate for loss of opportunity, nor for distress due to the loss (i.e. *solatium doloris*).[108]

In the 1928 decision of *Allard* v. *Monette*[109] a pregnant woman negligently injured in an accident was survived by her premature child, held to have been non-viable and therefore equivalent to having died *in utero*. She was held not entitled to damages for the loss of her unborn child. In *Lavoie* v. *Cité de Rivière-du-Loup, et al.*,[110] a woman suffered a miscarriage as a result of an assault by a police officer. In this case the court appealed to the definition of "human being" provided by s.206 of the Criminal Code, and held that because the unborn child was not a human being by that definition, the woman was not entitled to damages for the loss of her child.

Still more recently, it was held in *Julien* v. *Roy*[111] that such damages could only be awarded if such an award would be beneficial to the child. Since that could not be in such cases, no damages were justified.

More directly related to the question asked above is the decision in *Langlois* v. *Meunier*.[112] In this case as well a pregnant woman had a miscarriage (in the seventh month of her pregnancy) after being negligently injured in an accident. Damages seem to have been awarded obliquely on the basis of both a.1053 C.C. and a.1056 C.C., Judge Vallerand appears to have held that the wrongfully killed unborn child falls within

---

[108] See, J.-L. BAUDOUIN, *La responsabilité civile délictuelle*, Les Presses de l'Université de Montréal, 1973, at pp. 433-437.

[109] *Allard* v. *Monette, loc. cit., supra*, n. 11.

[110] *Lavoie* v. *Cité de Rivière-du-Loup, et autres*, [1955] C.S. 452.

[111] *Julien* v. *Roy*, [1975] C.S. 401.

[112] *Langlois* v. *Meunier*, [1973] C.S. 301.

"another" in a.1053 C.C., yet he explicitly denies that the unborn child had juridical personality. He also explicitly affirmed that a.1056 does not apply in this case, but nevertheless proceeded to award damage "on the analogy" of the wrongful death of a young child. As such, this judgment is an illustrative example of the degree of uncertainty and incoherence still existing in Civil Law regarding the status of the unborn child.

The following excerpt from the judgment of Judge Vallerand should suffice to make that point and to answer the question stated at the beginning of this section:

> Cet enfant à naître n'est certes pas une personne et les principes du droit civil concernant le décès ne peuvent s'y appliquer. Il n'est pas non plus une chose, non plus qu'un membre de sa mère. Il ne se situe, à vrai dire, dans aucune catégorie de biens ou de personne qu'identifie la loi. Cela ne signifie pas pour autant que sa perte ne constitue pas un dommage. L'article 1053 C.C. en effet parle "du dommage causé par sa faute à autrui ...", mais ne dit pas que ce dommage se limite à la perte ou à la dépréciation d'une chose ou d'une personne que la loi a cru utile d'identifier comme tel dans l'une ou l'autre de ses dispositions.[113]

One can only agree with the thrust of this comment by Deleury:

> Étrange réalité que le foetus, puisque, sans être une entité légale, il n'en mérite pas moins la considération de la loi! N'eut-il pas été plus logique, à tout le moins, de lui reconnaître une personnalité juridique au regard du concept de viabilité, puisqu'il avait atteint le stade où il pouvait être maintenu en vie en tant qu'entité séparée?[114]

Clearly then the Civil Law of Quebec does not recognize in the *full* sense actions for wrongful death when the negligently injured unborn child dies *in utero* as a result of the injury. To do so to the the extent that at least some American

---

[113] *Id.*, at p. 305. He goes on to hold that the loss of a child one hoped for, who one expected to bring joy, consolation and help, constituted an injury within the meaning of a. 1053 C.C.

[114] DELEURY, *op. cit.*, *supra*, n.6, at p.280. DELEURY also maintains (in note 47) that this decision is contrary to the tradition of Quebec civil law which does not grant monetary damages for *solatium doloris*.

jurisdictions at least implicity do, would be to acknowledge that the unborn child is a juridical person. *Langlois* demonstrates that compensation can indeed be awarded, but that laudable practical result is achieved at the expense of considerable doctrinal incoherence.

b) *Wrongful birth and wrongful life*

The Quebec Civil Law position on the issue of actions for wrongful birth and wrongful life is best illustrated by a decision which is in a sense a "hybrid" case, including as it does both sorts of actions. The particular decision is that of *Cataford, et al. v. Moreau*.[115] In brief, the facts involved in this case were the following: A woman underwent a sterilization for contraceptive purposes, after being assured by the surgeon that there would be no more children, and after both husband and wife signed a "sterilization request" form (which they did not understand). The document both stated that conception would be impossible afterwards, and absolved the surgeon from liability whatever the results of the operation. After the tubal ligation, Mrs. Cataford became pregnant and gave birth to a healthy child, her eleventh. The couple initiated an action claiming violation of contract, for an amount $25,000.00 It was decided by the court that the child's interests should be protected as well and that he should be personally represented. A tutor was appointed, who decided (without contest from the parents) that $20,000.00 of the parents claim should be claimed on behalf of the child. Judgement was rendered in favour of the plaintiff parents, but the claim of the child was rejected.

Not surprisingly the reason Chief Justice Deschênes gave for rejecting the claim of the child seeking compensation for his own unplanned but healthy birth (the "wrongful life" aspect of the case), was essentially the same traditional reason

---

[115] *Cataford v. Moreau,* [1978] C.S. 933.

given for rejecting such claims in American jurisdictions, the impossibility of assessing damages given the comparison involved.[116]

As for the claim of the parents (the "wrongful birth" aspect of the case), damages were awarded to compensate them for all injuries which could be directly and immediately attributed to defendant's fault. In this regard the court was applying the principle it stated clearly, namely that compensation **could** be awarded for damages resulting from the unplanned birth of a healthy child.[117]

Cataford did not (unlike the American decision of *Curlender* discussed earlier) involve a child born with defects. As Kouri notes, while the rejection of the healthy child's claim for damages in this case is justifiable, a claim by a child born with defects despite parental sterilization in order to avoid transmitting a hereditary disease, may well be worthy of approval.[118] This writer's research was able to uncover no Quebec jurisprudence as yet involving this latter situation.

It appears safe to conclude that the position of Quebec Civil Law as regards actions for wrongful birth and wrongful life is essentially the same as the Common law stance as demonstrated in American jurisdictions. One difference is

---

116 In the words of the court:

> La naissance d'un enfant sain ne constitue pas pour cet enfant, un dommage et encore moins un dommage compensable en argent. Il est bien impossible de comparer la situation de l'enfant après sa naissance avec la situation dans laquelle il se serait trouvé s'il n'était pas né. Le seul énoncé du problème montre déjà l'illogisme qui l'habite. D'ailleurs, par quelle perversion de l'esprit pourrait-on arriver à qualifier comme un dommage, l'inestimable don de la vie? *Id*, at p. 940.

117 The court established that principle in these words:

> ... la Cour ne se croit pas justifiée de conclure que la naissance non désirée d'un enfant sain, au surplus das une famille pauvre comprenant déjà dix enfants vivants, constitue un événement tellement heureux et normal que l'ordre public s'offenserait d'y avoir attacher une compensation pécuniaire dans un cas approprié. (*Id.*, at p. 940).

118 See KOURI, *op. cit., supra*, n.86, at p. 98.

that there has not yet been a *Curlender* type decision, but in principle there would appear to be no obstacle in Quebec jurisprudence or doctrine to the same decision being rendered in Quebec given similar facts. All of which allows us to conclude that in Quebec Civil Law as in Common law, nothing more is (or would be) contributed to clarifying and making more explicit the unborn child's legal personality and rights by allowing these actions. The traditional suspensive condition of live birth applies, and the goal of both actions is compensation (for parents, or child or both) but not prenatal protection.

c) *Preconception injury to parents*

As in the Common law jurisdictions of Canada, so in the Civil Law of Quebec, there appear to have been as yet no actions for preconception injury to the parents for the sorts of reasons referred to earlier. It has been suggested[119] that the *Léveillé* decision and the principle it established would rule out in Quebec an action for preconception injuries, since it was held in that decision that, "... a child, if born alive and viable should be allowed to maintain an action in the Courts for injuries wrongfully committed upon its person *while in the womb of its mother*".[120] [Emphasis added] But it is doubtful that the phrase "while in the womb of its mother" was meant to have the exclusionary effect of ruling out preconception torts, which were undoubtedly not even in the mind of Lamont J. in making that statement. As well, the real stress in that statement seems more likely to be on the phrase, "if born alive and viable".

---

119 The suggestion is by DICKENS, *op. cit., supra*, n.41, at p. 63, n.15.

120 *Montreal Tramways Co.* v. *Léveillé, loc. cit., supra*, n.10, at p. 464.

One is inclined to conclude that what the *Renslow* court said could apply equally in the Quebec Civil Law context, namely that, "... *Jorgensen* and the present case are simply cases involving actions for prenatal personal injuries."[121]

If that be so, then the significance for the unborn child's legal personality, rights and protection by the allowance of such actions in the Quebec Civil Law context, would add little or nothing to what is already affirmed about the unborn child in allowing actions for prenatal injury. Earlier we came to a similar conclusion regarding actions for preconception injury to parents in the Common law context.

---

121 See *supra*, p. 51 and n.102, 103. It is worth noting that in another Civil law jurisdiction, that of Germany, a claim has succeeded before the German Supreme Court for compensation for the injury of congenital syphilis contracted *in utero* and caused by a negligently administered blood transfusion administered to the mother before conception. See I. TEDESCHI, "On Tort Liability for 'Wrongful Life'", (1966) 1 *Is. L.R.* 513, at p. 523 and n.29.

Chapter II

JUSTIFYING AND DEFINING AN EXPANDED RIGHT TO PRENATAL CARE - THE MEDICAL EVIDENCE AND LEGAL PARAMETERS

To this point we have considered the legal actions available to the unborn child, its parents and other survivors in the event of negligent or delictual prenatal or preconception injuries. Two characteristics typified all these actions – the goal is compensation (of the child and/or its survivors) not prenatal protection, and the actions can only be brought once the child is born alive and viable, or (in the case of actions for wrongful death) has died.

In the first section of this Chapter the medical data will be summarized concerning the substances, acts and omissions which put the unborn child at serious risk. These prenatal threats to unborn health argue for the need to expand the law beyond providing only for postnatal compensation. In the second section of this Chapter we will propose in general terms what should be the content and scope of a right to prenatal care and protection, and address the contentious but inescapable problem of whether the mother-to-be should be included with those who have duties of care to her unborn child.

The medical data as to the vulnerability of the fetus has laid to rest older notions that the fetus was completely isolated from environmental harms, and spent its gestational period in protected bliss in the maternal womb. Not only was that never the case, but in our times there are man-made substances hazardous to the fetus which did not even exist a few years ago, or at least were not as widely used. Radiation is but one example.

It was the bombing of Nagasaki and Hiroshima which provided the strongest evidence to that point in time that environmental factors and substances are a major cause of congenital malformation. It was also that tragic event which therefore did the most to encourage research in this area. As we will indicate, there are now a vast number of chemical, physical and biological hazards to which men and women (and the fetus) are exposed daily in both the home and the workplace. Given those dangers, the need for effective legal protection of fetal health during the gestation period has become urgent.

1. *The fetus at risk - the medical data*

i) *Defects and deformities*

Brief reference should be made at the outset to the significance of the stages and development of the unborn child during its nine month gestational period. Directly related to these stages is the important distinction to be made between what are referred to as "structural defects" and "congenital deformities".[122] It is already in the earliest stages of pregnancy, especially during the first trimester, that the structural foundations of the various organs are established. It is also in this first trimester that the stages of embryonic differentiation take place. The significance of all this is that injury to the fetus in this differentiating and foundational stage is likely to be far more serious and permanent in effects than at later stages. Fetal abuse or neglect at this point is likely in other words to cause structural defects.

It is in this critical stage that the unborn child is most vulnerable. Environmental influences such as drugs or alcohol, which may cause only minor and temporary harm

---

[122] On this point and distinction and points to follow, see: J.WARKANAY and H. KALTER, "Congenital Malformations", (1961) 265 *N.E.J.M.* 1046; B. PATTEN, "Varying Developmental Mechanisms in Teratology", (1957) 19 *Pediatrics* 734; W.A. BOWES, "Obstetrical and Infant Outcome: A Review of the Literature", in W.A. BOWES, et al., *The Effects of Obstetrical Medication on Fetus and Infant*, Society for Research in Child Development, Monograph Series No. 137, 1970.

when the organs are developed, may do serious and permanent damage while the structures themselves are being established. It is essentially this fact which argues for the availability and use of appropriate anticipatory and protective legal mechanisms, if necessary and justified, already in the early stages of pregnancy. It is also the reason why the traditional point at which the law in some cases and jurisdictions begins to take an interest in the unborn child, namely at the time of viability, is no longer justified in view of present medical knowledge. By that time the period of greatest vulnerability has often long passed.

It is also concerning these earliest stages that medical knowledge about the effects of many acts, omissions or substances is most uncertain. Thanks to continuing research and medical experience, knowledge about the causes and effects of various acts, omissions and substances is expanding continuously.

It may also be appropriate at this point to indicate what the major medical theories have to say about the "mechanics" of prenatal defects and deformities. One of these theories of causation has identified *interferences with the fetal oxygen supply* as the mechanism whereby many injurious acts and substances cause prenatal anomalies.[123] These anomalies range all the way from fetal and neonatal death, to cerebral palsy and a large number of behavioural disorders. Another theory of causation applicable in some instances is that of the *developmental arrest theory*.[124] What this means essentially is that various maternal stresses during pregnancy cause congenital defects of varying severity by arresting the normal

---

[123] This theory was largely the outcome of research by Pasamanick. See, LILIENFELD and PASAMANICK, "Association of Maternal and Fetal Factors with the Development of Mental Deficiency", (1955) 159 J.A.M.A. 155.

[124] This theory now widely accepted, is often associated with the writings and research of Ingalls some years ago. See for example, T. INGALLS, "Causes and Prevention of Developmental Defects", (1956) 161 J.A.M.A. 1047. A somewhat similar explanation of the mechanisms of prenatal injuries is that which Warkany and others referred to as the theory of "borderline insult". See, J. WARKANY, "Etiology of congenital Malformations", (1947) 2 Adv. Ped. 1.

development of a particular organ or function. While these theories each have their various promotors and adherents, for the most part they are not mutually exclusive and the etiology of various prenatal anomalies are sometimes best explained by one mechanism, sometimes by the other, sometimes by a combination of both.

A last preliminary consideration is that of the importance of the hereditary make-up and predispositions of unborn children. It is well known that no two unborn children will be equally harmed by exposure to the same substance, act or omission. One of the reasons is that each fetus, as each child and adult, is differently predisposed, differently vulnerable. Birth defects and deformities may sometimes be the result of environmental factors, sometimes the result of hereditary factors, and sometimes a combination of both. While for purposes of determining responsibility in postnatal actions for prenatal injury, this can sometimes lead to serious difficulties in determining causality (and therefore responsibility), certain amounts of some substances and certain acts or omissions are predictably likely to be harmful to unborn children no matter what their individual hereditary predisposition.[125]

---

[125] The difficulties involved in establishing causality for prenatal injuries are, however, real and important. To deny legal relief to the child injured as the result of prenatal negligence would of course be unfair. But it could merely be transferring an injustice from the injured child to other parties to award damages to prenatally injured children when the evidence advanced to establish causality is inadequate. Especially in the context of this study, arguing as it does that the scope of duties owed to unborn children should be considerably enlarged, and the circle of debtors or those with such duties considerably widened, it is doubly important to promote adequate and fair standards for establishing causality-at-law. There is some reason to fear that potential defendants are at an unfair disadvantage in actions for for prenatal injury.

Space limitations preclude a detailed exploration of this complex issue. As well, this writer has already explored this issue at some length in an earlier (unpublished) paper, "Devising Fairer Tests for Proving Prenatal Negligence in Court", Institute of Comparative Law, McGill University, March, 1983.

A very brief summary of several points made in that paper might be in order at this point. The mere "possibility" of a causal relationship between an act (or omission) and injury is already in principle

In what follows in this and subsequent sections, three aspects are of particular interest. First of all, emphasis will be put on potentially harmful acts and omissions by mothers-to-be, rather than by third parties. Not because pregnant women are the only potential wrongdoers; of course they are not. The interest in mothers-to-be lies in the fact that nature has equipped, burdened or blessed them more than any other party with the capacity to do good or ill for their unborn children. As well, the duty and liability of pregnant women towards their unborn children remains an unresolved and

---

excluded by the rules of evidence on grounds of insufficiency of evidence. A standard based on "possible", "could" or "might" would encourage speculation and conjecture on the part of expert witnesses, juries and judges. But even if the rule already is that testimony as to causality should meet the "probability" level of certainty, the rule remains at too general a level to be applicable to the reliability of the medical / scientific theories of causation being relied on by expert witnesses and underlying their testimony. The "probability" rule, at least in the prenatal injury context, may need to be made more explicit and used more rigorously.

As long as a qualified witness expresses his testimony in terms of sufficient certainty, that assurance could be enough to lead to a finding against the defendant, no matter how invalid or un-tested the scientific premises on which that testimony is based. There is no rule at present which requires those premises themselves to be weighed.

Montreal Tramways Co. v. *Léveillé* may well be an instance of a decision rendered against a defendant on the basis of a medical theory of causation (in this case regarding club feet) which was largely un-tested and unreliable. The decision relied to a large extent on the use of presumptions. But the use of presumptions regarding causality (permitted by articles 1238 and 1242 of the Civil Code), were not intended to allow the plaintiff to escape the necessity of establishing a link of causality between defendant's act and his injury. There are grounds for concluding about the *Léveillé* decision, that the decision was based more on conjecture than reasonable probability.

In our view the American decision in *Puhl* v. *Milwaukee Auto Ins. Co., loc. cit., supra,* n.57 proposed a useful refinement of the probability test for application to medical theories of causation. Essentially that court proposed that unless a theory of medical causality is "*generally accepted*" by the relevant medical sciences, or is (in other words) acceptable to "*the consensus of medical opinion*", the opinions of experts based on them in court will be classified as only conjecture. Another proposal, somewhat more lenient and perhaps more equitable, is that the medical theory on which a case is based must be acceptable to a "*recognized school of scientific thought*". (For this latter proposal, see LINTGEN, *op. cit., supra,* no.58, at pp. 599-600.

challenging issue for law.[126] A second focus will be that of the similarity and continuity between unborn children and born children in the matter of vulnerabilities, needs and the effects of certain acts, omissions and substances. The stronger the link between unborn and born child in those respects, the stronger the case for similar legal protections for both. A third concern is the need to document the health and developmental effects on the unborn of acts or omissions not presently seen as being within the scope of even actions for prenatal injury.

ii) *Drugs*

It has been observed that given the vast increase in the use of prescription drugs by women, "...the fetus is potentially at greater risk from well intentioned medicaments than from the vicissitude of pregnancy and delivery".[127] The unborn is most vulnerable to the toxic effects of drugs early in the pregnancy, in which period even small amounts of any drug, even common over-the-counter ones such as aspirin can sometimes be harmful.[128] It has been reported that in the United Kingdom, 82% of pregnant women take prescription drugs during pregnancy, and 65% take various amounts of non-prescription drugs and other medicaments.[129] Occasional

---

In "Devising Fairer Tests... " *supra*, this writer examined a number of complementary mechanisms and made proposals in this context as well, partly with a view to obtaining a more objective and reliable picture regarding medical theories of causation. One mechanism was the use of court-appointed expert testimony. Another was the admission of medical tests as independent evidence.

126 The issue of maternal duty and liability will be addressed directly in a subsequent section.

127 BOWES, "Obstetrical and Infant Outcome: A Review of the Literature", *op. cit., supra*, n.122 at p.4.

128 See T. VERNEY, *The Secret Life of the Unborn Child*, Collins, Toronto, 1981, at p. 94. It is now known that the unborn child's brain is extremely sensitive to drug-induced imbalances in a blood waste known as bilirubin. Drugs can further inhibit the function of the still immature and inefficient liver of the unborn child, inhibiting the release of bilirubin and leading to excessive meonatal jaundice. Excessive jaundice can lead to an illness known as kernicterus which can produce permanent and serious brain disorders. On this point, see, R. GOTS and B. GOTS, *Caring for Your Unborn Child* (3rd Ed.) Bantam Books N.Y. 1981, at p. 82.

129 U.K. Law Commission, *Report, op. cit., supra*, n.61, at p.7.

taking of over-the-counter drugs could hardly be considered to put the unborn child at serious risk. But it does not seem farfetched to suggest that the excessive, careless and continual use of these drugs and medicines, in view of now generally available warnings about the risks of such habits to the unborn child, could constitute maternal breach of duty or obligation if established that such excesses could cause fetal defects.

There is little doubt or debate about the fact that once a drug is found to be a teratogenic agent (that is, one which causes gross structural defects), a duty is imposed upon physicians not to prescribe and advise it. But it is generally thought that there is no similar legal duty on pregnant women not to use it, an issue discussed below.[130]

As for specific prescription drugs known to be harmful, thalidomide is an obvious example, but there are many others which already do or possibly should fall into this category of teratogenic agents. Stilboestrol, or Diethylstilbestrol (DES), a drug once prescribed to pregnant women likely to miscarriage, can cause vaginal cancer later in adolescent daughters. Progestin, prescribed to treat those likely to spontaneously abort may cause the female fetus to become masculinized. Anti-convulsant drugs can cause cleft palates. Aminopterin, used to treat cancer, can cause serious congenital anomalies of the cranium and central nervous system. Some drugs show their harmful effects on children only months or years after their pregnant mothers took them. DES, referred to above, is an example.

Non-medical drugs can also do serious harm to the unborn and newborn if used to excess during pregnancy. Apart from having traumatic withdrawal problems after birth, newborns born of heroin addicted mothers may also have serious

---

[130] To date it apears that no pregnant woman who might have taken such drugs carelessly after being cautioned by her physician or against that physician's advice has been held liable for prenatal injury to her unborn child. Much legal opinion is against allowing maternal liability for prenatal injury, and in at least one jurisdiction (the United Kingdom) it is expressly excluded in the relevant statute. The pros and cons of maternal duties and liability regarding the health of their unborn children will be considered below. (see pp. 91-100).

behavioural problems for some time after birth. A large proportion of "methadone babies" are premature, stunted in development and have very serious respiratory difficulties and problems such as jaundice. In 1977 it was estimated that in the United States there was a fifteen to twenty percent rise in the number of infants born with drug addiction, approximately 800 (known) addicted infants being born to addicted mothers in New York City alone each year.[131]

Another example of a possibly serious effect of maternal drug addiction during pregnancy is the new and growing fear that newborns born of drug-addicted mothers with a particular virus infection, can induce in their unborn children what is referred to as an acquired immune deficiency syndrome (AIDS). Some of the resulting symptoms in the newborn child are: a failure to thrive, a recurrent infection, and interstitial pneumonia. In several cases, newborns so afflicted have died.[132]

iii) *Alcohol*

Alcohol, as well, can do serious harm to the unborn, harm which will in some cases amount to a permanent disability or defect. It is estimated that a pregnant woman's consumption of over two ounces of alcohol daily risks fetal alcohol syndrome (FAS) in the unborn child.[133] Among the possible symptoms of FAS are mental retardation, hyperactivity, heart murmur

---

[131] See V. FONTANA and D. BESHAROV, *The Maltreated Child* (3rd Ed.) Charles C. Thomas, Springfield, 1977, at p. 24.

[132] See A. RUBENSTEIN, *et al.*, "Acquired Immunodeficiency ... in Infants Born to Promiscuous and Drug-Addicted Mothers", (1983) 249 *J.A.M.A.* 2350. See also, J. OLESKE, *et al.*, "Immune Deficiency Syndrome in Children", (1983) 249 *J.A.M.A.* 2345.

[133] See, "The Fetal Alcohol Syndrome: Alcohol as a Teratogen", (1978) 11 *Drug Abuse and Alcoholism Newsletter*, 4

and facial deformities such as a small head or low-set ears.[134] It has been claimed that FAS is the third most common cause of mental retardation in Canada (after Down's Syndrome and spina bifida), and a medical geneticist at Queen's University has maintained that:

> ...in the long run, fetal alcohol syndrome will be a much bigger tragedy than thalidomide because not as much is being done to stop it.[135]

In the United States the U.S. Department of Health and Human Sciences has estimated that severe birth defects caused by alcohol occur in as many as one in 600 babies.[136] As for Canada, researchers who recently completed a two year study at Saskatoon's Alvin Buckwold Centre have concluded that the figures are similar for Canada, and that with an average Canadian yearly birth rate of 370,000, at least 600 new FAS babies are produced in this country each year.[137]

A recent report by a Committee of the U.S. National Academy of Sciences, National Research Council, concluded:

> Alcohol is a dangerous drug, not only for the mothers but also for their babies. Mothers should be cautioned against excessive alcohol consumption at any time in pregnancy. Women who are considering a pregnancy or are doing nothing actively to prevent one should avoid excessive alcohol intake at any time.[138]

---

134 VERNY, *op.cit., supra,* n.128, at p.92. Verny also notes that the United States National Institute of Alcohol Abuse and Alcoholism estimates that six or more strong drinks a day can cause the full range of deformities associated with FAS, and that the chances of the child being born with a serious defect are in the order of 50%.

135 *Globe and Mail*, February 17, 1983, at p.12. The medical geneticist quoted in the news report is Dr. Patrick McLeod.

136 *Ibid*.

137 *Ibid*.

138 "Alcohol a hazard during pregnancy", *Globe and Mail*, December 9, 1982, at p.18.

Finally, research at the University of Nebraska Medical Center suggests that infants born with FAS (or other abnormalities resulting from the ingestion of some drugs in excessive amounts) may predispose those children to cancer 10 - 20 years later.[139]

iv) *Cigarettes, exposure to infectious diseases, inadequate maternal diet*

Excessive maternal cigarette smoking is also hazardous to the health of the unborn child, both before birth and after birth.[140] As with drugs and alcohol, the greater the amount of intake, the greater the risk of harm. It has been estimated for example that a woman who smokes two packages a day is probably seriously risking her child's health. By cutting the supply of oxygen in the blood, the excessive smoker can slow the unborn child's growth, cause the birth of children who are small and in poor physical condition, many of whom by about the age of seven will have reading and learning difficulties and/or other psychological disorders. Some recent research at the Children's Hospital of Winnipeg suggests that children of mothers who smoked during pregnancy may suffer more severe heart attacks in later life than children of non-smoking mothers.[141]

Another source of potentially serious harm to fetal health is a pregnant woman's untreated infectious disease. Modern medicine has demonstrated that maternal infections during

---

[139] See, "Fetal Alcohol Syndrome May Increase Cancer Risk", (1983) N.S. 23 Am. Pharm. 8.

[140] See, J. FRAZIER, *et al.*, "Cigarette Smoking and Prematurity: A Prospective Study", (1961) 81 *Am. J. Obstet. Gynec.* 988; J. E. MURPHY, "The Effect of Age, Parity, and Cigarette Smoking on Baby Weight", (1971) 111 *Am. J. Obstet. Gynec.* 22. I.B. TAGER, *et al.*, "Effect of parental cigarette smoking on the pulmonary function of children", (1979) 110:15 *Am. J. Epidemiol.*

[141] "Smoke Harms Child's Heart, Doctor Warns", *Globe and Mail*, April 15, 1983, at p.14. Another recent study suggests as well that even if the pregnant woman herself does not smoke, smoking by other members in the home or environment exposes that child to an increase of a chemical by-product of tobacco smoke harmful to the fetus, namely thio-dyanate. See, S. BOTTOMS, *et al.*, "Maternal Passive Smoking and Fetal Serum Thiocyanate Levels", (1982) 144 *Am. J. Obstet. Gynec.* 787.

pregnancy such as, syphilis, measles, smallpox, chicken pox and influenza can all have serious teratogenic effects on the unborn child.[142] Maternal syphylis for example can cause mental retardation and congenital deafness in the unborn. It was recently reported by an epidemiologist at Health and Welfare Canada that in 1981 a number of babies were born with herpes contracted from their infected mothers during pregnancy.[143] If contracted before birth it is most commonly passed to the babies through direct contact with the mother's infected genital tract during birth. The study therefore recommends that if a mother has a positive herpes culture when ready to give birth, the baby should be delivered by caesarean section.

Still another source of potential harm to the fetus and child is that of inadequate maternal diet during pregnancy. Maternal diet can affect the health of the unborn child both directly (by the transmission of nutriment), and indirectly insofar as the effects on maternal health of a poor diet eventually influence the health of the unborn child as well. While there is much yet to be learned about this particular form of health threat, it has now been establised for example that a low protein diet by pregnant women can cause mental deficiency in children, and that chronic maternal malnutrition can induce premature labour, toxemia and other complications.[144]

---

[142] See, M. DESMOND, *et al.*, "The Relation of Maternal Disease to Fetal and Neonatal Morbidity and Mortality", (1961) 8:2 *Ped. Clin. N. Am.* 421, 423-24; POTTER, "Placental Transmission of Viruses", (1957) 74 *Am. J. Obstet. Gynec.* 505.

[143] "Herpes Disease Found in 16 Babies in '81", *Ottawa Citizen*, December 9, 1982, at p. 42; "Sexual Disease Epidemic Alarms Canadian Doctors", *Ottawa Citizen*, December 6, 1982, at p. 1.

[144] See for instance, W. TOMPKINS, *et al.*, "The Underweight Patient As An Increased Obstetric Hazard", (1955) 69 *Am. J. Obstet. Gynec.* 114; J. WARKANAY, "Congenital malformation Induced by Maternal Dietary Deficiency", (1955) 13 *Mutr. Rev.* 289.

It may not be unreasonable in view of these consequences of various transmissible maternal infections, to impose a legal duty on pregnant women to take available and reasonable steps to cure or protect their unborn children from these infections if known, to ensure an adequate maternal diet, and to be held liable for resulting injury if those steps are not taken.

v) *Workplace hazards*

In considering workplace hazards, it should be noted at the outset that the unborn child is not the only party at risk from the various substances and dangers to be referred to in this section. Working women themselves whether pregnant or not, are at risk in various ways when exposed to these same hazards, as are men as well. One way in which men and women are at risk when exposed to various chemical and other hazards, concerns their reproductive health - their ability to perform sexually, their ability to conceive healthy children, and the health of their reproductive organs. In the matter of their reproductive health, men and women excessively exposed to various hazards can for example become victims of the process known as "mutagenesis". What this means essentially is that exposure to these substances causes a change in the genetic material of genes or chromosomes, leading for instance to the sperm or ovum not being able to achieve fertilization. This same genetic change can also lead to spontaneous abortion or death of the fetus *in utero*, or serious structural defects in the child.

Another result for men and women workers exposed to various workplace hazards is increased incidence of cancer, including cancer of the reproductive organs. In such cases the process triggered by the hazards is that of "carcinogenesis".

But our concern here is mainly with the effects of workplace hazards on the unborn child, and therefore with the process of "teratogenesis" - the adverse development of the fetus itself in response to various environmental conditions. We have already examined some of these teratogenic hazards in what precedes, but now we will briefly consider still other dangers, now in the context of the workplace.

It is generally thought that in Canada at least three to four percent annually of all newborns are born with visible handicaps of one sort or another. The figure probably rises to something in the order of ten percent if one includes those born with physical or mental handicaps or developmental problems which only appear months or years after birth. An additional ten to fifteen percent of all pregnancies result in stillbirths or miscarriages.[145] There are no exact or even approximate figures as to what percentage of newborn disabilities are caused by workplace hazards, and there probably never will be given the remaining information gaps and the inherent complexities in making such determinations.[146] But it is increasingly thought that the workplace context accounts for a sizable number of newborn anomalies of various kinds, and that not enough efforts have yet been made either to study those causes or to provide adequate protections. One recent study observed that,

> ... the medical and scientific communities have made few efforts to link the incidence of miscarriages, stillbirths, birth defects, neonatal deaths or other reproductive problems with parental work histories. While public and professional interest in prenatal care for pregnant women appears to be extensive, the focus is primarily on life style, education and counselling for the expectant mother, and virtually ignores the effect of daily work conditions.[147]

---

[145] N. CHENIER, *Reproductive hazards at Work*, Canadian Advisory Council on the Status of Women, Ottawa, (1982) at p.9. See also, B.K. TRIMBLE and J. H. DOUGHTY, "The Amount of Hereditary Disease in Human Populations", (1974-75) 38 *Ann. Hum. Gen.* at p. 199.

[146] One of the many types of hazard about which there remains a general lack of information as to health effects is that of chemicals. In 1976 for example it was estimated that of the more than 400,000 chemical products used in the world to that date (and the number is growing continuously), only 13,000 had been examined and classified by the United States National Institute for Occupational Safety and Health (NIOSH), and only 400 were covered by U.S. occupational health standards. See, health and Welfare Canada, *Occupational Health in Canada - Current Status*, Ottawa, 1977, at p. 10.

[147] *Ibid.*

The workplace hazards of concern to us may be divided into three main groups - chemical, physical and biological.[148] Though the subject is a massive one, we must necessarily be brief and selective.

a) *Chemical hazards*

A large number of chemicals in the workplace are particularly hazardous, not only to men and women workers but to the unborn child. They can invade the body of men and women for example by ingestion, inhalation or absorption through the skin.

One such group of chemicals are *anaesthetic gases*, to which those in a number of occupations are potentially exposed on a regular basis. Among those so exposed are health care workers in hospitals and dental clinics, as well as those working as veterinary surgeons or assistants. Female workers exposed to excessive amounts of anaesthetic gases bear a higher than average number of children with congenital anomalies, and the children of male anaesthetists have a higher rate of birth defects than do other medical personnel not so exposed.

Another hazardous chemical is *benzene*, to which are exposed those making for example solvents, plastics, detergents, paints and petroleum. The fetus of pregnant women over-exposed to benzene develop various birth defects and have a higher incidence of leukemia. *Lead* is still another extremely hazardous workplace chemical. Both male and female workers develop various reproductive disorders, and the effects on fetuses of over-exposed parents can be stillbirth, neonatal death and mental retardation. Over-exposure of parents and the fetus to *mercury* can lead to severe fetal brain damage, mental retardation, and miscarriages. As for *pesticides*, to which are exposed for example farmers and those

---

[148] In what follows regarding workplace hazards and their effects on the unborn child, information has been drawn largely from two recent sources. One is the study by CHENIER, *op. cit., supra*, n.145, pp. 11-35. The other is the study produced by the Commission de la santé et de la sécurité du travail du Québec, *Les conditions de travail et la santé de la travailleuse enceinte de l'enfant à naitre et de l'enfant allaité*, Québec, 1982.

involved in their manufacture, these too can cause chromosomal changes in parents or potential parents, and miscarriages and birth defects to the fetus. *Vinyl chloride* is a particularly hazardous chemical to which are exposed those who work in its production or the production of the many products which use it. For the fetus, over-exposure of its mother-to-be can lead to fetal death or birth defects, and a greater than average risk of cancer.

b) *Physical hazards*

There are a number of physical hazards in the workplace potentially hazardous to the unborn child and to male and female workers. One of these is *ionizing radiation*, to which are exposed for example those who work in the atomic industry, dental workers and hospital employees. The developing fetus is particularly vulnerable to this hazard, and as a result of over-exposure is susceptible to death *in utero*, mental retardation, various birth defects and a greater likelihood of various cancers, especially leukemia. Another physical hazard is that of *non-ionizing radiation*. To this danger are exposed for instance pilots and flight attendants and health care workers. The fetus resulting may be retarded and can have other birth defects such as Down's Syndrome.

Noise and vibration constitute still another potential workplace hazard. The number of workers exposed to potentially dangerous levels of both is of course extremely large - it would include construction workers, assembly-line workers, garment workers, machinists and many others. Both male and female workers can be affected in their reproductive health, and the fetus as well is at risk, especially of miscarriage and perinatal mortality.

Another physical hazard, albeit a highly controversial one is that of *VDTs* (video display terminals). Though tests made of them for both ionizing and non-ionizing radiation have not detected dangerous levels of either, there continues to be a suspicion in many quarters that either the standards established are arbitrary or that standard monitoring equipment is inadequate to properly measure dangerous levels of radiation. Many health problems in users of VDTs and some reports of higher than average birth abnormalities in children born to users,[149] strongly suggest that real health dangers may exist both for workers who use VDTs for long periods and for the fetus so exposed. Given the large and fast-growing number of people who use them (100,000 according to one estimate in 1980),[150] there is an urgent need to develop still more sensitive testing methods, and better protections for workers.

c) *Biological hazards*

A last group of workplace hazards can be classified as *biological*. They exist in various forms, especially as contagious human diseases, fungi from vegetation and as harmful dusts. Workers can be exposed to them in a wide variety of ways and contexts, and very many of them are potentially harmful both to male and female workers and to the unborn child. *Chicken pox* is one such hazard, to which parents, day-care workers and pediatric nurses for example can be exposed. For the unborn child affected results may include skeletal defects, heart defects and a higher incidence of neonatal death. *Hepatitis* is another such hazard, an infection to which laundry workers, lab workers and kidney dialysis workers for instance are potentially exposed. For the fetus the risks if infected are many: miscarriage, prematurity, jaundice and an increased death rate. *Herpes* is still another such threat for the unborn child. As well as fetal death, one of the other dangers if affected is that of damage to the central nervous system. *Rubella, syphilis and tuberculosis* are still other biological workplace hazards with potentially serious dangers to the health of the fetus.

---

[149] See for example, "Work conditions Probed at Star as Defects Found in Four Employees' Babies", *Globe and Mail*, July 23, 1980, p.5.

[150] L. BLACK, "A Worrying case of the VDTs", (July 28, 1980) *MacLean's*, at pp. 42-43.

2. *The right to prenatal care defined and delimited*

Enough has been noted to this point about the hazards to which unborn children are exposed to establish that during gestation they have *needs*, specifically needs for care and protection. But do they have a *right* to that care and protection, not just a moral right to it but a legal right? And if they do have such a legal right, what ought to be the content, intensity and scope of that right? Who ought to be the debtors, have the duties, be the claimees with respect to such a right of the unborn child? These are the questions to be addressed in this section.

i) *From interests to (legal) rights*

It is arguable that the unborn child does indeed qualify as a right-holder of the *right* to prenatal care and protection, rather than just an entity with a *need* for that care and protection. In our view the strongest argument for the unborn child's right to prenatal care is one already referred to earlier -- the essential continuity between the child in its unborn and born states. But there are other related arguments which by analogy could also be used to support such a right. One of these is what could be called the "rights based upon interests" principle, used by Feinberg in discussing future generations.[151]

Whereas rights normally belong to competent adults, others can have rights as well. Children are acknowledged to have (legal) rights, since they can be represented, and the unborn child as well is acknowledged to have rights in that his interests can be represented by others for the purposes discussed earlier. Normally one should be able to instruct personally one's representative to be said to have a right, but children, incompetent adults and unborn children are all acknowledged to have rights though they cannot personally instruct those representatives.

---

151 J. FEINBERG, "The Rights of Animals and Unborn Generations", in, *Social Ethics - Morality and Social Policy*, T.A. Mappes and J.S. Zembaty, editors, McGraw-Hill, New York 1977, 350, at p. 356.

In other words, it is arguable that only those qualify as right-holders who have (or can have) interests. This is the view and analysis of rights compellingly argued by Feinberg, who maintains that this is so for two reasons. The first is that a right-holder must be capable of being represented, and it is impossible to represent a being that has no interests, and the second is because a right-holder must be capable of being a beneficiary in his own person. A being without interests is one incapable of being harmed or benefited, notes Feinberg.

Though Feinberg does not specifically apply the "interest principle" to the unborn child, he does apply it and grant rights to a class of beings not yet even in existence, namely, future generations. In this writer's view the same reasoning is even more applicable to unborn children and specifically to the right to care and protection. He writes about future generations:

Given that the unborn child can have no interests once born greater than their life and health, the "rights based upon interests" principle would appear to allow the conclusion that the unborn child does have a right to the protection of its life and health even before birth. Not to provide that right and appropriate protections of it would be invading now an interest all unborn children are "sure to have when they come into being".

> It is not their temporal remoteness that troubles us so much as their indeterminacy their present facelessness and namelessness ... Still, whoever these human beings may turn out to be, and whatever they may reasonably be expected to be like, they will have interests that we can affect, for better or worse, right now. That much we can and do know about them. The identity of the owners of these interests is necessarily obscure, but the fact of their interest- ownership is crystal clear, and that is all that is necessary to certify the coherence of present talk about their rights ... the vagueness of the human future does not weaken its claim on us in the light of the nearly certain knowledge that it will, after all, be human ... The rights that future generations certainly have against us are contingent rights: the interests they are sure to have when they come into being ... cry out for protection from invasions that can take place now.[152]

---

152 *Id.*, at p. 358.

Clearly this right to prenatal care cannot be absolute. The rights of other parties will often be in competition with it and must be balanced against it. As we will discuss later, one of those obvious parties is its mother-to-be, and one of her rights is the (also not absolute) right to abortion.

But the right to prenatal care we propose should be seen as inhering in the unborn child itself, not a "derivative right" in the parents or anyone else. For the legal right to lie truly with that unborn child, he must be acknowledged to have juridical personality from the moment the right exists. Gray is of course correct to note that:

> ... it is not only person which is protected from harm; property is protected, so also are parts of the body. So finding a duty upon others not to harm an unborn need not imply a right in the unborn nor his personhood, but only a right in his family.[153]

But it is our contention that *not* to acknowledge juridical personality (subject to the resolutory condition of live and viable birth)[154] would be to leave the unborn child and his interests in a most prejudicial position. Unless "armed" with juridical personality as the basis of his right to care and protection, the unborn child would be (as is now the case) unable to compete on a more or less equal basis with other parties with whom his needs and rights may be in conflict. They would be legal persons and he would remain more or less at the mercy of their ethics, whims or compassion. That would hardly constitute a basis on which to build the needed legal protections to promote his life-long health.

---

153 C. GRAY, "The Notion of Person for Medical Law", (1981) 11 *R.D.U.S.*, 341, at p. 371.

154 See, *supra*, n.20, and *infra*.

Our thesis is then that the unborn child's interest in and right to prenatal care and protection can only be secure if anchored in the acknowledgment of his juridical personality. A further and crucial factor supporting that thesis is that the unborn child can readily be shown to be essentially similar to and in continuity with the born child as regards vulnerabilities, health needs and development. The data examined in the previous section demonstrating the health effects of various hazards on the unborn child makes that conclusion inescapable. The various birth defects caused by prenatal hazards and abuses extend well beyond the prenatal stage into childhood and sometimes result in permanent life-long handicaps. To begin legal protection and comprehensive obligations towards human beings only at birth, is to assume that the most vulnerable period of all human life, the period during which the foundations of childhood and adulthood health are laid, is discontinuous with and of no influence on those later stages.

If the health needs and vulnerability of the unborn are essentially similar to and continuous with those of the child, then there are in principle no good reasons why the law should not recognize unborn and born children as juridical persons and provide legal protections, remedies, and mechanisms during pregnancy analogous to those already available to children. Some possible mechanisms will be examined and proposed in Chapters III, IV and V.

ii) *Narrowing the "right to be born healthy"*

In establishing the parameters, content and intensity of a right to prenatal care and the duties or obligations to which it gives rise, there are two obvious dangers. The first is to spread the net too widely, to be too general and all-encompassing. Writing of another though related issue (child abuse), Dickens has noted that:

> A paradox of legal definition is that the more comprehensive it appears, the less it may actually permit to be achieved ... All embracing definition may decay into mere description. Courts, especially when asked to intervene in protected human relations such as exist between parents and child ... require precision. The

precisely-sharpened legal scalpel may enter where the blunt-edged hatchet has no access ... A court may therefore treat a broad definition with caution, recognizing that indiscriminate words may not be sufficiently related to the specific incident or person charged.[155]

A number of formulations used in recent years which attempt to capture prenatal health needs within a rights formulation, appear to claim too much and to fall well within the "all-embracing" category referred to by Dickens.

One example is the formula used (and not defined) by Ament, namely, "the right to be well born".[156] He appears to have derived that formulation from another equally imprecise expression found in the American decision of *Smith* v. *Brennan*. In that decision it was stated that: "... justice requires that the principle be recognized that a child has a legal right to begin life with a sound mind and body".[157] Another formulation of this type is that found in the Ontario decision in *Re Brown*, in which the court listed among the basic rights that every child should have: "the right to be born healthy".[158] Yet another example of such a formulation comes from the context of wrongful life actions, examined earlier in this paper. In one wrongful life action the court held that: "The breach of this right may also be said to be tortious to the fundamental right of a child to be born as a whole, functional human being".[159]

The troubling aspects of all those formulations are that they appear to claim too much, and the claim is not specific enough as to the content, the intensity of the obligation and those with duties or obligations arising from the right. In

---

155 B. DICKENS, "Legal Responses to Child Abuse", (1978) 12 *Fam. L. Q.* 1, at p.4.

156 See, M. AMENT, "The Right to be Well born", (Nov. / Dec. 1974) *J. L. Med.* 25.

157 *Smith* v. *Brennan, loc. cit., supra,* n.59 at p. 503.

158 *Re Brown,* (1975) 21 R.F.L. 315 (Ont.), at p.323.

159 *Park* v. *Chessin, loc.cit., supra* n.93 at p. 114.

claiming for the unborn a right to *be* healthy one would in reality be claiming considerably more than is acknowledged for those already born, whether children or adults. Statutes and duties of care make claims to the right to *adequate* health *care* supportable, but not necessarily the right to health itself.

One of the difficulties arises from the use of the word "health" in such formulations. The word does not have an obvious or agreed upon definition, and therefore may not (yet) be a precise enough word used alone (without a qualifier such as "care") upon which to formulate an effective legal right such as the one being examined, proposed and fleshed out in this paper. A notable example of "health" defined in an excessively comprehensive and general manner is the much analyzed and criticized World Health Organization definition: "Health is a state of physical, mental and social well-being and not merely the absence of disease or infirmity".160

Callahan has observed about that definition of health that it clearly suggests:

> ... a conception of "health" which would encompass literally every element and item of human happiness. One can hardly be surprised, given such a vision, that our ways of talking about "health" have become all but meaningless.161

Callahan himself argues that a more acceptable definition of health would limit itself to: "a state of physical well-being". He goes on to add:

> ... that state need not be complete, but it must be adequate, i.e., without significant impairment of function. It also need not emcompass "mental" well-being; one can be healthy, yet anxious, well yet depressed. And it surely ought not to encompass "social well-being", except insofar as that well-being will be impaired by the presence of large scale, serious physical impairments.162

---

160 The World Health Organization's definition of health is the first "principle" of the preamble to the Constitution of the WHO. That Constitution was the outcome of an International Health conference in New York in June and July of 1946, and was signed by 61 nations. Constitution of the WHO, done in New York July 22, 1946, 14 UNTS 185; 4 Bevans 119; T.I.A.S. no. 1808.

161 D. CALLAHAN, "The WHO Definition of Health", (1973) 1:3 *H.C.S.* 77, at p. 80.

162 *Id.*, at p. 87.

With regard to the notion of health operative in a right to prenatal care, we would make it still more restrictive than does Callahan. Once one moves from simply defining health to incorporating it into a right, then one must consider not only what health *is*, but what others must *do* as a result. In other words both the right of the claimant to health and the duty of the claimee to provide it must be included in the concerns and formulation. Assuming (as is the case) that we do not intend to impose on potential right-owers of prenatal care a duty to *be successful* in every case in providing what Callahan calls an "adequate state of physical well-being, without significant impairment of function", then that duty or obligation should be formulated more restrictively than Callahan's definition of health implies.

The duty or obligation flowing from the right to prenatal care should in other words be a duty to *provide* adequate and reasonable prenatal *care* in order to best promote the level of *health* Callahan defines, namely an adequate state of physical well-being, without significant impairment of function. But right-owers would owe the adequate and reasonable care, not the level of health itself. There are, after all, too many factors beyond the control of the parties who could be said to have duties to provide prenatal care, to impose on them a duty to actually achieve a particular level of health in the unborn children to whom they owe a duty, to whom they are debtors of an obligation.

Put into legal terms, the only justifiable "intensity" of a duty or obligation to provide prenatal care is in civil law terms that of diligence, not result, and in common law terms that of the duty to take or provide reasonable care, not to warranty the results.

In the common law context, the best explanation of this duty of reasonable care which in our view should apply to the prenatal period is very possibly still that provided in the 1932 decision in *Donoghue* v. *Stevenson*:

> You must take reasonable care to avoid acts or omissions which you can reasonably foresee would be likely to injure your neighbour.

> Who then, in law, is my neighbour? The answer seems to be - persons who are so closely and directly affected by my act that I ought reasonably to have them in contemplation as being so affected when I am directing my mind to the acts or omissions which are called in question.[163]

In our view the unborn child fits within the class of "neighbour" as defined in that decision. The "definition" of neighbour provided in that decision also tells us which people or professions above all others should have such a duty of care towards the unborn child - doctors, hospital staff, parents and employers would be among those whose acts and omissions inescapably and closely affect unborn children.

In the Civil law context, Crépeau has written in a similar manner about the obligation of diligence or means:

> In such cases the duty of the debtor, whether it be contractual or extra-contractual, is to take the reasonable care and attention which the "bon père de famille" would ordinarily take so as not to cause damage to his neighbours.[164]

An expression of this same obligation of means in the Civil Code is to be found in a.1053 C.C.:

> Every person capable of discerning right from wrong is responsible for the damage caused by his fault to another, whether by positive act, imprudence, neglect or want of skill.

As indicated earlier in the book, the decision in *Montreal Tramways Co. v. Leveillé*[165] has already held that the unborn child fits within the meaning of "another" in that article, for purposes of actions for prenatal injury, if born alive and viable. The thesis of this study is that he should also fit within the meaning of "another" (or of "neighbour" in the common law decision of *Donoghue v. Stevenson*) for purposes of care and protection while still unborn.

---

[163] *Donoghue v. Stevenson*, [1932] A.C. 562, at p. 580.

[164] P.-A. CRÉPEAU, "Liability for Damage Caused by Things", (1962) 40 *Can. Bar. Rev.* 222, at pp. 223, 224. See also, P.-A. CRÉPEAU, "Des régimes contractuel et délictuel de responsabilité civil en droit civil canadien", (1962) 22 *R. du B.* 501.

[165] *Montreal Tramways Co. v. Léveillé, loc, cit., supra.* n.10.

As for the obligation of result, it is, "... a duty to achieve a definite result, for instance an obligation to deliver an object at a particular date and place.[166] A similar definition is the following: "... [l'obligation] pour la satisfaction de laquelle le débiteur est tenue de fournir au créancier un résultat précis fixé à l'avance."[167]

There is a very good reason why an obligation of diligence or a duty of care is appropriate for the obligation to provide prenatal care, for example on the part of hospitals, doctors, parents and employers. It is that this is already recognized in doctrine and jurisprudence, in both common law and Civil law systems, to be the "intensity" of the obligations of a physician to his patient, and of parents to their children. In the case of doctors, this was already affirmed in the 1939 Québec decision of *Nelligan* v. *Clément*, and often reaffirmed since then.[168]

There is every reason to insist that the burden on physicians and parents for example towards the unborn should be *as* onerous as their duties towards their patients or children. But there is no reason at all why that burden towards unborn children should be *more* onerous by positing in the unborn a "right to be born healthy", and thus in the right-owers an obligation of result or undertaking to warranty.

If there is to be a duty of reasonable care in common law terms, or an obligation of diligence or means in Civil law terms, there are important implications as well regarding the burden of proof. Mere proof of injury to the unborn resulting from the defendant's act or omission will not be sufficient to establish (in Common law terms) negligence, or, (in Civil law

---

[166] CRÉPEAU, "Liability for Damages Caused by Things", *op. cit., supra*, n.164, at p.224.

[167] J.-L. BAUDOUIN, *Les Obligations*, Les Éditions Yvon Blais Inc., Cowansville, 1983 at p.34.

[168] *Nelligan* v. *Clément* (1939) 67 B.R. 328. See also, *X v. Mellen* (1957),B.R. 389; *Beausoleil v. Communauté des Soeurs de la Charité de la Providence* (1965), B.R. 37. On the issue of medical responsibility see, P.-A. Crépeau, "La responsabilité médicale et hospitalière", (1960) 20 *R. du B.* 433, at p. 472.

terms) a *prima facie* in-execution or fault. As always in the cases of a duty of care or an obligation of diligence, here too the (unborn) plaintiff would have to prove fault, damage resulting and a causal connection between them. The (unborn) plaintiff would have to *prove* the absence of reasonable care or diligence, a considerably more onerous duty than if what was involved was an undertaking to warranty or an obligation of result.[169]

iii) *Expanding the "right to non negligent acts"*

If it is possible to spread the net of a right to prenatal care too widely, it is equally possible to spread it too narrowly. It is of course the thesis of this study that this is presently the case. In effect what the unborn child now has available to it by way of legal response to negligent injuries during the prenatal period, is only a legal action for *compensation once born alive* for *some* injuries inflicted by *some* third parties.

The other forms of action discussed earlier do not appreciably expand the protection available *to* the unborn child in the prenatal period, or even opportunities for compensation after live birth. The action for *wrongful death* is obviously only available in the event of the unborn child's death, and compensation if provided is to the survivors. Actions for *wrongful birth* usually seek damages for the parents for the birth of an unwanted, usually healthy child, not a birth with defects resulting from prenatal injury. Actions for *wrongful life*, if successful, only seek postnatal compensation, not prenatal protection. As for actions for *preconception injury* to parents, they are essentially reducible to standard actions for prenatal injury.

---

[169] On the other hand, in the Civil law context, because the plaintiff's burden of proof (when the obligation of the debtor is only one of diligence) is sometimes very heavy indeed, there is provision in Civil law for presumptions of law and of fact. These presumptions are covered in articles 1238, 1239 and 1242 of the Civil Code. That they can be applicable in actions for prenatal injury was demonstrated in *Léveillé* in which the court justified the application of a presumption of fact to draw a "reasonable inference" that there was a causal relationship between the accident ot the mother and the child's deformity. The common law doctrine of *res ipsa loquitur* is similar to these presumptions of fact, and could presumably also apply in actions for prenatal injury.

While negligence (in Common law) or delict (in Civil law) clearly include both acts and omissions, the emphasis to date concerning the unborn child has been on *positive* acts of negligence or delict rather than negligent or delictual *omissions*. Undoubtedly this is related to the fact that fetal injuries have been viewed as the indirect "by-products" of negligent acts which *directly* injure the mother-to-be. As noted earlier, the *Congenital Disabilities Act* in the United Kingdom is a clear expression of such thinking which it carries to the extreme in granting to the unborn child only a "derivitive" right to an action for prenatal injury, that is, only if the pregnant woman herself was owed a duty. The "classic" or normative action for prenatal injury therefore presently involves acts such as negligently pushing a pregnant woman from a tram,[170] or injuring a pregnant woman in an auto accident.[171]

But in view of the many health hazards now faced by the unborn child while unborn, and the certain knowledge in many cases that many of these forms of abuse and neglect will cause serious and often life-long injury, there is an urgent need to expand greatly the scope of the rights available to the unborn child. In particular the new emphasis must now be protective and anticipatory rather than just after-the-event and compensatory. Duties and obligations to be included in what we are terming a right to prenatal care should now include not only the *avoiding* of certain acts and exposures during the prenatal period, but also the affirmative *provision* of the basic care and protection needed by the unborn for its adequate health and development.

Failure to exercise reasonable care or diligence in providing for basic needs and avoiding known hazards, could lead to two legal responses. During the prenatal period itself it could trigger anticipatory and protective legal mechanisms to stop further abuse of the unborn child and provide needed care. If born with injuries resulting from negligent exposure of the unborn child to known hazards or from negligent deprivation during pregnancy of something needed for

---

170 For example, *Montreal Tramways Co.* v. *Léveillé, loc,cit., supra,* n.10.

171 For example, *Duval* v. *Séguin, loc, cit., supra,* n.49.

adequate health and development, then the party or parties responsible would be liable for that negligent exposure or deprivation, and such acts or neglects could be added to the expanded scope of actions for prenatal injury.

In the case of *physicians* then, their duty or obligation towards the unborn would not be to prevent or cure all injuries or disabilities, but to exercise reasonable skill, attention and care in the provision of adequate prenatal care, treatment and protection, of both the mother-to-be and her unborn child. Specific duties of physicians towards the unborn children of their pregnant patients would include for example: ensuring that medications provided are known by reliable tests to be safe for both the pregnant woman and her unborn child, informing mothers-to-be about the dietary needs of the unborn child, available prenatal care services, and the hazardous substances and environments to be avoided lest the child be put at serious risk, ensuring that any infectious diseases of the mother hazardous to the unborn child are adequately treated, reporting to child welfare authorities instances of persistent and serious abuse or neglect of an unborn child by a pregnant woman or other party (such as the father-to-be).172

---

172 The proposal that (at least) physicians should have a duty to report the serious and persistent abuse or neglect of unborn children, raises a number of difficult questions, too complex to adequately deal with given space limitations. Most of these questions and issues would be similar to those raised about reporting child abuse generally, and most of the same choices would seem to apply regarding unborn children. These questions are for example, who should report, should they have a legal obligation to report, and what should be reported. Provincial child welfare or child protection legislation generally makes specific provision for the reporting of child abuse. For example article 39 of Quebec's *Youth Protection Act*, R.S.Q. c.P-34.1, provides that *all persons* (child care professionals or lay persons) are *obliged* to report sexual or physical abuses of children; professionals are obliged to report all the other acts or omissions constituting threats to the safety and development of children (as listed in a.38); *all persons may* (not must) report those instances of abuse other than sexual or physical. In all cases the reporter must have a "reasonable belief" that the child's safety or development is compromised.

Ontario's *Child Welfare Act*, R.S.O., 1980, c.66, similarly provides in a.49(2), that professionals and officials are obliged to report any child who they have reasonable grounds to suspect is "abused". All persons have a duty to report any child falling within the definition of "child in need of protection" as defined in a.19.

A *hospital's* duty of care or obligation of diligence towards the unborn would include providing adequate prenatal care, facilities and equipment, skilled and available pediatric personnel and adequate observation of mother and child while in the care of that institution.

As for the *pregnant woman*, her duty of care or obligation of diligence towards her unborn child would include at least the following: taking reasonable precautions to avoid exposing the unborn child to infectious diseases (by avoiding contact with people, places or objects she knows or should know are likely to infect her, by reporting her infectious diseases to her doctor and following the treatment advised), avoiding excessive ingestion of or exposure to the various environmental hazards listed and discussed earlier, ensuring that her diet and nourishment are adequate for her own health and that of her unborn child. She would *not*, however, be obliged to produce a perfect baby!

Whereas the Quebec statute contains no sanction for non-reporting, the Ontario *Child Welfare Act* provides that a professional or official may be subject to a fine for failure to report an abused child, in a.94(1)(f)(ii).

It is arguable that in the specific context of reporting abuses of unborn children, the authorized or obligated reporters should be restricted to professionals (i.e. physicians, pharmacists, and others with child care or prenatal care training and duties). Given that in the case of unborn children one is faced with considerably more complex and uncertain causality factors, and no evidence of the effects of abuse visible to the naked eye, the "reasonable grounds" to suspect abuse to an unborn child would seem for the most part to be beyond the competence of the average "lay person". This would lessen the possibilities for frivolous and harmful interferences into the family by neighbours or others. There could perhaps be an exception made of flagrant, obvious and life-threatening abuse to the unborn child.

In this regard, the following caution noted by DICKENS regarding *child* abuse may be even more relevant to the reporting of *unborn* child abuse:

> While the care and vigilance of relatives, neighbours and benign strangers have much to offer the cause of child protection, and are to be both encouraged and protected, it may appear that a systematic legal approach to child abuse cannot give a primacy to reliance upon lay initiative. Child abuse must be rendered identifiable by tests that are meaningful to those with a trained competence in fields of child welfare and protection, and a professional or official duty of care. "Legal Responses to Child Abuse", *op, cit., supra*, n.155 at p.10.

That said, should professionals have a *legal* duty to report unborn child abuse, even if (as in the case of physicians) it may involve the violation of a confidentiality (i.e. towards a pregnant patient)? The provision of child

The duty or obligation of the *father-to-be* towards his unborn child would include at least the following: ensuring that he does not physically abuse the mother-to-be, providing adequate nourishment and health care for both the mother-to-be and unborn child, ensuring that he does not infect the mother-to-be with his infectious diseases, avoiding bringing into the home excessive amounts of any of the hazardous substances referred to earlier.

As for *employers*, it is arguable that they too have duties or obligations towards the unborn children of their female employees. We will consider in some detail in Chapter III some

---

welfare legislation to the effect that professionals have such a duty towards children even if they are linked to the person reported by obligations of professional secrecy, would seem equally arguable in the context of unborn children. In both cases there is the same justification - the protection of a child or unborn child exposed to serious harm or grave risk of harm should be favoured over the protection of confidentiality. The two American cases of *Landeros* v. *Flood*, 131 Cal. Rptr. 69 (1976) and *Tarasoff* v. *Regents of the University of California*, 551 P. 2d 334. could serve as precedents establishing such a duty and preference regarding both children and unborn children. The "good faith" qualification provided for in child welfare legislation, whereby those authorized or obligated to report abuse who do so in "good faith" are protected from civil and criminal liability, could presumably apply regarding the reporting of unborn child abuse as well.

Should such reporting of unborn child abuse be compulsory, with a sanction provided? Though much child welfare or child protection legislation does not provide for sanctions in the event of non-performance of a duty to report, sanctioning non-reporting in both cases may be necessary to have the duty to report taken seriously. Clearly, however, since the goal of such legislation should be primarily that of educating and reinforcing voluntary compliance, sanctions should be applied rarely and carefully. Especially is this so in order not to discourage *self-reporting* by parents aware that they require assistance to prevent further abuse or neglect to a child or unborn child, and are willing to seek it. If prosecution is the only and inevitable reaction to such abuse, then self-reporting would be deterred.

A last concern has to do with what should be reported and what standard of proof will suffice. To avoid harmful and unjustified interference in the family, reporting should be confined to instances when there are reasonable grounds to know or suspect *persistent or serious* abuse of an unborn child. There should be provision for reporting and intervention not only in the event of actual present abuse, but also for anticipatory neglect. The standard of proof for anticipatory neglect, in the event that a case of anticipatory neglect of an unborn child is brought to a court for disposition, should not be the Civil standard but the criminal one. To allow judicial intervention and protection on behalf of an unborn child, the initiating party or agency would have to establish that this unborn child is beyond a reasonable doubt at risk of serious and persistent abuse.

already existing or proposed legal duties towards and protections of unborn children in the workplace. Suffice it to say at this point that given both the control employers have over workplace conditions, and the workplace hazards to the unborn referred to earlier, there is every reason to assign to employers the duty to ensure that workplace conditions are not unduly hazardous to the health of both the adult workers themselves, male and female, and the unborn children of those workers. The obligation should extend to protecting workers against known harms to reproductive health. As indicated earlier, preconception injuries to parents can ultimately lead to serious defects in their offspring.

The fact that the obligations of pregnant women to their unborn children might include avoiding environments (including the workplace) known to put unborn children at serious risk, should not exempt the employer from having the prior and primary obligation to ensure that the workplace is free of such hazards in the first place, or that adequate protection is provided to both male and female workers. Given adequate protection in the workplace, pregnant women employees for example, would not need to exercise the right they should have to refuse to work and to be re-assigned to a workplace safer for their unborn child.

iv) *Expanding the circle of those with duties - the liability of the pregnant mother-to-be*

The previous section listed various potential duties of a pregnant woman towards her unborn child, and simply affirmed the fact that pregnant women *should* have such duties and obligations and be liable for failing to fulfill them. Present legal policy on that point and the various arguments advanced against maternal duties towards unborn children have yet to be considered. To that task we now turn.

It is interesting to note first of all, that the legal debate as to the liability of a pregnant woman towards her unborn child, appears to have taken place to date almost exclusively within

Common law contexts.[173] There appear to be no instances in Québec jurisprudence, doctrine or statutes in which this issue has been raised. On the other hand, there appears to be nothing in the Civil Code or Québec jurisprudence and statutes which would preclude the formulation of an explicit policy providing that pregnant women will have such obligations and liability in the extended sense proposed in this paper. Article 1053 C.C. after all affirms with no restrictions as to debtors that,

> *Every* person capable of discerning right from wrong is responsible for the damage caused by his fault to another... [emphasis added].

As earlier noted, the *Léveillé* decision had already ruled that the unborn child is to be considered as being within the meaning of "another" and therefore within the circle of creditors at least for purposes of maintaining an action for prenatal injury.

In the Civil law context, objections to expanding the circle of debtors as proposed, would have to be policy objections rather than strictly legal objections. That being so, the policy-oriented pros and cons of the discussion which follows now, though situated in the Common law context, would appear to be equally applicable in most respects to Civil law.

The first task is to determine if possible the state of the question in case law and statutes in the various Common law jurisdictions of interest to us - the United States, the United Kingdom and Canada.

The traditional rule in the United States apparently still followed, is that an unemancipated minor child is not allowed to sue a parent for what would otherwise have been tortious

---

[173] There have of course been discussions of the issue at national and international conferences in Civil law jurisdictions. An example of such an interdisciplinary symposium was one arranged in Sweden in 1980 by the Swedish Society of Medical Sciences, entitled, "Who is Responsible for the Unborn Child ?" Contributing to it were physicians, theologians and jurists. It was reported on by G. GIERTZ, "The Rights of the Unborn Child", *Proceedings of the Sixth World Congress on Medical Law*, Ghent, Belgium, 1982.

conduct, a rule essentially based upon a policy that to allow otherwise would threaten the harmony of the family.[174] However, some U.S. courts have opened the door slightly to such suits in several specific circumstances.[175] One American commentator concludes:

> The existing exceptions, together with the possibility that in the future the courts may see fit to discard the rule entirely, will present situations in which there is no substantive obstacle to the child's bringing an action against his mother for prenatal injuries.[176]

But though that commentator and others acknowledge both that the mother's act or omissions constitute the major immediate cause of birth defects, and that there may well be no "substantive obstacle" or legal doctrines opposing maternal liability, they propose a number of policy objections to it. They will be considered below.

As for the United Kingdom, the Law Commission which addressed the issue of maternal liability in some detail, observed in its Report that,

> We recognize that logic and principle dictate that if a mother's negligent act or omission during or before pregnancy causes injury to a fetus, she should be liable to her child when born for the wrong done.[177]

But it nevertheless concluded against allowing liability largely on the grounds that it would risk dispute in the family and such liability would be too onerous on the woman. Despite logic and principle, the Commission stated:

---

[174] See, LINTGEN, *op. cit., supra*, n.58, at p. 583. See also, *Redwine* v. *Adkins*, 339 S.W. 2d 635 (Ky. C.A. 1960); *Hastings* v. *Hastings*, 163 A. 2d 147 (N.J.S.C. 1960); *Parks* v. *Parks*, 135 A. 2d 65 (Penn. S.C. 1957).

[175] One such exception is when the parent's act caused the child's death, as in *Harlan Nat'l Bank* v. *Gross*, 346 S.W. 2d 482 (Ky. C.A. 1961). Another is when the parental misconduct was in the course of vocational and not parental activity, as in *Worrell* v. *Worrell*, 4 S.E. 2d 343 (Va. S.C.A. 1939).

[176] Lintgen, *op. cit., supra*, n.58, at p. 583.

[177] U.K. Law Commission, *Report, op. cit., supra*, n.61 at p. 22.

... we have no doubt at all that in any system of law there are areas in which logic and principle ought to yield to social acceptability and mutual sentiment and that this particular liability lies in such an area.[178]

The Congenital Disabilities (Civil Liability) Act resulting from that Report of the Law commission consequently did not allow claims by minor children against mothers for prenatal injury. The only exception allowed is for the mother's negligent driving of an auto.[179] That exception is based on the existence of a system of complusory auto insurance. Because these claims by the child against its mother will in practice be against the insurance company, resulting dangers of intra-familial disputes would be minimal.

It is worth noting however that the Act imposes no restrictions as to the liability of the father. Presumably, therefore, the father could be liable to his unborn child for prenatal injuries caused by his assault against the mother.

As for Common law Canada, the same traditional rule against mothers' liability for prenatal injuries to the unborn would seem to generally apply. However, the Ontario *Family Law Reform Act* of 1978[180] is an exception to that rule. That Act now includes these sections:

66. No person shall be disentitled from bringing an action or other proceeding against another for the reason only that they stand in a relationship of parent and child.

---

178 *Ibid.*

179 *Congenital Disabilities (Civil Liability) Act, 1976*, loc, cit., supra, n.62, S.2. That section reads:

A Woman driving a motor vehicle when she knows (or ought reasonably to know) herself to be pregnant, is to be regarded as being under the same duty to take care of the safety of her unborn child as the law imposes on her with respect to the safety of other people; and if in consequence of her breach of that duty her child is born with disabilities which would not otherwise have been present, those disabilities are to be regarded as damage resulting from her wrongful act and actionable accordingly at the suit of the child.

180 Now the *Family Law Reform Act*, R.S.O. 1980, C. 152.

67   No person shall be disentitled from recovering damages in respect of injuries incurred for the reason only that the injuries were incurred before his birth.

Wilson has noted that section 67 may apply for example to the situation in which a pregnant woman addicted to heroin or cigarettes gives birth as a result to an unhealthy child.[181] But there appear to be no cases as yet in Ontario where such an issue has been brought before a court. Wilson himself argues against allowing such liability, again on grounds of threat to family unity. As for section 66 and the matter of (born) children, Wilson also notes that at least two courts have already held that wrongdoers will not be relieved of liability for negligence only because the person injured was his or her own child.[182]

We will now consider the policy-oriented objections most frequently made against acknowledging maternal duties and liability to unborn children. A first group of objections is to the effect that to allow such legal duties and liability would be to impose an impossible burden on the mother because it would be equivalent to demanding that she produce perfect babies.

However, on examination it appears that his objection has in mind what we have earlier characterized (and ourselves rejected) as *extreme* claims and demands upon mothers-to-be. Against claims that mothers-to-be should have in effect a duty to more or less warranty their childrens' good health, this objection is strong and justified. Consider for example this claim by Shaw, that an injured child should be able to claim that, ..."its right to be born physically and mentally sound had been invaded."[183]

---

181 J. WILSON, *Children and the Law*, Butterworths, Toronto, 1978, at p.3.

182 See *Deziel* v. *Deziel*, [1953] 1 D.L.R. 651 (Ont. H. C.); *Young* v. *Rankin*, [1934] S.C. 499.

183 SHAW, *op.cit., supra*, n.82, at p. 225.

To this claim Capron responded, with some reason,

> The enforcement of such a rule by the State, through the courts and other agencies of social control, might even lead to unprecedented eugenic totalitarianism.[184]

Annas adds, in a similar vein,

> The most fundamental objection is that there is no 'right to be born physically and mentally sound' and should not be. Such a 'right' could turn into a duty on the part of potential parents and their offspring to make sure that no defective, different or 'abnormal' children are born.[185]

A similar expression of this same fear is to be found in the (U.K.) Law Commission's Report:

> Do smoking and gin-drinking count as negligence in a pregnant mother? Many doctors say that neither tobacco nor alcohol should be taken in a pregnancy. Must the mother follow always the most recently published ante-natal dietary or other regime in order to secure for her child the best possible mental and physical capacity?[186]

But none of these objections to what would be in effect an undertaking to warranty (or an obligation of result in Civil law terms) constitutes an objection to maternal duty and

---

[184] CAPRON, op. cit., supra, n.90 at p. 89.

[185] ANNAS, "Righting the Wrong of 'Wrongful Life'", op. cit., supra, n. 99 at p. 9.

[186] U.K. Law Commission, Report, op.cit., supra, n.61, at p. 22. The argument is in the first instance from the Bar Council in response to the Commission's Working Paper. But the Commission offers the point as one with which it is in total agreement.

This statement is not untypical of many objections to maternal liability (on grounds that it would impose an undue burden on the mother), in that it attempts to trivialize the whole range of potentially harmful maternal acts or omissions by fastening upon relatively minor every-day acts (i.e., "smoking and gin-drinking"). J. FLEMING does much the same when he rejects such liability by noting that, "... otherwise she might be made liable for her *indiscretions* during pregnancy, like excessive smoking, drinking or taking drugs". (*The Law of Torts*, 5th ed., Law Book Co. Ltd; Sydney, 1977, at p. 161). Labelling acts potentially harmful to the unborn child as merely "indiscretions" is an effective, though inaccurate, way of promoting the perception that such (and all other) maternal acts or omissions are by their very nature not really harmful, therefore maternal duties and liability would of course be unjustifiably onerous.

liability within reasonable bounds. It was noted earlier and bears repetition now, that there is indeed no justification for acknowledging in unborn children a "right to be born sound", or for obliging mothers-to-be to keep up with and understand the learned medical journals, or avoid cigarettes and alcohol within reasonable limits. But that said, it is quite another matter to absolve her from all (legal) duties and liability, including that involving the provision of *reasonable and adequate care* and protection.

The latter is after all the burden which most mothers-to-be take on willingly and perform well, without maintaining that it is unfairly onerous. The fashioning of an explicit legal duty and liability in this regard, and even more importantly, anticipatory and protective legal mechanisms for the prenatal period, would only be needed for the small minority of parents unwilling or otherwise unable to provide the minimal level of adequate care.

A second type of objection is a concern for the threat to family unity which might result from the existence of actions by children against parents for prenatal injuries. The Law Commission for example argued that,

> The relationship between mother and disabled child is one of the most stressful that can exist. To add to it a legal liability to pay compensation would be bound to increase the tension already existing between them.[187]

In a certain sense that Commission itself, in its earlier and tentative Working Paper on the same issue, already answered that objection when it originally opted for the opposite position:

> If a child is born with a disability due to his mother's negligent act or omission during pregnancy it seems at first sight socially unacceptable that he should have a cause of action for damages against her. On analysis, however, this situation is no different in principle from the cases where, by her negligence, a mother causes injury to a baby in arms, in which case, as the law stands, a cause of action would lie.[188]

---

187 U.K. Law Commission, *Report, op. cit., supra,* n.61, at p.22.

188 U.K. Law Commission, *Working Paper, op. cit., supra,* n.60, at p. 15.

An interesting version of the rationale behind the view that liability would disrupt family harmony, draws a comparison between the fetus in the womb and a passenger in a car who "assumes the risk". That commentator goes on to say that a person who bestows a benefit - in this case the mother bringing the child into the world - should not be held to the same high standard of care to the child-beneficiary as would a stranger.[189]

Another version of this concern about the disruption of family harmony is a fear that husbands may take unfair advantage of such liability of their wives. That was the point of this statement quoted in the Report of the Law Commission:

> ... it would be cruel to allow such an action against a mother, and even against a father. But the real danger is that it would give a new weapon to the unscrupulous spouse -and there are many. One knows from one's own experience the difficulties in married life which arise when a child is born with even a blemish... The vindictive father might be dissuaded in all but a few cases from seeking to take action on behalf of the child against the mother whom he is seeking to divorce and whom he now hates. But what of the father who is seeking custody of the child or children? An action against the wife for her supposed negligence while carrying the child would be a splendid additional weapon in his armoury...[190]

Several responses to the family harmony concern are possible. To begin with the statement just quoted, there is no denying that in the event of maternal liability some husbands could use the action "unscrupulously" or "vindictively". But that fear alone hardly argues against establishing maternal liability. After all, *any* legal action can be and sometimes is used unjustifiably against another party. And the position advanced in this paper (and in the Report itself) is that the father should also be liable. The wife could therefore also take action vindictively against her husband.

---

[189] LINTGEN, "The Impact of Medical Knowledge on the Law", *op. cit., supra*, n. 58, at p. 584. The same writer does however acknowledge that the driver *could* be liable by statutes in instances of *gross negligence*. Presumably by extending his logic further, he might grant that the mother who injures her unborn child by negligence which could be characterized as "gross", could in fact be held liable as can the driver.

[190] Statement of President of Family Division, Sir George Baker, quoted in U.K. Law Commission, *Report, op. cit., supra*, n.61, at p. 23.

The real test of the justice in establishing a new (or expanded) legal duty or obligation is, after all, the importance we assign to the interests and rights being thereby protected, and ultimately the importance we assign to the party claiming those interests and rights - in this case the unborn child. If the party and rights in question are judged to be worthy of legal protection and compensation when seriously threatened or injured, then a degree of risk that new or expanded liability and actions will sometimes be used vindictively or sometimes threaten family harmony can be tolerated. We do in fact have that tolerance *vis à vis* other legal actions because the rights and persons thereby protected appear to make the risk worthwhile.

There is some evidence available that the fundamental objection of many of those who oppose the maternal duty and liability in question, is to the status and importance of the unborn child as a being separate from its mother, with its own distinct and legitimate needs, interests and right. When that fundamental starting point is not acknowledged, then of course it follows logically that the unborn child cannot be allowed to compete with the rights and interests of others, and objections (such as risk to family harmony) to imposing duties and liability on other parties vis à vis that unborn child consequently become much stronger. The assumption would appear to be that the unborn child is not after all a member of the family himself, but an outsider. Members of the family such as the mother-to-be can injure the unborn child with impunity, but for the unborn child to legally respond would be a threat to the (real) family.

The Law Commission's Report is perhaps the most obvious example of this unacknowledged relationship between a rejection of the separateness and rights of the unborn, and the rejection of maternal duty on grounds of threat to family harmony. As already indicated earlier, that Commission adopted the most reductionist position of all jurisdictions on the matter of the legal existence of the unborn child while unborn - he quite simply has no such existence. He can recover damages only when a duty to the *mother* has been violated. Liability to the unborn child is to be (says that Commission) "derivative" only.

In conclusion, there may undoubtedly be some "cruelty" involved against mothers in the event of the imposition of maternal duty and liability towards her unborn child. But any "cruelty" to her must be weighed against the cruelty to unborn children which may result from the non-imposition of such duty and liability on her.

Chapter III

FROM POSTNATAL COMPENSATION TO PRENATAL PROTECTION

Having attempted to justify and define in general terms an expanded right to prenatal care, the next task is both to identify more precisely the main lines of the evolving and expanding legal interest in protecting the unborn child during the prenatal period, and in the course of doing so to put more flesh on the bones of the right to prenatal care under consideration.

To this point the legal responses considered (in Chapter I) have all had a goal of postnatal compensation. That goal, and the availability of corresponding legal actions, of course remains necessary and laudable for the most part. To anchor effectively duties of care and protection in the prenatal period requires and includes the right of the unborn child to claim compensation if injured once born. But compensation cannot be the only interest or right of the unborn child, given his needs and vulnerability.

The legal responses to be considered now (in case law doctrine, statutes, and the Civil Code) have a primarily protective thrust. That thrust is as yet somewhat hesitant and incomplete, and in some respects may not even be justified. But it is nevertheless identifiable, and it does provide the beginnings of a foundation on which a more explicit, coherent and comprehensive right to prenatal care may be built.

In this Chapter we will attempt to extend that thrust still further, mainly by building upon the rights and protective mechanisms already available to children, especially those felt to be in need of protection from abuse.

1. *Viable birth - from suspensive to resolutory condition*

It was argued above that the major legal reason for the unborn child's generally unprotected state is that his full acquisition and exercise of legal personality and the basic rights to life and inviolability, now only have practical effect upon viable birth. Legal personality and extra-patrimonial rights are in other words subject to the *suspensive* condition of viable birth. As long as that condition is in effect it would appear logically and practically impossible adequately to ground claims of the fetus to protective care *while still unborn*. The fiction of deeming the injured child, once born, to have been born at the time of the injury, already strains logic and coherence when at issue is only the question of postnatal actions for compensation. But that fiction can hardly apply *before* birth since its essential condition, viable birth, has not been fulfilled. And yet it is precisely during the prenatal period that protective legal interventions are needed.

Happily a doctrinal solution to this logical impasse has recently been proposed, one which is relatively simple, but has far-reaching implications. The proposal was made by Kouri, and is to the effect that the unborn child should be considered as a subject of rights on the *resolutory* condition of *not* being born alive and viable, rather than as present on the *suspensive* condition of being born alive and viable.[191] Though proposed by Kouri for the Civil law context, in our view it is equally applicable in the Common law context. The advantage for the unborn child of such a shift is obvious and important. Obligations or duties to the unborn child (including those of respecting its inviolability and providing prenatal care and protection) could now come into play immediately on conception. The suspensive condition approach makes the *granting* of legal personality and rights dependent upon the realization of a future condition (live and viable birth). But the resolutory condition approach would allow legal personality and rights to be *granted* at conception, but *lost* in the event a future condition is realized (not being born alive and viable).

---

[191] KOURI, "Reflexions sur le statut juridique du foetus", *op. cit., supra*, n.2, at pp. 196, and especially 197.

As Baudouin has noted on the subject of resolutory conditions:

> Lorsque l'obligation est contractée sous condition résolutoire, elle est immédiatement en existence. Le créancier a donc, comme le créancier d'une obligation pure et simple, le droit de requérir du débiteur l'exécution de l'obligation. Il peut ... aliéner l'objet, l'hypothéquer et l'utiliser généralement comme bon lui semble, étant dans une position juridique identique à celle d'un créancier ordinaire, avec la réserve toutefois que son droit peut être anéanti par la réalisation de la condition.[192]

Kouri has explained how such a resolutory condition would work in our context:

> De cette façon le foetus bénéficierait de la protection de l'article 19 C.C. Ainsi, advenant la réalisation de la condition résolutoire, ses droits acquis, tant patrimoniaux qu'extra-patrimoniaux, disparaîtraient rétroactivement. On ne se poserait plus la question académique de savoir si l'enfant conçu est une personne. Nous saurions que cet être, quel qu'il soit, jouirait de la protection accordée par le droit positif.[193]

In our view this proposal and doctrine if generally adopted in case law, doctrine and child welfare statutes, in both Civil law and Common law systems, would remove the major doctrinal obstacle to the provision of needed legal protection for the unborn child.

2. *The unborn as child - the common law perspective*

i) *Parental duties and childrens' rights*

Since the unborn child has health needs and vulnerabilities analogous to those of children, and since between the child when unborn and after birth there is continuity in all essential respects, then it would seem logical and just to assign to parents duties to their unborn children analogous (when applicable) to those they have to their children, and to recognize in unborn children analogous rights (when applicable) to those already granted to children.

---

[192] BAUDOUIN, *Les Obligations, op. cit., supra*, n.167 at p. 449, 450.

[193] KOURI, "Reflexions...", *op. cit., supra*, n.2, at p. 197.

In the matter of parental duties towards children, relevant legislation in the common law provinces does not provide a detailed and explicit picture of what those duties are. To a large degree these parental duties must be deduced from the criteria provided by child welfare legislation as to when a child is "in need of protection", criteria we will examine and apply to the unborn child in section (ii) below. It is clear from legislation and case law in the various provinces that (in law) parents have duties towards their children in at least the following ways and areas: support, supervision, provision for physical, emotional and moral needs, health care, education, affection and the provision of a family unit.194

The common law stance as regards parental responsibility for children is that the child is ideally and normally to be raised and cared for in the family unit, and according to a rule of equity, parents have an equal share in promoting the child's welfare and interests. This stance is typified for example in the *Infants Act* of Ontario:195

2. (1) Unless otherwise ordered by the Court subject to this Act, the father and mother of an infant are joint guardians and are equally entitled to the custody, control and education of infants.

3. In questions relating to the custody and education of infants, the rules of equity prevail.

---

194 WEILER & CATTON, (*op. cit., supra*, n. 7, at p. 648) suggest that it may already be the case that in Ontario and other provinces, when a child is *likely to be born* or is born out of wedlock and no agreement between the mother and the putative father for the maintenance of the child is in force, the order for *maintenance* which the Children's Aid Society may initiate may in reality be done in the interests of the unborn child and not just the mother. They suggest with reason that one could conclude that the unborn child has a right to maintenance in its own right. The operative section in the Ontario *Child Welfare Act,* (*loc. cit., supra,* n. 172) is s. 50(1).

195 *The Infants Act,* R.S.O. 1970, c. 222, subsequently sections 2 and 3 of the *Minors Act* RSO 1980 c.292 (save that the word "infant" was replaced by "minor" in them), since repealed by S.O. c.20, s.4. Now see *Children's Law Reform Act* RSO 1980 c.68 as amended by S.O. 1982 c.20 s.1.

Applied to the question of parental duties to unborn children, the fact that both parents (and not just the father), have an equal share in promoting their childrens' welfare and interests, may provide precedent and justification for assigning maternal duties and liability for the care of her unborn children.

It is infrequent indeed that common law child welfare or other relevant statutes refer in any explicit or detailed manner to the *rights* of the child. As we shall indicate below, largely thanks to the existence of the Civil Code, Quebec Civil law is considerably more emphatic and explicit as regards childrens' rights.

In the context of the Common law provinces, the rights of the child (as the duties of the parent) generally have to be deduced from the tests applicable to determining whether a child is "in need of protection". It is somewhat surprising that even the proposed *Children's Act* in Ontario, (intended to consolidate all Ontario legislation dealing directly with children), nowhere provided in any explicit and direct manner even a list of the basic right of the child.[196]

An exception to the general vagueness as to childrens' rights in statutes or proposals was the 1975 *Report of the (B.C.) Royal Commission on Family and Childrens' Law.* Among the rights listed which have potential relevance to both the child and the unborn child (though obviously not equally applicable to both in every detail), are these:

1. The right to food, clothing and housing in order to ensure good health and personal development.
2. The right to an environment free from physical abuse, exploitation and degrading treatment.

---

[196] See, *The Children's Act,* a Consultation Paper, (Ontario) Ministry of Community and Social Services, Toronto, 1982.

As with extant child welfare legislation, the proposed *Children's Act* does include a list of conditions for determining whether a child is "in need of protection". It also indicates what it calls the "rights and responsibilities of children in care", but these are not proposed as the rights of children as such, whether in their homes or in institutions, but only their rights if in residential care under the *Act.*

3. The right to health care necessary to promote physical and mental health and to remedy illness.[197]

Noteworthy for the concerns of this paper, is the *positive and affirmative* nature of children's rights listed in that Report. They obviously do not include only a right not to be harmed by positive acts of negligence. Rather they provide support for claims by children to affirmative acts of health care and support. It is this same affirmative thrust and some of these same rights to affirmative action, which, if extended to unborn children, would best protect their long-term interests and promote their health.

ii) *The unborn child as "child in need of protection" in statute and case law*

Before some form of protective care can be determined by a court at the dispositional stage, in the adjudication stage a Children's Aid Society (or equivalent) must prove the child to be "in need of protection". Before examining whether and how the various child oriented tests and protective mechanisms could apply to an unborn child, we should establish what those tests are.

A typical example of "child in need of protection" criteria in effect in the child welfare legislation of Canadian provinces, is the Ontario *Child Welfare Act*.[198] Of the twelve occasions which could lead to a child being held to be in need of protection, at least the following four could arguably be modified for application to an unborn child as well:

S.19 (1) (b):

"Child in need of protection" means...

> (iii) a child where the person in whose charge the child is, cannot for any reason care properly for the child,

---

197 B.C. *Royal Commission on Family and Childrens' Law*, Report V, Part IV, Special needs of Special Children, Vancouver, (1975), at p. 5.

198 *The Child Welfare Act* (Ontario), *loc. cit., supra*, n.172.

(iv) a child where the person in whose charge the child is neglects or refuses to provide or obtain proper medical, surgical or other recognized remedial care or treatment necessary for the child's health or well-being, or refuses to permit such care or treatment to be supplied to the child when it is recommended by a legally qualified medical practitioner, or otherwise fails to protect the child adequately,

(x) a child whose emotional or mental development is endangered because of emotional rejection or deprivation of affection by the person in whose charge the child is, or

(xi) a child whose life, health or morals may be endangered by the conduct of the person in whose charge the child is...

In the United States the various statutes involving judicial protection of children contain criteria very similar to the Ontario Act just quoted.[199] In the United Kingdom, the relevant subsection of the *Children and Young Persons Act* (of 1969) states that a child is liable to care proceedings if:

... his proper development is being avoidably prevented or neglected or his health is being avoidably impaired or neglected or he is being ill-treated;...[200]

While quite obviously an unborn child's "morals" could hardly be endangered by the conduct of another, it would not be at all difficult to bring an endangered unborn child within the meaning of one or more of these criteria, and hence being "in need of protection" for purposes of this or a similar Act.

An important and very relevant aspect has to do with the standard the Family Court (the Court which administers the Child Welfare Acts) should use in deciding whether any of the reasons quoted are serious enough in specific instances to justify considering that child to be "in need of protection".

---

[199] See S. Katz, *When Parents Fail*, Beacon Press, Boston, 1971, at pp. 57-58. See also The Model Child Protection Act proposed by FONTANA and BESHAROV, *op. cit., supra*, n.131, at pp. 90-118.

[200] *Children and Young Persons Act*, U.K. Statutes, 1969, c. 54, s. 1 (2)(a), and "care proceedings" defined in s.1 (6).

While High Courts, guided as they are by the rules of equity and exercising their *parens patriae* jurisdiction, may act according to a child's best interest standard, it is not so for Family Courts. They must act strictly according to the provisions and definitions of the Act, and cannot bring into play any child protection only because someone establishes that someone other than the parents *could do a better job or the best job* for a child. As Wilson has noted,

> The criteria underlying the definitions provided for in (s.19) should not be based on what is "in the best interests of the child", but rather what is necessary to raise the child's standard of care back to an acceptable minimum level.[201]

A similar point was made by Dickens:

> A child is not shown in need of protection simply because an agency can satisfy a judge that it can offer the child preferable circumstances to those provided by the parents. Before the question of disposition can arise, a child must be shown to be in need of protection or care according to objective standards. Judicial recognition of the good intentions ... of welfare personnel and of their capacity to improve the child's material and other conditions of life is not itself a sufficient basis for intervention between parent and child.[202]

If the child-oriented criteria of "in need of protection" are to be applied or adapted to unborn children, then the fact that the basic standard in both cases would be an objective and "acceptable minimum level" assessment (rather than the "best possible"), would serve as yet another response to those who object that providing new legal interventions to protect the unborn would amount to demanding too high a level of parental care and promoting a further meddling by the law into the family. Parents could not be held to do the "best job" for the unborn child any more than for the child - an adequate

---

[201] WILSON, *op, cit., supra,* n.181, at p. 49. On this point see also *Re G* (unreported) May 6, 1976 - B.C. Provincial Court [Family Division]; *Re Brown, loc, cit., supra,* n. 158.

[202] DICKENS, *op. cit., supra,* n. 155, at p. 24. For further explorations and support of this view see the books by J. GOLDSTEIN, A. FREUD and A. J. SOLNIT, *Beyond the Best Interests of the Child,* MacMillan, New York, 1973; *Before the best Interests of the Child,* MacMillan, New York, 1979.

job would do. It is, after all, a fact that:

> The unborn child is far too resilient to be put off by a few set-backs. The danger arises when he is shut off from his mother or when his physical and psychological needs are consistently ignored.[203]

Coming now to the question of the appropriateness of the court-ordered or statutorily supported but voluntary child protection mechanisms if applied to unborn children, it should be noted at the outset that some of them are clearly not applicable. One obvious reason is that because the unborn child cannot be separated from the (pregnant) woman, it cannot have recourse to those protective mechanisms involving placement away from the family. But it is arguable that at least some of the available child-oriented legal protections could be extended (with modifications in some instances) to the unborn child in need of protection. Obviously if the principle were to be acknowledged that unborn children need and merit legal protections analogous to those available for children, nothing would preclude the fashioning of interventions specifically adapted to all the special circumstances of the unborn child.

Once found by a court in the adjudication stage to be "in need of protection" according to the terms of a *Child Welfare Act*, or in the case of High Courts that on equity grounds there are good reasons to intervene beyond just the criteria of such statutes, then a number of both court-ordered and voluntary interventions are available depending on the degree of protection desired.

Among the court-ordered and involuntary protections applicable to children and potentially (with modifications) to unborn children, might be the following:

(i) the granting of *injunctions* against certain acts being done or decisions taken;

---

[203] VERNY, *op. cit., supra*, n. 128, at p. 94.

(ii) the appointment of *guardians* (or tutors in Quebec) to make certain decisions on behalf of an endangered child;

(iii) *supervision orders*, according to which the child remains where he is but custody is granted to a child welfare service to officially supervise;

(iv) the child is temporarily removed from parental care and made a ward of a child welfare service.[204]

The granting of injunctions and the appointment of guardians for purposes of protecting the unborn child, have already been granted by courts in two cases to be considered below.[205] As for the application of a supervision order exercised by a child welfare service, the child continuing to remain at home, it could be very appropriately applied to the unborn child needing protection.

Clearly in this case the supervision order would for all practical purposes be directed to and exercised over the mother-to-be, though in the interests of the child. It would acknowledge and effectively respond to two realities. One is that much abuse or neglect of unborn children might be lessened if more help, advice and supervision were available. A second such reality is that it would be unreasonable, counter-productive and a grave injustice to involuntarily place pregnant women in an institution except perhaps as a last resort.

As for (iv), it is of course impossible to temporarily "remove the unborn child from parental care". However, if it is established that the father's physically abusive or otherwise seriously endangering conduct towards the pregnant woman poses a serious risk to the physical or emotional health and development of the unborn child, this type of mechanism could

---

[204] The last three of the protective orders listed, typical of Child Welfare Acts in the common law provinces, are found for example in s.30 of the *Child Welfare Act* (Ontario) *loc. cit., supra,* n.172.

[205] *Hoener* v. *Bertinato,* 171 A. 2d 140, (N.J.J.D.R.C. 1961) and *Raleigh Fitkin - Paul Morgan Mem. Hospital* v. *Anderson,* 201 A. 2d 537 (N.J. Sup. Ct. 1964). See below, pp. 118-121.

be modified to have the *father* (temporarily or permanently) removed from proximity to his wife and unborn child, whether or not the child is then made a ward of the child welfare service.

As well as court-ordered legal protections, there are several others available to children which, though legally supported, are either voluntary or at least do not (initially) require court orders or court findings of neglect. Some of these could be particularly justifiable and effective for the unborn child as well. They reflect an important reality, namely that both child and unborn child proceedings need not always be contentious and involuntary. Many parents are quite prepared to acknowledge that they need assistance and that their children are at risk.[206] Presumably the same could be true regarding unborn children.

In this category are especially two mechanisms provided by, for example, the Ontario *Child Welfare Act*, though equivalents are found in some other jurisdictions as well. Neither requires an initial court order or a court finding that the child is in need of protection. The first involves the placement of a "homemaker" in the home in which a child has been discovered to be apparently neglected (s.23). It is seen as an alternative to taking a child to a "place of safety", and may be continued and renewed as long as necessary by court permission. This form of protection and care would undoubtedly be one of the most applicable and effective in cases of "unborn neglect" as well, since the unborn child obviously cannot be taken to "a place of safety" without the mother. The assistance of a homemaker with special skills and training in prenatal care and nutrition could provide the most effective protection against neglect or abuse.

A second such measure is that of the "non-ward agreement", a written agreement between the parents (or parent) and the child welfare society for the care of a child for an agreed upon period (s.25). It was a measure enacted

---

[206] See DICKENS, *op, cit., supra*, n.155, at p. 23.

especially for parents who for circumstances of a temporary nature are not able to provide adequately for a child, or who cannot provide the services needed because of the special needs of a child. One adaptation of this measure to make it apply as well to unborn children could be that the non-ward contract be made with a prenatal clinic attached to or recognized by the local Children's Aid Society or equivalent.

The use or adaptation of child-oriented protections for unborn children in some of the ways suggested above is consistent with a direction encouraged by the (B.C.) Royal Commission on Family and Children's Law, when it recommended:

> Therefore, in new child legislation we think that the future infant should be protected ... The definition of children who are "in need of care" should extend to these unborn children ... As a result, a disposition could be made which places the mother under a supervision order. In this way, the child's future growth and development could be protected at the earliest stage.[207]

Some courts have already held that to one extent or another an unborn child merits legal protection in the prenatal period, by finding for example that for a particular purpose an unborn child should fall within the meaning of "child" or "dependant". Decisions of this type are rare. An early American example is the 1931 California decision in *People* v. *Yates*,[208] in which the unborn child was brought within the meaning of child by applying an unusual provision in the California Penal Code. It provides that a child conceived but not yet born is to be deemed a person insofar as that section concerning support is concerned. Since the father was found to have failed to provide food and care to his unborn child "through its mother", liability followed more or less automatically.

---

[207] B. C. Royal Commission on Family and Children's Law, Fifth Report, Part V, *The Protection of Children (Child Care)*, Vancouver, 1975, at p. 66.

[208] *People* v. *Yates*, 298 P. 961 (Cal. App. Dep't. Super. Ct. 1931).

In a 1943 Canadian decision, an unborn child was brought within the meaning of "dependant" in a Workmen's Compensation Act. In *Chapman* v. *C.N.R.*[209] a judicial interpretation of a Workmen's Compensation Act held that an unborn child was a "dependant" and entitled to share in damages for wrong done to the family provider.

A more recent example was the 1979 Nova Scotia decision in *Re Simms and H.*[210] In this instance the Family Court appointed a guardian *ad litem* for an unborn child since the father was seeking an injunction to prevent the mother from having an abortion. One of the questions the court felt obliged to answer was whether an unborn child of 18 weeks gestation is a child within the meaning of the *Children's Services Act*. The relevant section of that Act states, "... 'child' means a boy or girl under sixteen years of age, unless the context otherwise requires". (s.2(i)). The court answered in the affirmative.

Two Canadian courts still more recently held that an unborn child can indeed be a "child in need of protection" before birth. One of these was a 1981 Ontario Family Court decision, *Re J.L.*[211] In this wardship application a girl was born suffering from fetal alcohol syndrome. It was held that the mother's use of alcohol constituted physical abuse of the child before birth, and the fact that she refused to obtain help was a denial of adequate care needed for the child's health. The court declared the newborn baby a "child in need of protection" and a ward of the Crown.

---

209 *Chapman* v. *C.N.R.*, [1943] O.W.N. 47 aff'd at 297. For comments on this case, see WEILLER and CATTON, *op. cit., supra*, n. 7 at pp. 650, 651.

210 *Re Simms and H*, (1979) 106 D.L.R. (3d) 435 (N.S. Family Ct.).

211 *Re Children's Aid Society for the District of Kenora and J.L.*, (1981), 134 D.L.R. (3d) 249 (Ont. P. C. Fam. Div.).

The medical evidence established that:

> ... the fetal alcohol syndrome had been wilfully inflicted upon Janis L. by the mother, Catherine L., who refused to seek help for her alcohol problem despite the entreaties of Doctor Bevridge.[212]

In the light of these circumstances the court went on to state:

> Accordingly, the child was a child in need of protection *prior to birth*, at birth and on May 24, 1981, being the time of apprehension, pursuant to sections 19(1)(b)(ix) and (xi) of the *Child Welfare Act*, ... by reason of the physical abuse of the child by the mother in her excessive consumption of alcohol during pregnancy, which conduct endangered the health of Janis L....[213] [Emphasis added]

Two factors should however be noted which somewhat qualify the originality of this decision, neither factor having received much attention at the time of the decision or subsequently. One is that the statement that the child was a child in need of protection prior to birth may well have been obiter rather than an element of the ruling itself. As Judge Bradley himself stated:

> The finding with respect to the child being a child in need of protection prior to birth is not essential to the finding that the child was in need of protection at the time of the apprehension and at the time of the hearing...[214]

A second qualification is that even though the child was said to be (though not "held" to be) "in need of protection" prior to birth, actual legal intervention only took place, as usual, *after* the birth of the child. It could hardly have been otherwise given that no statutory or other authority yet exists to permit a court to "apprehend" a mother-to-be and provide legal protection to an unborn child in the position of Janis L.

---

212 *Id.*, at p. 252.

213 *Ibid.*

214 *Ibid.* It is therefore strictly speaking inaccurate to imply that it was "held" by that court that the unborn child was a child "in need of protection". A recent example of such an implication is to be found in the *Advocates for Human Life Newsletter*, January, 1983, at p.2.

That said, the decision is nevertheless a big step forward. It was at least stated that Janis L. was "in need of protection" prior to birth, even if not a necessary element of the actual judgment. Such an admission and recognition is a *sine qua non* condition before any actual prenatal intervention can be authorized by statute. Judge Bradley himself noted that the finding that Janis L. was "in need of protection" before birth was at least "... an important factor to be considered in determining the best interests of the child".[215] He also added:

> Needless to say, it also raises a number of issues, which are not required to be determined at this time, and in particular the issue as to the responsibility of the Children's Aid Society *in protecting an unborn child.*[216] [Emphasis added]

The second of these cases was the 1982 British Columbia decision in *Re McDonald*.[217] In this instance because of the addiction of her mother, a child ("D.J.") was born drug addicted and the court held that abuse can indeed occur during the gestation period. Judge Proudfoot held in part that:

> From the evidence before me of the physical problems that a baby born drug addicted has to endure it would be incredible to come to any other conclusion than that a drug addicted babe is *born abused.* That abuse *has occurred during the gestation period...* She continues to suffer pain and, in addition, is susceptible to a myriad of life threatening health problems. Her safety and well-being, *has been and continues to be* endangered. D.J. falls within the definition under s.1 (of the *Family and Child Service Act*, S.B.C. 1980, c.11) of a "child in need of protection" as would any other child born drug addicted.[218] [Emphasis added]

Once again, this decision was to the effect that the child in question was abused before birth, and the implication is that therefore she was already "in need of protection" before birth. Even though this decision, like the previous one, did not involve protective legal intervention in the prenatal period

---

215 *Ibid.*

216 *Ibid.*

217 *Re Superintendent of Family and Child Service and McDonald*, (1982) 135 D.L.R. (3d) 330 (B.C.S.C.).

218 *Id.*, at p. 335.

itself, it nevertheless constitutes a further preparation and stage towards that eventuality.[219]

(iii) *Court-ordered medical interventions on pregnant women for the sake of the unborn child - from transfusions to fetal surgery*

In the United States, recent decisions have in several instances gone still further in the direction of protecting the unborn child. There is a growing class of cases which can best be classified as court-ordered medical interventions on

---

[219] It should not of course be assumed that recent decisions involving issues relevant to unborn children have all gone in the same direction as the cases just reviewed. A recent example of another direction is to be found in the Alberta decision of *Fitzsimonds* v. *Royal Insurance Co. of Canada*, (1983) 24 Alta. L. R. (2d) 200 (Q.B.). At issue was a claim by a daughter for insurance benefits as a result of her father's death in an automobile accident. When her father died she was only a one-month old fetus. The relevant regulation stipulated that payment shall be made only to "a person who is alive 60 days after the death of the insured person". The daughter was at that point a fetus of three months. The court held that this did not constitute being "alive" and therefore she could not collect death benefits. (at p. 202).

Somewhat surprisingly, by the (dictionary) definition of the word "alive" used by the court, the daughter would seem to have been very much "alive" indeed. That definition used of "alive" was, " . . . marked by a state in which the organs perform their vital functions". Judge Bowen went on to add, "It is the mother's organs that are performing the vital functions and not those of the child". That would indeed be news to physicians and others. If Judge Bowen were correct, then anyone whose organs are being supported by heart, lung or other organ supports, would not be "alive".

But whatever the justification or lack of it for this particular decision, it does at least illustrate that it is probably too early to identify a definite and fixed trend in the jurisprudence of the common law provinces involving unborn child issues. There are definite indications that there may be a trend in Canada in the direction of an increasing jurisprudential interest in protecting the rights and health of the unborn child, but time will tell whether this is really so and remains so.

On appeal the trial judgment in *Fitzsimonds* was overturned (1984) 29 Alta. L.R. (2d) 394 (C.A.). The court stated (at p. 399):

> "I find nothing in the statute or regulations which indicates that a child *en ventre sa mère* [sic!] should be treated differently than a child living at the date of death of his father."

The court implicitly, however, seems to have agreed with the trial judge's interpretation of the word "alive". It preferred to rely on what it called a "legal fiction" (at p. 397):

117

pregnant women for the sake of the unborn child, usually for the sake of saving its life. The interventions so ordered range from court-ordered blood transfusions to caesareans. Courts have not yet gone so far as to order fetal surgery without the pregnant woman's consent, but that eventuality is at least being seriously discussed in legal and medical literature.

Court-ordered medical interventions for the sake of the fetus raise serious policy issues, especially the obvious one of just how far a court can go in ordering such interventions without violating the pregnant woman's rights to refuse treatment and to inviolability. In our view there should be very definite limits and clear criteria regarding such interventions, and hopefully they will begin to be formulated and refined both by case law and in statutes. Case law decisions made to date in this class of case are not encouraging in this respect. For the most part they were decided in great haste and with little or no analysis of precedents and principles. After a brief description and analysis of these decisions, we will propose some basic criteria and tests which courts and statutes should apply when there is a clear conflict between the life or health of the unborn child and the inviolability of the pregnant woman.

Generally speaking and at least in principle, the right of competent adults to refuse treatment even to save their lives, at least when no higher interests of others are involved, is well established in common law. In the United States, the 1965

A fiction has developed in the law that in respect of property rights, an unborn child who is subsequently born alive is in the same position as a child living at the time of the death of the benefactor. This fiction has existed for over a century and is so well established that for a statute conferring property rights on children to be interpreted as excluding a child who was *en ventre sa mère* [sic!] at the time of the death of the father would require specific words of exclusion. In interpreting statutes, such as the Insurance Act I think cognizance must be taken of this fiction. It would be known to legislative draftsmen and legislation would be passed with this fiction in mind.

The decision specifically avoided the issue of a child's juridical status and its basic rights by stating (at p. 400) the "legal fiction applying to property rights for unborn children . . . had nothing to do with the arguments either of the 'Pro-Life Group' or the 'Pro-Abortion Group'".

decision *In Re Brooks Estate*[220] clearly underlined that principle. A lower court granted authorization to a physician who had sought court permission to give a blood transfusion to his life-threatened woman patient who had refused it. But the Illinois Supreme Court reversed that decision, holding in part the following:

> No minor children are involved. No overt or affirmative act of appellant offers any clear and present danger to society - here only a governmental agency compelling conduct offensive to appellant's religious principles. Even though we may consider appellant's beliefs unwise, foolish or ridiculous, in the absence of an overriding danger to society we may not permit interference therewith ... for the sole purpose of compelling her to accept medical treatment forbidden by her religious principle and previously refused by her with full knowledge of the probable consequences.[221]

But what if minor children *are* involved? That court implied that the decision would have been otherwise if "minor children" or other "overriding dangers to society" were involved. What if those minor children were unborn children? That question was in fact raised and answered in two other decisions.

a) *Maternal transfusions*

The first was the 1961 New Jersey case of *Hoener* v. *Bertinato*.[222] In view of the pregnant woman's RH negative blood condition, the medical evidence seemed to establish that unless a blood transfusion was given soon after birth the child would die. A previous child had in fact required just such a transfusion. But the Jehovah Witness parents refused consent on religious grounds. The court therefore took jurisdiction over the unborn child while still unborn under a child protection statute. It awarded custody of the child, when born, to the County Welfare Department and authorized it to consent to the transfusion. But, while injunctive relief was granted to the unborn child *in utero*, that relief was of course

---

[220] *In re Brooks Estate*, 205 N.E. 2d 435 (Ill. Sup. Ct. 1965).

[221] *Id.*, at p. 442

[222] *Hoener* v. *Bertinato, loc, cit., supra*, n. 205..

to be applied and to be effective only *after* birth and *if born*. What the court was really ensuring was the well being of the child once born - without live birth the injunction would of course have no effect. As such this decision stopped short of ordering actual medical intervention in the prenatal period.

Another New Jersey decision however did order a transfusion to be given to a pregnant woman before the birth of her child. That was the 1964 decision in *Releigh-Fitken - Paul Morgan Memorial Hospital*.[223] Once again the pregnant woman was a Jehovah Witness, in this case about eight months pregnant. The physicians thought that at some point before giving birth she might hemorrhage severely and that both she and the unborn child would die unless a blood transfusion was given. The mother refused. The hospital sought court authority to administer the transfusions. Whereas the trial court upheld her refusal, the New Jersey Supreme Court decided that the child was entitled to the protection of the law, and held that the blood transfusion could be given to the woman if it became necessary, "... to save her life or the life of her child, as the physician in charge at the time may determine." The court reasoned that:

> ... the welfare of the child and the mother are so intertwined and inseparable that it would be impracticable to attempt to distinguish beween them.[224]

As it turned out, the transfusion was never carried out. In fact the woman had left the hospital against the advice of her physicians before that judgment.

These judgments, especially *Raleigh-Fitken*, have obviously elicited a great deal of analysis and criticism, some of it justified; some of it less so. In the latter category is this comment by Crockett and Hyman, "... despite the difference in the focus of the courts in *Raleigh-Fitkin* and *Hoener*, intervention by the court in either case would serve no

---

223 *Raleigh Fitkin - Paul Morgan Memorial Hospital* v. *Anderson, loc, cit., supra,* n. 205

224 *Id.,* at p. 538

purpose absent the subsequent live birth of the child".[225] In fact there is a crucial difference between the decisions, and precisely in the matter of live birth. In *Hoener* the transfusion could be provided only after birth; but in *Raleigh-Fitkin* it could have been provided to the mother before birth, for the sake of the fetus. As such, *Raleigh-Fitkin* is clearly an example of the court-ordered provision of protective intervention in the prenatal period. The fact that the treatment was not in fact given does not change the fact that it was allowed and available.

But *should* it have been allowed, and what weight should be assigned to *Raleigh-Fitken* by way of precedent? As to its value as a precedent, Annas[226] for one is of the view that the decision is only of limited value, partly because the judgment itself gives hardly any reasons able to be evaluated, partly because no one was actually forced to do anything as a result, and partly because it was decided eight years before the United States Supreme Court decision in *Roe* v. *Wade*.[227]

As Annas noted, *Roe* v. *Wade* stands for the proposition that the State does have a compelling interest in preserving the life of the viable fetus, but if the mother's life or health is thereby endangered, that compelling interest of the State can give way. Because the *Raleigh-Fitken* decision did not offer any such calculation or reasons in coming to the conclusion it did, it is both difficult to evaluate and of limited value as a precedent.

Presumably in Canada there is the same need and obligation to balance the interest of the State in preserving the life of an unborn child on the one hand, and on the other hand the risk imposed on the pregnant woman's life or health by the contemplated intervention to save that child's life. In Canada the interest of the State in preserving the life of the

---

[225] CROCKETT and HYMAN, *op, cit., supra*, n.70, at p. 832.

[226] G. ANNAS, "Forced Cesareans: The Most Unkindest Cut of All", (1982) 12:3 *H.C.R.* 16, at p. 17.

[227] *Roe* v. *Wade, loc, cit., supra*, n. 71.

fetus is undoubtedly even more compelling than that applicable in the United States. The life of the unborn child is after all protected during the whole period of gestation by s.251 Criminal Code, and not just or especially after viability.[228] But on the other hand and by exception, again according to s.251(4) Criminal Code, the State does not have that compelling interest if the continuation of the pregnancy puts the pregnant woman's life or health in danger.

b) *Caesarean sections*

Before attempting to formulate a test by which to determine the legitimacy of court-ordered medical interventions for the sake of the unborn child, two more decisions merit evaluation, both of them allowing medical intrusions much riskier than that involved in *Raleigh-Fitkin*. In both instances the court-ordered medical intervention was that of a caesarean section.

The first of these was the 1981 Georgia decision in *Jefferson v. Griffin Spalding Co. Hospital Authority*.[229] A hospital sought a court order allowing it to perform a caesarean section if necessary on a woman about to give birth in about four days. Her doctors felt that there was a 99 percent certainty that the baby would not survive vaginal delivery, and a 50 percent chance she would not survive it herself. She had previously told the hospital that she did not plan to make or allow intervention if anything went wrong, but would accept whatever happened as God's will. The court decided the unborn child deserved legal protection, authorized all medical procedures deemed necessary by the physician and granted a petition requiring the mother to submit to a caesarean section. The basis given for granting the petition was the State's interest in preserving the unborn child's life,

---

[228] See KOURI, *op. cit., supra*, n. 2, at pp. 198-199. Kouri has said in this regard: "Il y a lieu de noter enfin que l'article 251 C. cr. s'applique de la même façon à tous les enfants conçus, c'est-à-dire, sans faire de nuances quant à l'époque où en est la gestation".

[229] *Jefferson v. Griffin Spalding Co. Hospital Authority*, 274 S.E. 2d 457 (Ga. 1981).

and it's duty to do so, outweighs the intrusion involved. The parents petitioned the Georgia Supreme Court to stay the order but the court denied the motion. After all this, the pregnant woman delivered a few days later, without complications and without any surgical intervention, a healthy baby.

The second case[230] involved a pregnant woman with a strong fear of surgery who refused to consent to a caesarean section. A fetal heart monitor indicated fetal hypoxia and the need for the caesarean. But despite the efforts of relatives and physicians, she continued to refuse. The hospital petitioned the (juvenile) court to find that the unborn child was a dependant and neglected child, and to order the caesarean section in order to save its life. After an emergency hearing was held in the patient's room the court ordered the surgery. The caesarean section was performed but to the physician's surprise the child was born healthy and without complications.

Several points merit attention concerning these cases. The first is that just as in *Raleigh-Fitkin,* no effort was made to identify, consider and weigh the rights of the pregnant woman along with the State's right and duty to protect the unborn child. Secondly, both of these last two cases depend heavily upon the *Raleigh-Fitkin* decision and thus share its shortcomings. Thirdly, the court-ordered intrusion in those last two cases was considerably more intrusive and dangerous to the pregnant woman than is a transfusion - a further reason why *Raleigh-Fitkin* is an inappropriate precedent for these last two cases. Fourthly, the medical prognosis in both cases turned out to be quite inaccurate and unduly alarmist.

A fifth point worth considering is how far a hospital could really go in carrying out a court-ordered intervention if the

---

[230] The decision has apparently not yet been reported, and in the two accounts of the decision read by this writer, the case was not named. Two sources which refer to the case are: G. ANNAS, *op. cit., supra,* n. 226, at p. 16, and W.A. BOWES and B. SELGESTAD, "Fetal Versus Maternal Right: Medical and Legal Perspectives", (1981) 58 *Am. J. Obstet. Gynec.,* at pp. 209-214.

woman in question continued to refuse, even physically. That eventuality did not in fact arise in any of these cases, but the prospect underlines an obvious limit to court-ordered interventions of this kind - should a woman struggle and resist (for example the administration of anaesthesia), it is highly doubtful that the physicians would or should restrain her if it involves serious risk of injury to her.

c) *Fetal surgery*

A still further escalation of the level of intrusiveness merits some consideration as well - namely that of (involuntary) fetal surgery. Recent medical literature indicates that there are a number of congenital defects which are not only diagnosable *in utero* but that some already are or soon might be treatable and correctable *in utero* as well.[231] Some of these are malformations which influence the timing of delivery, indicating early and induced (often caesarean) delivery since they require correction as soon as possible. They are detectable *in utero*, but are best corrected after induced pre-term delivery and birth. But a number of other deficiencies, malformations and anatomical lesions already are or may eventually be treatable and correctable before birth.

Among the latter are the following:

- fetal RBC (red blood cell) deficiency, requiring transfusion of red blood cells into the fetal peritoneal cavity;

- growth retardation of the fetus, requiring the injection of nutrients into the amniotic fluid;

- obstructive hydrocephalus (accumulation of fluid in the cranial vault, compressing the brain and eventually destroying neurological function), requiring decompression of the cerebrospinal fluid, or shunting of the fluid into the amniotic fluid;

---

[231] See for example, M. HARRISON, *et al.*, "Management of the Fetus With A Correctable Congenital Defect", (1981) 246 *J.A.M.A.*, 774-777.

- congenital hydronephrosis (obstruction of the ureter), requiring early decompression of the fetal urinary tract and drainage of urine from the bladder into the amniotic fluid;

- congenital diaphragmatic hernia (causing a compression of the lung), requiring surgical relief of pulmunary compression.

The required techniques are not yet sufficiently developed or safe in some cases to make the risks to pregnant woman and/or the unborn child worth the hoped for benefits. Some forms of fetal surgery have been so far successfully performed only on the fetuses of sheep, not yet on the human fetus or the fetus of any primate for that matter. Such is the case for example with the fifth problem listed above, congenital diaphragmatic hernia. The uterus of the sheep is considerably less sensitive than that of the human.

On the other hand it should not be thought that *in utero* interventions per se are futuristic or experimental. In fact the first four of those listed above have now been successfully performed on unborn children in the womb, the first since the 1940's, and the next three more recently. The surgery to relieve fetal hydrocephalus by inserting a shunt into the fetus was performed succesfully only in 1982.[232] As for the surgical relief of congenital nephrosis, that was successfully achieved only in 1982 as well.[233] When the procedures are available and used, in those cases the risks are judged acceptable for *consenting* pregnant women. A leading perinatologist has summed up the state of the question this way:

> Our ability to diagnose fetal birth defects has achieved considerable sophistication. Treatment of several fetal diseases has proved feasible, and treatment of more complicated lesions will undoubtedly expand as techniques for fetal intervention improve. It seems likely that the fetus with a treatable birth defect is on the threshold of becoming a patient.[234]

---

[232] See W. H. CLEWELL, *et al.*, "A Surgical Approach to the Treatment of Fetal Hydrocephalus", (1982) 306 *N.E.J.M.*, 1320-1325.

[233] See M. HARRISON, *et al.*, "Fetal Surgery for Congenital Hydronaphrosis", (1982) 306 *N.E.J.M.*, 591.

[234] HARRISON, *et al.*, *op. cit.*, *supra*, n. 231, at p. 777.

The ability to provide prenatal diagnoses of many fetal malformations or genetic defects has already led to a medical alternative to bringing those pregnancies to term, namely selective abortion because of the defect. But now, thanks to ever-improving methods of prenatal diagnosis and fetal and neonatal treatment, an alternative to delivery at term is induced pre-term delivery for early correction; and an alternative to selective abortion is increasingly likely to be *in utero* fetal treatment, including surgery on the fetus.

It would therefore seem none too early to begin the necessary and urgent task of debating and determining the *ethical and legal* implications, principles and criteria which should apply in decision-making involving fetal surgery.

What especially requires addition to the ethical and legal equations is the crucial fact that while some of these *in utero* fetal interventions are necessary to correct non-life threatening disabilities (the fetal interest therefore being a "quality of life" one), others are necessary for the purpose of saving the unborn child's life. In other words, if not performed, the unborn child will die, either *in utero* or shortly after birth.[235]

---

[235] For example, prior to the development and use of intrauterine transfusions (in the later 1940's), approximately 45 percent of RH complicated pregnancies resulted in intrauterine or neonatal death, whereas recent studies indicate a lowered perinatal mortality rate of 8 percent thanks for the most part to these transfusions. See, J. T. QUEENAN, "Intrauterine Transfusion, A Cooperative Study", (1969) 104 *Am. J. Obstet. & Gynec.*, 397 at p. 397.

The under-developed lungs of those afflicted with congenital diaphragmatic hernia causes 50 percent to 80 percent of infants affected to die at birth. While the less serious instances of this defect can be readily corrected at birth, the 50-80 percent who die could only be saved if the defect is corrected before birth, so that the lung will grow and develop sufficiently to support life at birth. A technique to surgically provide the needed correction *in utero* has now been developed experimentally. See M. HARRISON, *et al.*, "Correction of Congenital Diaphragmatic Hernia in Utero. III. Development of a Successful Surgical Technique Using Abdominoplasty to Avoid Compromise of Umbilical Blood Flow", (1981) 16 *J. Ped. Surg.* 934.

The legal issues raised by fetal surgery could be expressed in the following questions:

- what, if any, court imposed medical interventions *in utero* upon the unborn child and in that child's interest, could be considered morally and legally acceptable in the event of a refusal by the pregnant woman?

- what moral and legal principles and priorities require consideration and balancing?

- if involuntary court-ordered fetal surgery is ever acceptable, what limits should be imposed on such intrusions in view of the pregnant woman's rights to life, inviolability and her own health?

These ethical and legal issues are not of course essentially different from those already alluded to earlier in discussing cases involving court-ordered maternal transfusions or caesarean sections. From the point of view of legal and ethical criteria, the only real difference between *in utero* fetal surgery, and maternal transfusions or caesareans for the sake of the fetus, is that the former will often involve a greater degree of intrusiveness and risk for the pregnant woman. If that is so, then it ought to be possible to formulate a single set of general guidelines or criteria applicable to *all* instances of contemplated court-ordered medical interventions on the mother for the sake of her unborn child.

d) *The candidates for court-ordered interventions*

A first task is to identify those who would be the likely subjects of such interventions. It could be argued that any eventual legal policy allowing court-ordered surgical interventions on the fetus *in utero* and / or on pregnant women for the sake of the fetus, would potentially include within its net vast numbers of non-consenting pregnant women. But such a fear is hardly justified in the light of several realities and arguable assumptions.

First of all, the unborn children at issue would arguably be only those presumed to be *wanted*, those in other words for whom pregnant women have ruled out abortion. This would considerably narrow the field of those unborn children whose lives or health could constitute an interest to be protected by the state even to the extent of involuntary fetal surgery. To limit the field in this manner is inescapably imposed by and consistent with the fact that s.251 of the Criminal Code in effect extends to pregnant women a qualified and exceptional right to abortion. That means that the interest of the State and the duties of pregnant women and others to provide adequate prenatal care gives way in the event of the woman's decision to undergo a legal therapeutic abortion. Otherwise, that interest and duty continues until the child's birth.[236]

It follows that even if a case could be made out for court-ordered surgical interventions on the pregnant woman for the sake of the fetus in the event of her refusal, that would *not* mean that a woman could also be legally ordered to let the pregnancy go to term. For example, a woman who is informed that an ultrasonography test of the fetus reveals a serious but correctable *in utero* malformation, would still be allowed the option of selective abortion at that point if she is able to establish to the satisfaction of a therapeutic abortion committee that the abortion is justified to save her life or protect her health.[237] If we accept the present abortion law and practice as a given (whether one is in agreement with it or not), then we must conclude that the legal status and claims of a *wanted* fetus with a defect (treatable and correctable by maternal transfusion or after caesarean section, or *in utero*) outweighs that of the *unwanted* fetus with the same defect.[238]

---

236 The need to balance the right of the fetus to prenatal care with the woman's right to abortion, will be addressed in greater detail below.

237 It is of course true that genetic or other defects of unborn children, do not *per se* fall within the explicit exceptions permitting abortion in s. 251 of the Criminal Code. But as the Badgely Committee and other studies point out, in practice defects of the fetus are a major motive for abortion, and it is apparently not difficult to convince therapeutic abortion committees that giving birth to a defective child would constitute a threat to a pregnant woman's (physical or psychological) health.

238 In this writer's view the *moral* status of the two unborn children is equal. After all, moral status should not turn on a factor as extraneous and variable as whether another party happens to, or continues to, want one or not.

While in some cases the availability of fetal surgery or precipitated early birth to correct a defect might encourage fewer abortions, it is probably equally likely that the threat of court-ordered medical interventions of this kind may sometimes encourage or precipitate decisions to undergo an abortion. Abortion may appear to some for various reasons to be a more acceptable option than unwanted surgical intrusions for the sake of the unborn child.

There is another factor which would undoubtedly limit the number of cases at issue. One could reasonably assume that many if not most pregnant women who want to continue the pregnancy, on being informed that their unborn child has a serious problem correctable only by pre-term delivery or some other form of prenatal surgical intervention, would consent to it. Their consent is all the more likely if the potential benefit to the child were great (especially life-saving) and the risk to the woman minimal. Some would undoubtedly consent even when the risks to themselves are serious, in order to provide the best possible chance of a healthy start for their child.

However, though the number of pregnant women who opt to continue the pregnancy but refuse surgical intervention for the sake of the child would probably not be great, one can readily imagine several motives leading some to adopt that course. A feminist might for example argue that no one is going to violate her body to operate on her unborn child, voluntarily or involuntarily. After all, (she might say), the fetus is only an extension of her body, and it will just have to take its chances without violating her physical integrity. Another might base her refusal on religious motives - whatever happens is God's will and she is ready to accept it without interfering with God's plans by consenting to a prenatal intervention. This was in fact the motive of the pregnant woman in the *Jefferson* case referred to above. Still another motive for refusal could be fear of the surgery, either for herself or for the fetus or both. This was the motive in the Colorado case also referred to above. Still another motive could be simple disbelief of the physicians' medical prognosis, and a conviction that all will be well despite their dire predictions of fetal damage or death if the prenatal intervention does not take place. As noted above, in both the cases just referred to the medical prognoses turned out to be excessively pessimistic. The court-ordered interventions were very likely unnecessary in the light of the actual outcome.

e) *Weighing benefits, risk and prognosis*

Obviously a first criterion should focus on the potential *benefits of intervention for the unborn child*. The strongest justification for intervention by the State in this manner would of course arise if the benefit sought was that of saving the life of the unborn child. Another benefit would be that of correcting a serious disabililty, in other words a "quality of life" reason.

A second criterion should consider *benefits to the pregnant woman and family*. An obvious gain resulting from the successful treatment *in utero* of a serious fetal disability would be that of thereby obviating the great and potentially life-long costs to the parents and family in terms of money, care, time and many other sacrifices. However, it is difficult to see how such a motive could justify court-ordered surgical intervention if the pregnant woman and family are in fact willing to bear those burdens.

A third criterion and consideration could arguably be that of the potential *benefits to society*. If determined that without prenatal intervention on the pregnant woman, a wanted child once born will very likely impose heavy financial and care burdens on public resources for many years to come, a refusal of such intervention when the risks to the woman are minimal could be held to be unjustified. Some might feel that her refusal would in effect be imposing potentially heavy costs on unconsenting parties, not only the child but society generally.

Fletcher has written in this regard:

> The great appeal of fetal therapy is the promise of earliest possible treatment to correct diseases that result in a life-time of physical suffering and economic burdens. The economic considerations should be secondary to the opportunity to relieve or prevent suffering, but the economic question should not be passed over

lightly. From here it appears that the most difficult moral dilemma in medical ethics in the United States in the near future will be the influence of cost considerations ... Fetal therapy may, in fact, represent one example where treatment is indeed prevention.[239]

But fourth, against possible benefits must be weighed the *potential risks to the fetus and pregnant woman*. A court should want to be assured that the risk to both is "minimal", or, in the case of the fetus, "acceptable". Since the hoped-for therapeutic benefits would normally all go to the unborn child and not the pregnant woman, the risks to the woman in court ordered treatment should never be more than minimal. They may be considerably greater for the unborn child. For example, if a particular prenatal intervention offers the only hope for saving an unborn child's life, then a relatively high degree of risk to that child may well be acceptable.

At present, the degree of risk involved in some prenatal interventions is fairly well known and not always encouraging. About *caesarean delivery* for example, one recent study reports that:

> Despite improvement in surgical technique, anaesthesia, blood replacement and post-operative care, mortality following caesarean section is four times that following vaginal delilvery.[240]

As for *intrauterine transfusions*, given that they have been successfully performed for some forty years now, there is some useful data about risks and efficacy. The risks of complications for both fetus and pregnant women are not inconsiderable. For the fetus the major complications are trauma and hemorrhage, mainly due to inadvertent piercing of various organs and tissues during the transfusion. One study showed that of 591 fetuses transfused, 59 (10%) suffered

---

[239] J. FLETCHER, "The Fetus as Patient: Ethical Issues", (1981) 246 *J.A.M.A.* 772, at p. 773.

[240] H. AMIRIKIA, *et al.*, "Cesarean Section: A 15-Year Review of Changing Incidence, Indications and Risks", (1981) 140 *Am. J. Obstet. Gynec.* 81, at p. 86. On the ethics and practice of caesarean delivery generally, see J. GUILLEMIN, "Babies by Cesarean: Who Chooses, Who Controls ?" (1981) 11:3 *H.C.R.* 15.

such traumas.[241] No firm data is yet available as to long term development and growth of those who survived and were born healthy. Though the risks may appear high for the fetus they really are not when balanced against the fact that only those likely to die are considered candidates for the procedure. At least from the unborn child's point of view, the court-ordered use of this procedure appears quite justifiable.

But maternal risks are another matter, especially since she receives no therapeutic benefit from the intrauterine transfusion. The study in question reported that 175 of 584 pregnant women (33%), went into premature labour, and 70 of these had premature rupture of the membranes. Ten percent had infections, 4 of the 58 requiring hysterectomies as a result. Clearly and rightly physicians feel that these percentages of maternal risk justify the intervention if *consented* to by the pregnant woman. But would the risks of this intervention also be acceptable if she refuses? It would of course depend upon what is to count as "minimal risk", but it is difficult to construe the percentages and types of risk indicated as being only "minimal" for the pregnant woman.

A further risk factor to be weighed involves the *diagnostic tests* themselves. If a court considers authorizing an involuntary diagnostic test to determine fetal health in a high-risk pregnancy, then the risks involved in the particular test in question would also merit consideration by the court before any such authority is granted.[242]

---

241 The study in question is by QUEENAN, *op. cit., supra*, n. 235.

242 In general, the risks of prenatal testing techniques are thought to be minimal, particularly for the pregnant woman. See HARRISON, *et al., op. cit., supra*, n. 231, at p. 776. On the other hand, much depends on the pregnant woman's state of health and the degree of intrusiveness of the test. Even for amniocentesis, the most intrusive of the tests available, the risks to the pregnant woman appear to be minimal. At a recent International Conference attended by this writer it was reported that the reported incidence of amnionitis is about 1 per 1,000, and a Working Group could identify only one maternal death directly attributable to the complications of genetic amniocentesis. See (unpublished) Report of an International Workshop, *Prenatal Diagnosis - Past, Present and Future*, (Val David, Quebec, November 4-8, 1979, 1980) at p. 5. See also, Report of a Consensus Development Conference, *Antenatal Diagnos*, U.S. Dept. of Health, Education and Welfare, Public Health Service, National Institutes of Health, NIH Publication No. 79-1973, April, 1979.

A final consideration regarding risks is the matter of their *fair distribution*. In the event of a court-ordered intervention for the sake of the unborn child it may well be that the pregnant woman could have risks and burdens imposed on her which are not imposed on parents vis-à-vis their born children. As Annas notes:

> No woman has ever been legally required to undergo surgery or general anesthesia (e.g. bone marrow or kidney transplant) to save the life of her dying child. It would be ironic, to say the least, if she could be forced to submit to more invasive surgical procedures for the sake of her fetus than for her child.[243]

As well, it could be argued that such court-imposed interventions are unfairly distributed in that the burdens would fall only on mothers but not on fathers.[244]

A fifth criterion concerns the *accuracy of the diagnosis*. Prenatal diagnostic procedures and tests are continually improving, but there remain uncertainties in some cases involving the use of amniocentesis, fetoscopy, ultrasonography and various forms of fetal monitoring.[245] The Colorado case referred to above demonstrates what Bowes, *et al.*, have referred to as, "... the limitations of continuous fetal heart monitoring as a means of predicting neonatal outcome".[246] The same writers acknowledge that,

---

[243] ANNAS, *op, cit., supra*, n. 226, at p. 17.

[244] W. RUDDICK and W. WILCOX for example have observed the following with some justification:

> "It might be argued that all parents have an obligation to submit their bodies to surgical invasion in order to prevent their children from suffering a life of significantly low quality; hence gynecological intervention could be ordered by the court. But ... fathers are not currently required to give blood, bone marrow or kidneys to spare their children a life of significantly low quality. Until such mandatory donations are standard practice, this argument seems prejudicial". (From, "Operating on the Fetus", (1982) 12:5 *H.C.R.* 10 at p. 12.

[245] Some of these uncertainties were noted for example by M. HARRISON and A. de LORIMIER, "Management of the Fetus with Hydeonephrosis", Mimeograph, Fetal Treatment Program, Dept. of Surgery, University of California, San Francisco.

[246] BOWES, *et al., op, cit., supra*, n. 230, at p. 211.

"The long-term mobility of infants surviving prolonged periods of presumed uteroplacental insufficiency is not well known".[247] In many cases therefore there may be good reasons for a court to be at best hesitant to accept at face value the medical testimony of a physician or agency as to the certainty of the diagnosis upon which they base their request for authority to proceed with the intervention.

A sixth criterion should be that of the *prognosis for success*. A "minimal" risk to the pregnant woman, an "acceptable" risk to the unborn child and a high probability of success might contribute to a strong *prima facie* case for court intervention in the event of a woman's refusal. But the *extent* of the hoped-for success must be weighed as well. It should not be considered sufficient justification that appropriate tests for a particular problem demonstrate that the proposed treatment has an excellent chance of correcting it. That fetus may well have other problems as well, which in the aggregate considerably lessen the chances of real success. As Harrison, *et al.*, have noted:

> Since it is known that malformations often occur as part of a syndrome, a search for associated abnormalities is necessary to avoid delivering a neonate with one corrected anomaly but other unrecognized disabling or lethal abnormalities.[248]

When one applies the efficacy criterion to intrauterine transfusions, the study referred to earlier[249] reported that of 591 fetuses transfused, 203 or 34%, survived. Fifty-one percent of those not surviving were intrauterine deaths and

---

247 *Ibid.*

248 HARRISON, *et al., op. cit., supra*, n 231, at p. 776. RUDDICK and WILCOX (*op, cit., supra*, n. 244, at p. 11) have made a similar point in this observation:

> "Fetal surgery may salvage a fetus whose prospects prove to be dismal. Rather than death in the womb or shortly after birth, it will survive only to face a series of painful operations, institutional existence or perpetual childish dependence on parents or others. To the extent that life-preservation is a worthy pursuit, such results may be counted successes; but this success must be balanced against the cost in lives of low quality."

249 QUEENAN, *op, cit., supra*, n. 235.

15% were neonatal deaths. At first sight this does not seem the sort of success rate likely to encourage court-ordered intrauterine transfusions when otherwise indicated. But when one recalls that the technique is used only when the unborn child is in danger of dying and that most would have died without this procedure, the 34% success rate may in fact be acceptable not only when elective but also when court-ordered, assuming of course that the other suggested criteria have also been met.

A seventh and last criterion could be that of the *gestational age or viability* of the unborn child. Strictly speaking the fact that the unborn child in question has reached the stage of viability should not establish any new or stronger right to prenatal care. As already proposed earlier in this study, that general right and the duty of the State and others to protect it should exist from conception.[250] But as regards *particular* types of care or intervention, the viability or non-viability of the fetus in question obviously does give it a stronger or weaker claim to have correctable defects prenatally treated, by court order if necessary. Viability strengthens such claims mainly because the chances of successful treatment are greater, but also because some other options may be more or less ruled out because of that gestational age.

As it happens, several corrective prenatal interventions for the sake of the fetus are best performed about the time of viability - generally thought to be about 25 weeks at present.[251] This is past the point at which abortions are thought to be safe for the pregnant woman. For example, life-saving intrauterine transfusions are apparently most

---

[250] For a proposal as to the point at which the right to prenatal care and the duty to provide it arises, see below.

[251] On the issue of the relationship of gestational age and birth weight to neonatal mortality, see L. O. LUBCHENCO and J. V. BRAZIE, "Neonatal Mortality Rate: Relationship to Birth Weight and Gestational Age", (1972) 81 *J. Ped.* 814. Thanks largely to evolving technology and care, the time of viability can already be earlier than 25 weeks in some cases.

successful in the 25-32 week gestational period.[252] Since the options for a fetus diagnosed to require the intrauterine transfusion to save its life, are reduced to either having that corrective intervention done or allowing it to die (*in utero* or neonatally), court-authorization of that or similar interventions in the face of maternal refusal may perhaps be justified. Once again of course, the other proposed criteria would also have to be met, particularly that of minimum risk to the mother.

Having proposed a number of criteria which courts could apply in all cases involving prenatal intervention on the fetus or on the pregnant woman for the sake of the fetus, it may be useful to classify the defects and corresponding interventions:

- prenatal diagnostic tests (amniocentesis, fetoscopy, ultrasonography, amniography and various forms of fetal monitoring) to provide information for decision-making.

- serious defects not correctable *in utero* or *ex utero*;

- defects detectable *in utero*; but correctable after term delivery;[253]

- defects requiring induced pre-term delivery for early *ex utero* correction;

- defects requiring surgical intervention on the fetus *in utero*.

Further comment is in order about the first two "classes" listed above. As regards *prenatal diagnostic tests*, these are not all surgically intrusive, but they do nevertheless involve some degree of intrusiveness and some degree of risk. When performed on an elective basis, it is usually because the

---

252 QUEENAN, *op. cit., supra*, n. 235, at p. 403.

253 Among such problems best corrected after delivery are for example, cystic fibrosis, spina bifida and many others. HARRISON, *et al., (op. cit., supra,* n. 231, at p. 774) have observed about this class of defect:

"... most correctable malformations that can be diagnosed *in utero* are best managed by appropriate medical and surgical therapy after delivery at term. The term infant is a better anesthetic and surgical risk than the preterm infant ... knowing that a fetus has one of these anomalies may not alter the timing or mode of delivery, but it does allow preparation for appropriate prenatal and postnatal care."

pregnant woman in question is in a high risk pregnancy bracket due to her age or her medical or genetic history or that of her male partner.

When performed electively, these tests are undergone for various motives. They provide needed information upon which to base an eventual decision to do one of the following:

- have the fetus treated *in utero* if correctable in this manner; or

- undergo an induced pre-term delivery for early *ex utero* correction if indicated; or

- have an abortion if the problem is not thought to be correctable *in utero* or *ex utero* and the birth of the child can be construed as a threat to the pregnant woman's life or health; or

- have the neonatal staff forewarned and alerted to be prepared to correct the malformation after term delivery; or

- provide the pregnant woman and family with time to adjust and plan for long-range care if the fetal defect is not correctable and selective abortion is ruled out.

Some of these reasons and potential benefits to the fetus could also conceivably merit consideration by a court being requested authority to proceed with a diagnostic test in the event of maternal refusal. But whether elective or court-ordered, there should be no obligation on the woman's part to agree in advance to any particular course of action if the test demonstrates some form of serious fetal defect. For example, some women do not consider selective abortion an acceptable option for one reason or another, no matter what the disability of their unborn child.

As for the second class, a number of fetal defects are not correctable *in utero* or *ex utero*, among them: anencephaly, serious chromosomal anomalies such as trisomy 13, renal agenesis (kidney growth failure), Tay Sachs disease, and many others. In these cases the available options are limited to selective abortion or term delivery without correction. Should courts be allowed to authorize that non-consenting pregnant women be compelled to undergo abortions in such cases, either on grounds of benefit to the unborn child (thereby saved from suffering), or for the benefit to society thereby saved from paying the costs of long term care? Apart from the fact that courts would have no legal authority at present to grant such requests,[254] the very request itself is unjustified. In the first place, serious and non-correctable defects are often diagnosed too late for safe abortion. But more to the point, court-ordered abortions would be a big step on the road to a "eugenic" society, one which might thereby become increasingly intolerant of imperfections and handicaps. Such court orders could all too easily move from an initial interest in protecting the defective unborn child from suffering (by being born), to a largely economic motive based on the financial costs of caring for these newborns. It could become increasingly and dangerously tempting to broaden the number and type of prenatal defects which could expose an unborn child to the possibility of court-ordered abortions.

f) *A formula for decision making*

In view of all the considerations and criteria just analyzed, we propose the following by way of a general and summary formula incorporating all the essential tests:

In the event of a pregnant woman's refusal, there are only two prognoses which could justify a court-authorized surgical intervention before birth for the sake of a wanted child. One such prognosis would be that there is a reasonable hope of saving the life of the unborn child who would otherwise probably die. The other prognosis would be that it would represent the only reasonable hope of correcting disabilities likely to result, once born, in intractable and continuing pain and/or in a seriously diminished quality of life.

In both cases such a court order could not be provided unless all the following conditions or criteria are met:

— *the pregnant woman intends to continue the pregnancy but refuses the needed intervention;*

— *the diagnosis and prognosis can be shown to be accurate and reliable;*

---

[254] As already indicated, Section 251 Criminal Code does not include fetal defects as one of the exceptional justifications for abortion. It is true that in practice therapeutic abortion committees often consider such defects in the fetus to constitute a threat to the life or health of the woman, and thus within that provided-for exception, but that is a far cry from a policy whereby a court could order such abortions over the objections of the woman in question. It could hardly be argued despite such refusals that her life or health are endangered by continuing the pregnancy. That being so, such requests would constitute asking the court to order something which is a criminal act.

- *the deficiencies or organic lesions and malformations are such that they require early ex utero correction after a caesarean section, or they cannot be corrected after birth and must be corrected in utero;*

- *the risks to the pregnant woman are minimal;*

- *chances of success are good;*

- *the risks to the unborn child are acceptable in view of the benefits to be gained, and in view of the alternatives to treatment, death or serious and possibly life long pain or disability; the claim of the unborn child to such an intervention, and the interest of the State in ensuring that form of care, increases as the fetus approaches and reaches the stage when it is probably viable and when an induced selective abortion is no longer safe;*

- *any forcible restraint and medication required in order to perform the court-ordered intervention, will not pose a serious risk of injury to the pregnant woman; the mere fact alone that physical restraint and forced medication are required in a given case may not be reason enough not to enforce a court order. But if that required restraint risks injury to the still-resisting woman, that should justify a delay in executing the court order in order (for example) to find another and safe method of restraint;[255] if there is no such method the order should not be enforced.*

Given these rather stringent criteria, it seems reasonable to conclude that court orders authorizing the interventions in question would and should be rare indeed. In principle, court orders permitting even surgical interventions for the sake of the fetus in the event of a woman's refusal would seem to be legitimately included within a right to prenatal care, provided a number of criteria are met. But one proposed criterion in particular is likely to defeat most if not all requests for such authorizations - that of ensuring minimal risk to the non-consenting pregnant women. In our own analysis of the risk factor involved in interventions which could perhaps meet all the other criteria, we could find none which presently passed the minimal risk test, not even intrauterine transfusions.

---

255 It should be noted that in the Colorado case referred to earlier, in which instance a cesarean section was authorized by the court, the pregnant woman in question did not continue to resist, physically or otherwise, after the court order. BOWES, *et al.*, report that after the court's decision, "... the patient, although still reluctant, became more cooperative and agreed to the induction of general anesthesia" (*op. cit., supra*, note 230, at p. 210.)

In that light, one can only disagree strongly with Lieberman, *et al.*, who maintained that all maternal refusals to allow for example medically recommended caesarean sections for the sake of the fetus, are felonies.[256] In their view the physician has the responsibility to try to persuade such women to consent, and if unsuccessful, to warn them they are breaking the law. But in fact they would not presently be breaking the law in the United States or any other jurisdiction. In our view courts *should* be able to grant these authorizations in the rare case which meets, or might in the future meet, the proposed criteria. But one cannot agree with those like Lieberman that the law should be routinely and frequently used in this manner. One cannot but suspect that for some physicians, too ready access to such court authorizations might constitute a new and dangerous license to expand medical paternalism and pressure.

3. *The unborn as child - the Civil law perspective*

This section will be considerably shorter than the previous one which considered the unborn as child from the Common law perspective. The reason for the relative brevity of this section from the Civil law perspective is simply that the basic principles, policies and medical data involved in providing legal protections for unborn children, have already been examined in the previous section. Since for the most part those principles, policies and tests are sufficiently general to be compatible with both legal systems, they need not be considered again in detail here. What remains to be identified are the particular formulations and mechanisms specific to the Civil law of Quebec.

This will necessitate consideration of the Civil Code (including Book Two of the New Civil Code of Quebec, "The Family", introduced as Bill 89);[257] the Draft Civil Code; Bill

---

[256] J. R. LIEBERMAN, *et al.*, "The Fetal Right to Live", (1979) 53 *Obstet. Gynec.* 515.

[257] Bill 89 came into force (April 2, 1981) as Book II of the *Civil Code of Québec*. Since the existing Code is entitled, *The Civil Code of Lower Canada*, there are two Civil Codes presently in effect in Quebec. See on

106 ("An Act to add the reformed law of persons to the Civil Code of Quebec"); the *Youth Protection Act*; the *Public Health Protection Act*.

The goal of this section is essentially the same as that of the previous one - to indicate specific legal doctrines and mechanisms which could be used or expanded as appropriate vehicles to provide anticipatory prenatal protections to unborn children, on the analogy of those already available to children. The general contents of this section will be similar to that of the previous one - the rights of the child as rights of the unborn, the unborn as child whose "safety and development" is compromised, court-ordered medical interventions for the sake of the unborn child.

i) *Rights of the child as rights of the unborn*

It is our general thesis that because unborn children have health care interests and vulnerabilities analogous to those of children, they should be acknowledged to have essentially the same health care rights as those of children, rights which could entitle them to analogous protective legal mechanisms. The first step is to determine what those existing health and protection rights of children are in Quebec Civil Law.

There is an important evolution to be noted since the formulation of the first Civil Code of 1866. That evolution is striking if we compare the Civil Code to the Draft Civil Code completed in 1977. There is first of all a new emphasis on both *persons* and the *protection* of persons, including children. For example, the Preface of the Draft Code states the following:

> It has often been said that the Civil Code was designed for landowners and those in a position to live off their investments, that it is more concerned with the protection of property than with respect for human rights. It was for this reason that there existed a desire that

---

this point, P.-A. CRÉPEAU, *The Civil Codes*, A Critical Edition, Centre of Private and Comparative Law, McGill University, Montreal, 1983, at pp. XI-XIII. Since the article numbers of this new Civil Code of Quebec are not concordant with the article numbers of the earlier and still extant Civil Code (of Lower Canada), in order to avoid confusion we will refer to that Book in what follows as Bill 89.

the recognition of the role of the human person, along with the affirmation and protection of human dignity, be one of the main features of the Draft." [258]

The Draft Code began its emphasis on persons, personal rights and protections, already in its first article, "Every human being possesses juridical personality". In the clear affirmation of children's rights and protections in the Draft Code, the *Youth Protection Act,* and even Bill 106, that goal of protecting human dignity is clearly enshrined. There is no denying that Bill 106[259] blunted and limited that strong and general affirmation by adding another sentence to its article 1: "He is the subject of rights from birth till death". But as already indicated above in this study, there was a chorus of opposition to that quite unjustified addition. That addition is not only out of step with jurisprudence and doctrine of the past many years, but also out of step with a.123 of the same Bill 106 and a.664 of Bill 107.

A second new emphasis apparent in recent times is the shift from a stress on parental rights to a stress on parental duties. Generally speaking the Civil Code has contented itself with an affirmation of parental rights:

a.242. A child, whatever may be the age, owes honour and respect to his father and mother.

a.243. He remains subject to their authority until his majority or his emancipation.

While the Draft Code included those duties of children to parents (in 11.350, 352 Draft Code), it displayed a radical shift away from parental rights and authority for their own sake, to a stress on parental rights and authority being vested in them to better perform their protective roles for their children.[260]

---

[258] P.-A. CRÉPEAU, "Foreword" in *Report on the Quebec Civil Code* 1977 Vol. 1, Draft Civil Code, Éditeur officiel, Québec, 1978 at p. XXIX.

[259] Bill 106, *loc. cit., supra,* n. 23.

The following two articles from the Draft Code make that clear:

> 11.351. Authority is vested in parents so that they may execute their obligations towards their children.
>
> 11.353. Parents have the rights and duties of custody, supervision and education of their children.
>
> They must maintain their children. They represent them in all civil acts.

This same obligatory character of parental duties to children was adopted (with slightly different wording) in Bill 89, and is now law:

> a.647. The mother and father have, with regard to their child, the right and duty of custody, surveillance and education.
>
> They must nourish and maintain their children.

A further aspect to this evolution is the move from paternal authority and duties to those of both parents. This emphasis on shared *parental* authority is evident in the Draft Code (11.350, 354) and finally in Bill 89 (articles 640, 641, 642). In V. 97 Draft Code it is clear that the intensity of the parental obligation to children is one of diligence:

> Parents are bound to ensure with prudence and diligence the education and supervision of their minor children.

Two conclusions can be drawn from the above with relevance to the unborn child. The first is that the shift from a stress on the authority and responsiblity of the father alone to the responsibility of the mother as well, can serve as a remote support for proposals to attach liability to the pregnant mother for violations of her own obligations to her unborn children. The second is that since the unborn child has similar needs for nourishment and maintenance as do children, these

---

260 In the Draft Code itself it is noted that, "The suggested changes are in keeping with the spirit of the *Declaration of the rights of the Child* adopted by the United Nations". Civil Code Revision Office, *Report on the Québec Civil Code*, 1977, Vol. II, Commentaries, Tome I, Éditeur officiel, Québec 1978, at p. 120.

same duties could readily apply to them as well.

The specific health and welfare rights of children are referred to in various places, and most of them could be equally applied to the health and care needs of unborn children as well.

The guiding principle for the rights and protections of the child was clearly spelled out in Bill 89 in what has now become a.30 of the Civil Code:

> In every decision concerning a child, the child's interest and the respect of his rights must be the determining factors.

A similar principle was enunciated in 1.25 Draft Code, and still earlier in a.3 of the *Youth Protection Act*.[261] The same principle is now to be found in a.31 of Bill 106.

Still more specifically we find the following in 1.24 Draft Code:

> Every child is entitled to the affection and security which his parents or those who act in their stead are able to give him, in order to ensure the full development of his personality.

A similar provision is stated in a.30 of Bill 106:

> Every child has a right to the protection, security and attention that his parents or the persons acting in their stead are able to give to him.

More specifically still, we find this provision in a.8 of the *Youth Protection Act*:

> A child is entitled to receive adequate health services and social services and educational services, on all scientific, human and social levels, continuously and according to his personal requirements account being taken of the organization of the resources of the establishments providing such services.

---

261 *Youth Protection Act, loc, cit., supra*, n. 172.

Two conclusions may be drawn from the above with relevance to the unborn child. First of all it is clear that for (born) children, much more is provided for than simply a right not to be harmed by positive acts of negligence. The rights provided for call for positive and affirmative acts of health care and support, matched by obligations of parents to provide that care. It is this same positive thrust and these same affirmative rights which would best promote the interests and health of the unborn child as well.

Secondly, the interests of the unborn child, just as of the child, because of the essential continuity between the child in its prenatal and postnatal state, can be at least "a" determining factor in decisions affecting him. As already conceded, the unborn child's interests cannot be the "only" determining factor, as there are rights of the pregnant woman to be balanced with his.

ii) *The unborn as child whose "safety and development" is compromised*

A number of the circumstances indicating that, "the safety or development of a child is compromised" according to a.38 of the *Youth Protection Act*,[262] could readily apply as well to unborn children. Those which could, in whole or in part, are the following:

> a.38 For the purposes of the present law, the safety or development of a child is considered compromised if:
>
>> (a) his parents are deceased, no longer able to take care of him, or seek to be rid of him and no other person is taking care of him;
>>
>> (b) his mental or emotional development or his health is threatened by the isolation in which he is maintained or the lack of appropriate care;
>>
>> (c) he is deprived of the material conditions of life appropriate to his needs and to the resources of his family;

---

262 *Ibid.*

(d) he is in the custody of a person whose behaviour or way of life creates a risk of moral or physical danger for the child;

(f) he is the victim of sexual assault or he is subject to physical ill treatment through violence or neglect.

Obviously not every aspect or those endangering circumstances could apply to the unborn child. Unborn children clearly cannot be sent away or kept in isolation (at least not from their pregnant mothers), or sexually abused or exposed to moral risk. But considering the vulnerability and health and development needs of the unborn child, adaptations of the other circumstances to the prenatal period would be appropriate.

A point made earlier should be recalled here as well. The protective intervention of a social service or court should only be invoked when parents have failed to provide *adequate* support and care in the various respects indicated by a.38. The violations or suspected violations of maternal or parental obligations to their unborn child (as to their born child) should be serious and continuing before potentially disruptive interventions are allowed. Pregnant women and others should not, after all, be held to do the *best possible* job (in the objective sense) for their children, but only held to the provision of (objectively) *adequate* support and care. The obligation is one of diligence, not result.[263] That an agency might be able to provide better care than parents cannot be a sufficient reason for the state to intervene to protect children.

---

263 This is already recognized to be the case in Quebec regarding children. C. BOISCLAIR for example makes the following assessment of child-welfare decisions by Quebec courts:

Une jurisprudence importante nous indique que seules des causes graves ou exceptionnelles, désignées sous le terme générale 'd'indignité' peuvent faire échec à l'autorité parentale et au droit de garde. (*Les droits et les besoins de l'enfant en matière de garde: réalité ou apparence?*, Publication de la Revue de Droit de l'Université de Sherbrooke, 1978, at p. 28.

As for the specific and protective mechanisms which could be made available to unborn children when needed, here too the analogy with those available for children is relevant. Clearly not all of them are equally appropriate to both children and unborn children, but adapted and revised when necessary, at least some of them could be. Some of these are *voluntary* protections, and some can be *ordered* by a court.

Article 54 of the *Youth Protection Act* provides for a number of voluntary protections for the child. Those readily applicable to the unborn child as well, could be the following:

> a.54 In the form of voluntary measures, a director [of a social services centre] may recommend:
>
> a) that a child remain in his family environment and that his parents present a report periodically on the measures they apply in their own or in the child's regard to correct a previous situation;
>
> b) that a person working for an establishment or body provide aid, counsel or assistance to the child and his family;
>
> e) that a child be referred to a hospital centre, a local community service centre or to an organization in order that he may there receive that care and assistance he may need;
>
> g) that the child receive certain health services.

All of these voluntary mechanisms could be applicable to the unborn child. Obviously it cannot be separated from its mother and sent to a "place of safety", and effective protections would have to assume that physical inseparability. Therefore the home is the natural and best environment in which to provide the specified aid and supervision. Removal of mother and child to a hospital, clinic or another institution, should only be proposed as a last resort, to lessen unbearable pressures of home (e.g. husband or other children), or to provide aid and health services not otherwise available.

The voluntary character of these protective measures would acknowledge (as they already do in the case of children) that protection of the unborn child in the prenatal period need not be contentious and adversarial. Many pregnant women are more unable than unwilling to cope with the stresses of pregnancy and the nutritional or other needs of their unborn children. There is every reason to believe that many pregnant women are ready to acknowledge their need for help when their unborn children are at risk, and that they will ask for it or at least accept it voluntarily if offered.

The *Youth Protection Act* also provides in a.91 that if the security or development of the child requires it, the protective measures listed in a.54 can be *ordered* by a court. A court may also order other measures proper to a.91. Two of these could perhaps be applied to the protection of unborn children. One of these, a.91(a), provides that a court may withdraw from parents their parental authority if they cannot or will not look after their children. Article 91(b) provides for the naming of a tutor for the child.

Though this tutorship is strictly speaking to *the child*, in the case of an unborn child, given its location in the womb of the mother and its dependance upon the mother, the tutorship would in effect have to take the form of a supervision of the mother for the sake of her child. The interest and purpose of the tutorship could nevertheless remain the health and welfare of the endangered unborn child.

Given the new *protective* emphasis of the mechanism of tutorship, it could be a particularly apt legal response to the endangered health of an unborn child. That protective emphasis was already evident in 1.125 Draft Code: "Tutorship is intended to ensure protection of the person and of the patrimony, or of the patrimony only". It is equally evident in a.140 of Bill 106, which reads in part:

> The director of youth protection may also apply for the institution of tutorship ... to a child whose father and mother or tutor fail to fulfill the obligations of maintenance and education...

iii) *Court-ordered medical intervention for the sake of the unborn child*

We already examined above the various types of possible surgical interventions on the fetus or on the pregnant woman for the sake of the fetus, and the responses of Common law courts to date to requests for authorization to proceed with such interventions over the objections of pregnant women. A number of criteria were then proposed for use by courts in considering such a request. It was proposed that if the contemplated intervention represented the only hope of saving the unborn child's life or of correcting serious disabilities likely to result in continuing and intractable pain and/or a very diminished quality of life once born, then, if a number of stringent tests are met, such court authorizations could be justifiable.

Our next question is whether those same criteria and the proposed decision-making formula could not be equally applicable in the context of (Quebec) Civil law. What remains to be examined then are some of the particularities of the (Quebec) Civil law system to determine whether those criteria are compatible with the Civil Code, doctrine, jurisprudence, statutes and the provisions of the Bill 106.

Just as in the Common law, so too in the Civil law, the apparent obstacle to court ordered treatment of the fetus or pregnant woman for the sake of the fetus, is the pregnant woman's inviolability and right to refuse treatment. That fundamental rule of inviolability is affirmed in a.19 of the Civil Code:

> The human person is inviolable. No one may cause harm to the person of another without his consent or without being authorized by law to do so.

It is also affirmed in a.1 of the *Charter of Human Rights and Freedoms*;[264]

> Every human being has a right to life, and to personal security, inviolability and freedom...

149

In Bill 106, articles 11 and 12 propose a more detailed formulation regarding inviolability, including (in a.12) a new and direct reference to the right to refuse treatment:

> a.11 Every person is inviolable and is entitled to his physical integrity.
>
> No harm may be done to the physical integrity of a person without his free and enlightened consent given according to law, or unless it is authorized by law.
>
> a.12 No one may subject a person to an examination, a treatment or an operation required by his physical or mental state of health, or keep him under care in a health establishment, without his consent.
>
> No consent is required in an emergency if the life of the person is in danger, or if his physical integrity is in danger and his consent is not obtainable in time.

The context in which this rule is usually considered is one in which there are no third party interests to be considered, and the issue in effect is whether any other individual or the State may interfere with that person's physical integrity, *in that patient's interest*, and without consent. For that context, two different approaches can be found regarding inviolability.[265] The first is that a competent person's decision as to whether or not to allow a physical intrusion proposed for her benefit, must *always* be respected, no matter what the results for herself and her health. This (majority) view proposes inviolability and its consequence, the right to refuse treatment, as in effect absolute and unassailable.[266]

---

264 *Charter of Human Rights and Freedoms*, R.S.Q., c.C-12.

265 Regarding these "schools of thought" on inviolability, see, R. KOURI, "Blood transfusions, Jehovah's Witnesses and the rule of inviolability of the human body", (1975) 5 *R.D.U.S.*, 156. See also, R. KOURI and A. BERNARDOT, *La Responsabilité Civile Médicale*, Les Éditions Revue de Droit, Université de Sherbrooke, 1980, at p. 133.

266 For a doctrinal justification of this position, see for example R. DIERKENS, *Les droits sur le corps et le cadavre de l'homme*, Masson et cie., Paris, 1966, at p. 42: "Le droit sur le corps n'est pas seulement un droit de défence contre le monde extérieur. Il se rapporte aussi et même primordialement au droit de l'homme de pourvoir librement et souverainement à sa propre destinée". In *Hôpital Notre-Dame* v. *Dame Villemure*, Owen J. opted for this same position: "From a legal point of view, as distinct from a religious point of view, it may be asked whether a

A second view or school of thought holds that the rule of inviolability is only relative. The most articulate representative of this view is A. Mayrand, who wrote:

> C'est précisément dans le principe de l'inviolabilité de la personne que l'on puise la justification d'une intervention imposée. L'inviolabilité de la personne aurait pour but sa protection; or, les droits doivent être exercés dans le sens de leur finalité. Ce serait fausser le droit à l'intégrité corporelle d'un malade que de lui permettre de l'invoquer pour faire échec à ce qui peut conserver sa vie et, par là même, son intégrité essentielle.[267]

In effect this view holds that the relative right to refuse treatment should give way to the absolute duty of others to provide life-saving assistance. Kouri has compellingly criticized this view and opted for the first school of thought:

> ... our objection to the theory of relative inviolability goes deeper than to mere issues of difficulty in application; it strikes at the problem of individual liberty and its constant erosion .... We prefer to think that in drafting article 19 C.C., the Quebec legislator has not abridged a right but rather, has made a clear statement of principle which can be set aside only in formally recognized exceptional circumstances, i.e. when the person *consents*, or when the *law* distinctly allows encroachments upon one's corporal integrity without the necessity of consent.[268] [Emphasis added]

Essentially the same criticism can be levelled at a.12, paragraph 2 of Bill 106, which reads:

> No consent is required in an emergency if the life of the person is in danger; this is also the case if his physical integrity is in danger and his consent is not obtainable in time.

---

person has the legal obligation, or even the right, to prevent another person from shortening or terminating his own life". [1970] C.A. 538, at p. 552.. See also, *Laporte* v. *Laganière, J.S.P., et. al.,* (1972) 18 C.R.N.S. 357 (Que Q.B.), at pp. 368-369; *Beausoleil* v. *Communauté des Soeurs de la Charité de la Providence* [1965] B.R. 37, at p. 41.

267 MAYRAND, *op, cit., supra*, n.1, at p. 48.

268 KOURI, "Blood Transfusions, Jehovah's Witnesses and the rule of inviolability of the human body", *op. cit., supra*, n. 265, at pp. 161,162.

It should be noted that Kouri suggests in this same article (at p. 164) that there is also a third "school of thought" regarding the extent of inviolability, namely, the so-called "expedient" view. To this school would belong those who feel that if a patient refuses tratment, then loses consciousness and becomes critically ill, one could be justified in proceeding with the refused operation because the patient is no longer in

151

This paragraph appears to have been directly inspired by the relative view of inviolability, as exemplified in the position of Mayrand quoted above. Not surprisingly, a number of submissions to the Legislative Committee on the subject of Bill 106 were strongly critical of this paragraph. One such submission had this to say:

> ... le principe du "noli me tangere", la thèse du caractère absolu du droit à l'inviolabilité et sa conséquence normale, le droit de refuser des soins, admis par la doctrine et la jurisprudence, n'existe plus. Par voie de conséquence, il est permis de traiter une personne malgré elle en vue de la sauver.[269]

The submission of the Quebec Human Rights Commission also opted for the absolute point of view, and criticized a.12, paragraph 2 of Bill 106 in part as follows:

> La Commission est d'avis que, même en cas d'urgence, une personne majeure peut, en connaissance de cause, refuser pour elle un traitement même si cela peut entraîner la mort. Il s'agit du respect de l'autonomie de la personne et de son inviolabilité. Prendre parti pour la vie, c'est prendre partie pour la liberté de la personne, ce qui ne signifie pas que la personne en état d'urgence doive être privée du droit au secours car le droit au secours ne signifie pas l'obligation d'être secouru.[270]

---

a position to be consulted and is faced with a life-threatening illness which he was not actually faced with when he refused treatment. Kouri rightly rejects this view by noting that, "strictly speaking, if we were to follow [this viewpoint] with regard to transfusions, would it not necessarily follow that all authorizations, consents or decisions destined to take effect while one is incapacitated would be invalid ?".

Two proponents of the "expedient" view are: W.C.J. MEREDITH, *Malpractice Liability of Doctors and Hospitals*, Toronto, Carswell, 1956, at pp. 155-156; L.E. ROZOVSKY, *Canadian Hospital Law*. Canadian Hospital Association, 1974, at pp. 39-40.

269 BERNARDOT, KOURI and NOOTENS, *op. cit.*, *supra*, n. 24, at p. 4.

This submission proposes replacing a.12, paragraph 2 with the following:

> Nul consentement n'est requis en cas d'urgence, lorsque la vie ou l'intégrité physique de la personne est en danger et que son consentement ne peut être obtenu en temps utile. (p. 6).

270 Commission des droits de la personne du Québec, *op. cit.*, *supra*, n. 28, at p. 7.

The Commission therefore proposes (p. 8) that paragraph 2 be replaced with a text very similar to that proposed by the Professors of the University of Sherbrooke, that is:

In the context of treatment alleged to be in the patient's own interest then, the only exception generally recognized by present law in the absence of that person's consent is when the life or physical integrity of that person is endangered and consent cannot be sought in time.

But if we widen the focus to consider treatment possibilities *not* in the interest of the person for whom the treatment is contemplated, but in the interest of third parties (whether individuals or the State), there are several other exceptions to inviolability to be noted in Quebec Civil law.

There are first of all obligatory medical examinations according to a.399 of the Code of Civil Procedure, which allows a party to an action, "... when there is in issue the physical or mental condition of any party or the victim of the offence which has given rise to the action ... (to) summon at his expense such person by writ of subpoena to have a "*medical examination*". Article 399a of the same Code allows a judge to order that person to have *another* medical examination. On the basis of this article a variety of involuntary interventions have been allowed such as electro-cardiograms[271] and X-rays.[272]

It should be noted that the principle has been established that no one should be obliged to submit to long or painful examinations. An imposed stay of two days, according to one judgment, would be too long because it is close to a form of imprisonment.[273]

En cas d'urgence, nul consentement n'est requis lorsque la vie de la personne ou son intégrité physique est en danger et que son consentement ne peut être obtneu en temps utile.

[271] *New York Life Ins. Co.* v. *Desbiens*, [1942] B.r. 749.

[272] *Lorquet* v. *Sun Life. Ass. Co*, [1938] 2 D.L.R. 777 (Qué. K.B.)

[273] *Toro* v. *Dental Co. of Canada Ltd.*, (1936) 40 R.P. 121 (Super. Ct.)
MAYRAND wites that a. 399 could be very widely interpreted and applied. For example in an action for annulment of a marriage, the plaintiff wife could force her husband to have a medical examination to prove his impotency. *(Op. cit., supra,* n. 1, at p. 110).

An application of article 399 to the prenatal child context could perhaps justify ordering a pregnant woman to undergo a medical examination to verify prenatal abuse and determine appropriate remedial and protective care. Should she refuse, she could then be guilty of contempt of court according to a.50 C.C.P. If she were to be held in contempt of court, it would be important to tailor the sanction to what is best for the health of the unborn child. Obviously imprisonment would not fit that bill, but confinement in an appropriate health services institution might - for example in a detoxification unit if that is what is called for for the sake of her child.

A second form of legal exception to absolute inviolability has to do with imposed medical examinations and treatment on grounds of protecting the health of others. For example, the *Public Health Protection Act*[274] provides for: compulsory immunizations (a.8); treatment for venereal disease (a.10,11); court orders for immunizations, treatment or examinations if refused. According to the *Mental Patients Protection Act*,[275] there can be court-ordered psychiatric examinations and confinement in an institution for persons appearing to be deranged (a.13), if the mental state of the person makes it likely he will endanger his own health or safety or that of others (a.11). And according to the *Workmen's Compensation Act*,[276] the Commission is authorized to compel medical examinations of workers exposed to silicone dust (a.114).

Insofar as these provisions allow imposed examinations or treatment mainly on the grounds of protecting third parties or the public (i.e. from infectious diseases), they may not be completely apt precedents for imposed treatment or examinations of pregnant women for the sake of the fetus. On the other hand, the serious risk of permanent disability to one identifiable victim (of a woman's infectious disease for example), namely her unborn child, may justify the same sort of legal concern and mechanisms.

---

[274] *Public Health Protection Act*, R.S.Q., c.P-35.

[275] *Mental Patients Protection Act*, R.S.Q., c.P-41.

[276] *Workmen's Compensation Act*, R.S.Q., c.A-3.

But could a Québec court order medical intervention on an unborn child or on a pregnant woman for the sake of that child in the event of a refusal by the pregnant woman? An affirmative answer may well be justified. Once again we may refer by analogy to provisions directly intended for minor children. The provisions are articles 42 and 43 of the *Public Health Protection Act*.[277] These articles provide for court-authorized treatment for minor children in the event of parental refusal. Article 42 states, in part,

> Where a minor is under fourteen years of age, the consent of the person having parental authority must be obtained; however, if that consent cannot be obtained or where refusal by the person having parental authority is not justified in the child's best interest, a judge of the Superior Court may authorize the care or treatment.

The test then for court-ordered treatment in the absence of parental consent is that it is either impossible to reach the parents for their consent, or, though refused, the refusal is not in the child's best interests.

Article 43 addresses the specific eventuality of a danger to the minor child's life:

> An establishment or a physician shall see that care or treatment is provided to every person in danger of death; if the person is a minor, the consent of the person having parental authority shall not be required.

Crépeau has argued compellingly that these provisions could also be made to apply to the *unborn* child:

> Une personne majeure peut, en connaissance de cause, refuser pour elle un traitement même si cela peut entraîner la mort; mais peut-elle entraîner aussi dans la mort l'enfant qu'elle porte? Ne jouit-il pas, lui aussi, ainsi que le proclame l'article 18 C.c., du plus fondamental des droits: le droit à la vie? Il y a ici un tel conflit d'intérêts que l'un doit céder devant l'autre. Lequel? Nous optons pour le droit à la vie. En ce qui concerne l'enfant, ce refus est aussi injustifié que celui prévu à l'article 36 [now article 42] de la Loi pour

---

277 *Public Health Protection Act, loc. cit.*, n. 274. These provisions have been available only since 1972, though judicial authorizations for treatment of minors had been granted prior to that date, without explicit legislative support.

> la protection de la santé publique et nous croyons que le curateur (au ventre) pourrait, par analogie, s'adresser à la Cour supérieure en vue de faire autoriser les traitements malgré l'opposition de la mère.[278]

As Crépeau himself implies, the argument for such an intervention on behalf of the unborn child ultimately depends upon whether that child is acknowledged to have legal personality or not, the necessary basis for the right to life to which he explicitly refers. The access of the unborn child to needed treatment, despite maternal refusal, is yet another instance of how, absent the acknowledgement of legal personality for the unborn child, that child would lack the necessary foundation on which to base his claim to a needed protective intervention.

Finally, what is the position of Bill 106 on this matter? Of all the articles of Bill 106, the ones which were targeted as the most confusing and badly drafted, are the articles which might be most relevant to the court-ordered treatment issue. These are articles 13, 14 and 15:

> a.13 Consent is given for a minor by the person having parental authority, or, in the case of impediment, by his tutor.
>
> a.14. Consent is given for a person of full age and incapable of discernment by his tutor or curator; if he is not so represented, it is given by his spouse or, if he has no spouse or his spouse is under an impediment, by a close relative.
>
> a.15 The authorization of the court is required if the minor capable of discernment objects, if the consent of the representative, the spouse or the close relative cannot be obtained, or if the refusal to consent is not justified in the interest of the person.

With a degree of understatement, one of the submissions on Bill 106 stated the following about article 15: "L'article 15, tel que formulé dans le projet, présente une grande difficulté

---

[278] P.-A. CRÉPEAU, "Le consentement du mineur en matière de soins et traitements médicaux ou chirurgicaux selon le droit civil canadien", (1974) *Can. Bar Rev.* 247, at p. 251, n.10.

KOURI *(op.cit., supra,* n. 265 at p. 171) agrees with that analysis by Crépeau.

de compréhension".[279] As it stands now, it is not at all clear to whom the court-authorized treatment could apply, and the age of the minors is not specified. The article refers to "discerning minors", but is the possibility of court-authorized treatment also meant to refer to minors "generally", as in a.13, making it thereby more readily adaptable by extension to the *unborn child* as well? Such a meaning would seem to be compatible with the text in its larger context.

An excellent proposal has been made for reform of the present a.15 of Bill 106. The proposed re-wording brings it very close to the wording of a.42, paragraph 2 of the *Public Health Protection Act*, and thus makes a.15 potentially applicable to the context of children (a.13) and unborn children. It reads:

> Dans le cas des arts. 13 à 15 qui précèdent, s'il est impossible d'obtenir le consentement du titulaire de l'autorité parentale ou du représentant, ou si le refus de consentir n'est pas justifié par l'intérêt de la personne, l'autorisation d'un juge de la Cour supérieure est requise.[280]

In conclusion then, at least the principle is established in Civil law that in the case of minors, when parental refusal of an examination, treatment or operation is not in the interests of that child, a Court may authorize it. By analogy this protective mechanism could perhaps also be applied to *unborn* children in the event of a maternal refusal of medical treatment or surgery on the fetus or herself for the sake of the fetus. But finding support for the principle obviously does not mean that authorizations to treat should be granted without further consideration. Decisions as to whether or not a particular proposed treatment or operation really is in the best interests of the unborn child, *and* does not expose the unconsenting pregnant woman to unjustified risk, require careful application of the criteria and formula proposed in the previous section.

---

279 BERNARDOT, KOURI and NOOTENS, *op. cit.*, *supra*, n. 24, at p. 8.
280 *Id.*, at p. 9.

4. *Protection of the unborn child in the workplace*

Earlier in this study a wide variety of substances hazardous to fetal health and development, divided into chemical, physical and biological hazards, were identified and discussed. It was also noted that not only actually pregnant women and their fetuses are at risk from these substances, but women who are not pregnant, and men as well. Those hazards (and others) are therefore rightly identified as "reproductive hazards", and not just as hazards to the fetus.

That being so, it would be unrealistic and artificial to explore and prepare workplace protections for the fetus in isolation from the wider context which includes men and women among the threatened parties.

There are five major players or parties to be acknowledged in this issue, each with its own interests, sometimes complementary and mutually supportive, but sometimes in conflict. Those five players are: the unborn child, the pregnant or potentially pregnant women, the labour union, the employer and the state. The growing concern to protect fetal health in the workplace is often perceived to be in potential conflict with a major interest of women, namely that of equal and continuing employment. As far as employer and employment policies are concerned, efforts to protect fetal health to a large extent appear to constitute a defensive measure protecting against the threat of subsequent law suits for prenatal injuries allegedly the result of exposure to workplace hazards. As for the state, its efforts to balance competing concerns vary according to the jurisdiction in question, as will be indicated below. Its role in this regard is generally expressed in the form of occupational health and safety legislation, human rights legislation and human rights commissions.

As with other aspects of the right to prenatal care and protection already considered, workplace hazards too call for the balancing of both fetal protection and women's rights. Obviously the goal of policy making in this area, by employers, workman's compensation boards, legislatures and human rights commissions, is to protect both equality and health, the latter including not only the health of the fetus, but that of both men and women as well. In reality, such policies have not been notably successful either in achieving the needed balance, or in protecting either side of the equation, equality or health.

In the past few years, however, there have been some positive signs that policies or policy proposals are now evolving in the direction of a healthy balance between fetal protection and women's rights. Both the achievements to date and the distance yet to go can best be identified by considering separately what appear to be the three types of workplace policy relevant to the concerns of this study:

i) *exclusionary employment policies*, according to which employers do not hire pregnant women, or women with the capacity to become pregnant, for jobs involving exposure to hazards at levels thought to be dangerous to the fetus; or, if already employed, they are removed;

ii) policies granting women the right, at their own initiative, *to refuse work* hazardous to the fetus, combined with a right to reassignment and wage protection;

iii) policies by which employers establish a *single standard of exposure* in the workplace for the substance in question, at a low enough level to ensure full protection for the fetus and *all* workers, especially the most vulnerable workers of both sexes and all ages; to the extent that this policy could be put in place, it would lessen the necessity for both exclusionary employment policies directed only against women, or the need for women to request reassignment.

i) *Exclusionary employment policies*

Of relatively recent origin, exclusionary policies represented a step forward in the protection thus afforded unborn children, but a step backwards with respect to women's rights. And even with respect to the fetus, the resulting protection is incomplete since for the most part only women and not men are barred from jobs hazardous to the fetus and reproductive health.

159

Such policies are sometimes quite overt and explicit, sometimes less so. For the most part they are to be found in company policies, but sometimes they are supported by occupational health and safety legislation as well. An example of an exclusionary company policy, one which led to tragic results, is that of the General Motors plant in Oshawa, Ontario. In 1975 a woman working in a lead storage battery division was asked to give evidence that she was sterile, failing which she would be transferred to a lead-free area of the factory to protect her fetus from exposure to lead. She would have had to work a different shift, resulting in her not being able to be with her children during the day-time. As a result she had a tubal ligation, and commented afterwards: "If you want your job badly enough, you'll do anything". There was good evidence available that exposure of male workers to the same level of lead could be equally hazardous to their reproductive health, and thus to their offspring, but men were not excluded from that division.[281]

Another and similar policy, also involving lead, and with even more tragic results, was that of the American Cyanamid Corporation Plant in West Virginia in 1979. The Company informed its women employees that those working with substances which might endanger the health of a fetus if they become pregnant, would have to be transferred to other jobs. The Company argued that it was impossible to eliminate the risk and only removal would provide the protection needed for the sake of the fetus. The new jobs were lower paying and did not offer the opportunities presently available for overtime. As a result five women chose to be sterilized in order to keep their present jobs. Here too there was evidence that the exposure level in question was equally dangerous to male reproductive health and their future children.[282]

---

[281] Saskatchewan Dept. of Labour, Women's Division, (1979) 3 *About Women*, p.2.

[282] "Company and Union in dispute as Women undergo Sterilization", *New York Times*, Jan. 4, 1979, p. A7. See also, R. BAYER, "Women, Work and Reproductive Hazards", (1982) 12:5 *H.C.R.*, 14. Bayer and others report that such exclusionary employment policies have been adopted in very many corporations, especially those in the petrochemical sector. Among firms with such policies are for example: Dupont, General

Another, though less overt, example of an exclusionary policy, in this case a legislative policy, is to be found in the regulations attached to the (Ontario) *Occupational Health and Safety Act*.283 In 1981 the Ontario government filed a regulation under that Act setting limits for the exposure of workers to lead, and called for regular medical examinations of those exposed. Men and women were not treated differently in the regulation itself. But incorporated in the regulation as a legally binding document is a Code for medical surveillance, and in that Code is a section titled, "Action Levels" which does require that men and women be treated unequally. The section states that workers must be removed from exposure to lead if his or her blood lead concentration exceeds 0.70 mg/L. But if the woman is capable of bearing children, she must be removed when her blood lead concentration exceeds 0.40 mg/L in order to protect the fetus.284 Swinton concludes:

> Such a regulation will undoubtedly result in the exclusion of women from certain places of employment where lead is used, indirectly sanctioning a staffing practice of some employers who have barred women of child-bearing capacity from manufacturing processes using lead.285

Predictably, exclusionary policies have come under attack by many groups and individuals, especially (but by no means only) feminists. in a 1979 edition of *Feminist Studies* for example, it was stated that the focus on fetal rights in such policies, "... brought us back to the Victorian notion that woman's childbearing capacity - in short her biology - should determine where and whether she should work".286

Motors, B.F. Goodrich, Sun Oil, Gulf Oil, Union Carbide, Allied Chemical and Monsanto (Bayer, p. 15). Bayer claims that given the list of industrial chemicals with fetotoxic potential, exposure to which these and other companies are seeking to exclude fertile women, they could (if such policies were consistently applied) be excluded from as many as 20,000,000 jobs in the U.S. (p.15).

283 *Occupational Health and Safety Act*, R.S.O. 1980, C. 321.

284 Code for Medical Surveillance, s. 4(1) (a) (i). Cited by K. SWINTON, "Regulating Reproductive Hazards in the Workplace: Balancing Equality and Health", (1983) 33 *U. Toronto L.J.*, 45.

285 SWINTON, *id.*, at p. 45.

The (U.S.) Coalition for the Reproductive Rights of Workers has stated:

> Exclusionary policies are discriminatory because they deny women equal employment opportunity and they ignore the fact that reproductive hazards threaten men as well. Companies should clean up the workplace instead of forcing workers to pay the price of management's negligence.[287]

Employers and business interests give several responses in defence of these exclusionary policies. They deny first of all that anyone is required to be sterilized and take no responsibility for the women who did so.[288] Others claim that the exclusion of all fertile women is "necessary" because of the high costs involved in reducing exposure levels to the point that the fetus would not be endangered.[289] Most employers also acknowledge that exclusionary policies for fertile women are used as a shield against potential actions for prenatal injury to a child injured prenatally by exposure to hazardous substances in the workplace.

As already indicated above, actions for prenatal injury have long been recognized now, both in Common law jurisdictions and in the Civil law of Quebec. On the basis of decisions such as *Jorgensen* and *Renslow*,[290] both involving actions for preconception injury to parents, there is every reason to include employers among those with duties and obligations of prenatal care towards unborn children of their

---

[286] R. PETCHESKY, in (summer, 1979) *Feminist Studies*.

[287] *CRROW Newsletter*, Spring 1981, at p. 1.

[288] See for example R.B. GOLD, "Women Entering Labour Force Draw Attention to Reproductive Hazards for Both Sexes", (February, 1981) *Family Planning Population Reporter*, at p. 11.

[289] An example is this statement by P.J. Gehring, the Director of Health and Environmental Services at Dow Chemicals:

> "The difficulty and cost of implementing good industrial hygiene shouldn't be used as a blanket excuse to exclude women, But if the cost is going to rise exponentially to reach a certain level for uniquely fetal toxins, it's justified to take a woman out of the workplace then." *(Wall Street Journal.* Feb. 9, 1981).

[290] *Supra, pp. 51-53*

employees, and they should indeed be liable if they fail to perform them. But (as will be argued below) there may well be a better and fairer expression of that duty or obligation than merely the application of blanket exclusionary policies.

But is that fear of employers that they are exposed to actions for prenatal injury and staggering judgments against them, realistic? Probably not. If not, since one of the pillars of their case for exclusionary employment policies is considerably weakened, so too is the case itself. One tends to agree with Swinton when she observes the following:

> Even with a recognized duty of care to a child for pre-natal injuries, recovery in tort is far from easy. There are difficult problems of causation in any case of industrial disease, for 'cause' is often established by a lengthy process of acquiring statistical evidence connecting exposure to disease. Even if an individual contracts a disease, he or she must show the cause was workplace exposure rather than the environment. A child born deformed will thus have to show a link between the injury and maternal exposure to a toxic substance in the workplace of the employer sued. Often the mother will not know the substances to which she was exposed or their concentration and her length of exposure ....[291]

Are these exclusionary policies discriminatory in Canada? Neither legislation nor case law are entirely clear in the matter. It is of course a fact that the Canadian Human Rights Act, the ten provincial Human Rights Acts and the two territorial Fair Practices Ordinances prohibit discrimination in employment on grounds of sex, race, religion and various other factors. But what is yet to be clearly and finally determined is whether the exclusionary employment policies in question constitute "discrimination on the basis of sex".

The relatively little case-law dealing with discrimination in the context of health and safety issues appears for the most part to have adopted the analysis and conclusion of the 1978 Supreme Court of Canada decision in *Bliss* v. *A.-G. of*

---

[291] SWINTON, *op. cit.*, *supra*, n. 284, at p. 66. See also T. ISON, "The Dimensions of Industrial Disease", Queen's Industrial Relations Centre, Reprint No. 35, 1978, at pp. 3-4.

163

Canada.[292] The issue involved a challenge to the pregnancy benefit scheme in the *Unemployment Insurance Act,* and it was decided under the equality provision, s.1 (b), of the *Canadian Bill of Rights.*[293] Though the *Unemployment Insurance Act* imposed a higher standard of work on pregnant women to qualify for benefits than it did on other workers, in a unanimous judgment, Ritchie J. held that any discrimination there may have been was not on grounds of sex, but of pregnancy, since non-pregnant women were treated in the same way as men. In the words of Ritchie J., "... any inequality between the sexes in this area is not created by legislation but by nature".[294]

In a 1979 Ontario arbitration case involving the policy of General Motors to exclude all women of child-bearing capacity from its battery division, the claim was that it was discriminatory because men with child-bearing capacity were not similarly excluded. The arbitrator concluded, as did the Supreme Court in *Bliss,* that because of their procreative function (not their sex), women can be treated differently from men, and since there was evidence that exposure to lead can harm fertility and fetal health, putting women at greater risk than men, the policy of the employer was legitimate in this instance.[295]

In Quebec, two complaints of this sort were brought before the Quebec Human Rights Commission alleging sex discrimination contrary to sections 10 and 16 of the Quebec

---

[292] *Bliss* v. *A.-G. of Canada,* (1978) 92 D.L.R. (3d) 417 (S.C.C.)

[293] *Canadian Bill of Rights,* R.S.C. 1970, Appendix III.

[284] *Bliss* v. *A.-G. of Canada, loc. cit., supra,* n. 292 at p. 422.

Swinton writes the following about that decision: "The interpretation [of s.1 (b) of the Bill of Rights], however, is unduly restrictive, for it permits widespread discrimination against women on the basis of pregnancy or the ability to become pregnant, conditions which men can never experience". *Op. cit., supra,* n. 284, at p. 58.

[295] *Re General Motors of Canada and United Automobile Workers, Local 222* (1979) 24 L.A.C. (2d) 388 (Palmer).

Charter of Human rights and Freedoms.[296] However, in both decisions it was held, again as in *Bliss*, that the Charter does forbid discrimination between males and females, but not between women on the basis of pregnancy.[297]

On the other hand, a recent decision by a federal board of inquiry came to the opposite conclusion, that discrimination based on pregnancy really is in effect discrimination on the basis of sex in view of the more onerous impact of this sort of policy and discrimination on women.[298]

A last case worthy of mention at this point is the 1981 decision of a (federal) board of inquiry in *Bhinder* v. *Canadian National Railways*.[299] Though the specific issue did not involve fetal health, the principle therein established could perhaps be applied to the issue we are considering. The issue in that case involved a conflict between an employer's rule which required the wearing of a hard hat, and the Sikh religious rule that men are obliged to wear turbans. It was held by the board that an employer may not exclude an employee on the basis of a prohibited ground of discrimination (in this case religion) only because the *employee himself* was at greater risk as a result (i.e. wearing a turban instead of a hard hat). The board also said that it is up to the *employee* (not the employer) in such cases to assess the risk and make his or her own choice.

The decision is in accord with other decisions and with the thrust of occupational health and safety legislation generally, which allows employers to exclude a worker from employment

---

[296] *Charter of Human Rights and Freedoms, loc, cit., supra*, n. 264.

[297] *Breton* v. *La société Canadienne des Métaux Reynolds Ltée* (1981), 2 C.H.R.R. D532 (Que. Prov. Ct.); *Nye* v. *Burke*, (1981) 2 C.H.R.R. D538 (Que. Prov. Ct.). Both cases (and that in the following note) first came to this writer's attention in Swinton, *op. cit., supra*, n. 284, at p. 61.

[298] *Tellier-Cohen* v. *Treasury Board*, (1982) 82 CLLC, 1055 (Dion), (paragraph 17, 007).

[299] *Bhinder* v. *Canadian National Railways*, (1981) 2 C.H.R.R. D 546 (Cummings).

on the basis of a prohibited ground of discrimination only when that characteristic would endanger *other workers* or the *public*.

If one applied the *Bhinder* decision to the exclusionary policies used to protect only the health of *women* (not the fetus), then one could conclude that such policies were discriminatory. After all, the matter of sex alone does not affect performance, and any risks she herself may be incurring do not endanger other workers or the public. One is inclined to agree with Swinton that in cases where only her own health is at issue, where she is not pregnant, does not intend to become pregnant and practices a reliable form of birth control, then,

> The woman's freedom to choose would govern, rather than employer paternalism. This would be particularly true if male reproductive capacity was equally at risk with female reproductive capacity, for where both sexes are at risk but only one sex is 'protected', there appears to be discrimination.[300]

But what if the woman is pregnant or is trying to become pregnant? In the interest of protecting the existing or future fetus, the employer may well have a right or even a duty to exclude such pregnant women or those likely to be so from workplaces which continue to be hazardous to unborn children. Once we add the fetus to the equation, then it is no longer only the (woman) employee herself who is at risk, but the unborn child. But acknowledging such a right or duty in the employer should not in our view absolve that employer from what we shall propose below as his *primary* duty or obligation - to take reasonable measures to ensure that the workplace is sufficiently safe that women, whether pregnant or not, and men as well, can work there without the need for exclusionary policies. Nor does the right or duty of the employer to exclude pregnant women from a hazardous workplace necessarily absolve both women and men from exercising their legal right to refuse work and request reassignement when they know that work is hazardous to their existing or future unborn children. It is to this second type of policy that we now turn.

---

300 SWINTON, *op. cit., supra*, n. 284, at p. 63.

ii) *The woman's right to refuse work and be reassigned*

To one extent or another all workers in Canada, with the exception of Prince Edward Island, the Yukon and the North West Territories have a statutory right to refuse work. In some cases the work may be refused only when the work is dangerous to the *worker's own health or safety* (Manitoba and New Brunswick); in some other cases it may be refused also when *another employee's* health or safety is endangered (Canada, Ontario and Alberta); in some cases the right is wider still, allowing refusal of work when the health or safety of *any person* at the workplace is threatened, whether employee or not (Saskatchewan, Newfoundland); in still other cases the refusal appears to be permitted even when the health or safety of any person may be endangered (British Columbia, Quebec and possibly, Nova Scotia). In these cases, the person endangered presumably need not be an employee or even be at the workplace. In the case of Nova Scotia the relevant legislation (*Industrial Safety Act*, R.S.N.S. 1967, c.141, s.15) is somewhat vague about whose health and safety must be endangered.

Of interest to this study is the fact that those endangered according to the last two categories (any person at the workplace, or any person) could in principle include the unborn children of pregnant employees. As we shall indicate below, only Quebec's statute makes specific provision for the endangered fetus, but the wording of the right to refuse in the other provinces indicated would at least appear to be open to this possibility. Whether for example Labour Relations Boards would be likely to accept such an interpretation is of course another matter, one which will be addressed below. The fetus is not yet generally included within the meaning of "person" for such purposes.

Only the federal government, in the *Canada Labour Code*,[301] and Quebec, in its *Act Respecting Occupational*

---

301 *Canada Labour Code*, R.S.C. 1970, c. L-1.

Health and Safety[302] explicitly provide for no loss in pay as a result of the refusal. The relevant statutes of the other provinces have no explicit provision to cover the question of pay. The initiative to refuse the work is the worker's, and the burden of proof that there are "reasonable grounds" to believe there was such a danger, is on the worker as well.

Our first question is, does this right to refuse hazardous work, where it exists, also provide a pregnant woman with the right to refuse work she fears might endanger her unborn child? Our second question will be, even if she does have that right, are there obstacles and conditions involved in its exercise such that it may not be the victory it appears?

A comparison between the occupational health and safety legislation in Quebec[303] and Ontario[304] will take us a long way towards answering both questions in at least a general manner. Of all the relevant provincial occupational health and safety legislation, only that of Quebec provides not only the general right available to all workers to refuse dangerous work (s.12), but also the statutory right of pregnant women and nursing mothers to be reassigned and to the continuance of salary (ss.40-48). In particular, section 40 of Quebec's Act states:

> s.40 A pregnant mother who furnishes to her employer a certificate attesting that her working conditions may be physically dangerous to her unborn child, or to herself by reason of her pregnancy, may request to be re-assigned to other duties involving no such danger that she is reasonably capable of performing ...

Section 41 permits an immediate refusal to continue working in that dangerous position if not immediately re-assigned:

> s.41 If a requested re-assignment is not made immediately the pregnant worker may stop working until she is re-assigned or until the date of delivery.

---

302 *An Act Respecting Occupational Health and Safety*, R.S.Q., c.S-2.1.

303 *Ibid.*

304 *Occupational Health and Safety Act, loc. cit., supra*, n. 283.

Section 43 provides for the continuance of benefits:

> s.43 A worker who exercises her rights under sections 40 and 41 retains all benefits attached to her regular employment before her re-assignment to other duties or before her work stoppage.

As far as salary is concerned, sections 36 and 37 apply, which provide that if not re-assigned immediately her full salary is protected for five working days. Following that period, she may apply for an indemnity to the Commission de la santé et de la sécurité du travail under the *Act Respecting Indemnities for Victims of Asbestosis and Silicosis in Mines and Quarries*.[305]

Section 46 grants the same rights to nursing mothers:

> s.46 A worker who furnishes to her employer a certificate attesting that her working conditions involve risks for the child she is breast-feeding may request to be re-assigned to other duties involving no such risks that she is reasonably capable of performing ...

In Ontario, however, refusal by pregnant women of work dangerous to the fetus, and re-assignment, does not appear to be provided by the *Occupational Health and Safety Act*, even by the widest interpretation of its provisions. In the first place the *Act* itself makes no explicit reference to pregnant women or unborn children. Only in the Code for Medical Surveillance attached to the Act's regulations does one find reference to the exposure of pregnant women to lead (in s.4 of the Code), and the exposure of "females capable of bearing children" to mercury (in s.5 of the Code). But, as already noted above, that Code does not grant pregnant women or woman capable of bearing children the right to refuse work and be re-assigned, rather it provides only for their removal.

The pregnant woman in Ontario *may* be able to invoke section 23 of the *Occupational Health and Safety Act* to refuse work unsafe to *her* and to be re-assigned. But neither that section nor any others in that *Act* provide any statutory

---

[305] *Act Respecting Indemnities for Victims of Asbestosis and Silicosis in Mines and Quarries*, R.S.Q., c. 1-7.

support at all for a refusal and re-assignment based upon fears of endangering her *fetus*. Section 23 itself allows workers to refuse work if they have reason to believe that any equipment or thing used in that work is likely to endanger *herself or another person*, or if the physical condition of the workplace is likely to endanger *herself*. Swinton notes with reason, that:

> An interpretation of section 23 of the Act which extends the right of refusal to the susceptible worker, including the pregnant woman, seems consistent with the legislative objective of individual initiative in protecting health and safety.[306]

But extending that interpretation still further to include endangering the fetus as a ground for refusal would not appear to be justified. One could perhaps construe danger to her unborn child as constituting danger to herself, but whether that construction would stand up to the required investigation by the employer, or arbitration by the Labour Relations Board in the event of a grievance, is doubtful.

The test itself which has been applied by Labour Relations Boards when the right to refuse work and be re-assigned has been invoked is further reason to doubt that extended interpretation. A decision by a Labour Relations Board in Ontario held that the test is whether:

> ... the *average employee* at the workplace, having regard to his general training and experience, would, exercising normal and honest judgment, have reason to believe that the circumstances presented an unacceptable degree of hazard to himself or to another employee.[307] (Emphasis added)

Swinton notes that, "The words are not supportive of a pregnant woman's right to refuse work which she fears might endanger a fetus, for she is unlikely to be an 'average worker', particularly in a predominantly male environment."[308]

---

306 SWINTON, *op. cit., supra*, n. 284, at p. 70.

307 *Re Pharand & Inco Metals Ltd.*, [1980] 3 Can. L.R.B. Rep. 194 (O.L.R.B.), at p. 208. For details and comment regarding this decision, see M.I. NASH, *Occupational Health and Safety Law*, CCH Canadian Ltd., Don Mills, Ontario, 1983, at p. 106.

308 SWINTON, *op. cit., supra*, n. 261, at p. 70.

170

In fact a recent ruling by the Ontario Ministry of Labour was to the effect that a pregnant woman exposed to diseases or substances hazardous to her fetus, does not have the right to refuse work because she is not in imminent danger and there is no specific protection for the unborn child under the law.[309] In this instance the seven month pregnant woman was a counsellor in an institution for the mentally retarded and was working with a patient who was a hepatitis carrier. She was told by physicians that if she were infected in the last two months of pregnancy, her child would have a 75 percent chance of becoming a hepatitis carrier. In fact the centre did transfer her as requested, but it was made clear that she had no actual right to such transfer. A report of this event concludes with the following:

> Labour Ministry officials, after poring over the law governing the right to refuse work, solemnly pronounced that while Mrs. Ruttan might enjoy protection from health hazards in the workplace, her baby did not. The fetus was not covered in the legislation.[310]

We come now to our second question - even if or where (as in Quebec) there is a right to refuse work and be re-assigned on grounds of danger to the fetus, is this necessarily in practice the victory it might appear? There is little doubt that the availability of such a right is indeed a victory in terms of the woman's autonomy and initiative. As such this second policy option if generally enacted, should help to prohibit exclusionary employment policies. However, without questioning the real gains of such a policy, there are at least three remaining problems with this approach, all of which raise questions as to whether such policies would really represent in practice a victory for women and unborn children.

---

[309] "Pregnant Woman couldn't shun work despite health risk,", *Globe and Mail*, Dec.9, 1982, at p. 4. The same report states that a recent Ontario public service arbitration board ruled that the belief that radiation from video display terminals can harm an unborn child, gave a pregnant Government employee reasonable grounds to refuse work. The decision is referred to as "unprecedented", which in a sense it is. But in reality this decision was made under the terms of the union contract, and not under the provisions of the Occupational Health and Safety Laws.

[310] "Fetus at Risk", *Globe and Mail*, Dec. 10, 1982, at p. 6.

One of these problems has to do with the information needed by a pregnant and potentially pregnant woman in order to make decisions to refuse work hazardous to unborn children, and to make that case strong enough to convince for example inspectors and Labour Relations Boards. Such information is not generally available or easily obtained, even though one of the goals of recent occupational health and safety legislation is to ensure the workers' rights to information about workplace hazards.[311] As Chenier for example has noted:

> While the problems of identifying the general health concerns associated with many workplaces are great, trying to identify reproductive hazards is an enormous task. Most workers do not have access to full information about potential workplace hazards. Many reproductive problems are difficult to link directly to the workplace.[312]

There is a second and still more fundamental problem involved in placing the whole burden of protecting fetal health on the pregnant woman's initiative. It could make it too easy for employers to leave in place otherwise correctable hazardous workplace conditions, hazardous not only to pregnant women and their fetuses but to the reproductive health of men as well, and thereby to the health of their future children. It could be tempting for employers to either remove susceptible pregnant women from hazardous conditions (as present exclusionary policies dictate), or encourage the exercise of womens' initiative to refuse hazardous work, rather than incur the expenses of lowering the release of dangerous substances to a level safe for everyone.

A third problem or limitation about work refusal, re-assignment and wage protection is that they are directed only to those presently employed. They do not necessarily attack the aspect of discriminatory employment policies whereby those susceptible to certain hazards are simply not hired at all.

---

311 For example ss. 8 (6) (d), 9, 14 (2) (a) of the (Ontario) *Occupational Health and Safety Act, loc, cit., supra*, n. 283. and ss. 10 (1), 51 (9) (10), 52 of the (Quebec) *Act Respecting Occupational Health and Safety, loc. cit., supra,* n, 302.

312 CHENIER, *op. cit., supra*, n. 145, at p. 57.

iii) *Single exposure standards to protect all workers of both sexes and the fetus*

This third type of policy is still the furthest from realization. Essentially it would involve setting workplace exposure levels low enough, or providing sufficient protection, to protect the fetus and all workers, including the most vulnerable workers of both sexes and all ages. But as already indicated earlier, employers generally object on grounds of the expenses involved, many of which would be passed on to consumers. There is, however, some evidence to the effect that many industries or agencies do not even seriously consider this alternative in planning company or legislative policy. This appears to have been the case for example in the establishment of levels of lead exposure in Ontario workplaces, an issue referred to above. The Ministry of Labour apparently never seriously considered the economic or technological feasibility of adopting the lower level of lead exposure decreed for pregnant woman (0.40 mg L), for *all* workers.[313]

By contrast, a large step in the direction of establishing single standards and removing discriminatory procedures, was recently agreed to by the Atomic Energy Control Board. Present Atomic Energy Control Board regulations stipulate that for both pregnant women and women of reproductive capacity, the abdominal dose limit of radiation is 0.2 rem per 2 weeks. For male workers the restriction is that they should not receive more than 3 rems in 3 months. A recent ruling by the Canadian Human Rights Commission lead to the announcement by the Atomic Energy Control Board that it will modify its regulations to place the same dose limit on male and female workers regardless of reproductive capacity, and the lower dose rates will apply only to pregnant women.[314] Employers will now find it far more difficult to

---

[313] See SWINTON, *op. cit., supra*, n. 284, at p. 54.

[314] See, Canadian Human Rights Commission, *Summary of Decisions*, October/November, 1981.

justify exclusion of women when it comes to hiring for jobs involving exposure to radiation.[315]

But even this step, despite its positive aspects in moving towards a single standard for men and most women as well as attacking discriminatory employment policies and promoting the autonomy of women, is not pure gain. The burden will now be more obviously and onerously on the pregnant woman to protect the fetus, since the woman will have the burden of informing the employer if she is pregnant or plans to become pregnant.

And there is a curious irony in the fact that the desirable goals of the autonomy and equal access of women to jobs, have in this instance to some extent been purchased at the expense of putting themselves, their unborn children and future children at greater risk of radiation damage than they already were. For instead of lowering the permissible radiation exposure level for *everyone* to the stricter dose limit of 0.2 rems per 2 weeks, everyone except pregnant women (those, that is, who notify the employer), will now be exposable to the higher and less strict limit of 3 rems in three months. There is little doubt that the biggest single reason why this state of affairs is nevertheless acceptable to and even sought after by women, is the unequal employment opportunities for men and women. In the interest of equalizing those opportunities, even health does not seem to some of them too high a price to pay. Bayer has observed the following in that regard:

> In the name of equal opportunity, the defenders of women's rights have demanded the freedom to take on those risks. In the name of fetal health, corporations have sought to restrict the liberty of working women. Uniting the two sides of the conflict over reproductive hazards in the workplace is a recognition that the American economy so limits the possibilities of its women workers that they would demand, as a sign of liberation, the right to share with men access to reproductive risks.[316]

---

[315] Ontario Hydro for example has announced as a result of the imminent AECB change in regulations that it will modify its discriminatory hiring policies based upon the earlier AECB regulations. See M. LANGTON, "Double Exposure: The Fight Against Reproductive Hazards in the Workplace", (1980) 1 *Health Sharing*, 14. See also N. CHENIER, *op. cit., supra*, n. 289 at p. 44.

[316] BAYER, *op. cit., supra*, n. 282, at p. 19.

We are now in a position to make some summary conclusions. First of all, there can be little doubt that from the perspective of the protection of fetal and reproductive health, the most attractive policy is one which establishes single and strict exposure standards for workplace hazards, at a level low enough to ensure the fullest possible protection even for the most vulnerable workers, men and women. When feasible, such levels should be formulated, made mandatory and periodically revised in the light of new evidence and research. As such the primary duty for protecting the fetus in the workplace would fall upon the legislator and the employer. Since workplace hazards are, after all, a societal problem, it is manifestly unfair to place the burden for reproductive and fetal health entirely on the shoulders of parents or prospective parents by leaving it entirely to their initiative whether to refuse work or not. Single and strict exposure levels are also the best protection of equal job opportunities for women not yet hired.

In the event that such single and strict standards are not feasible, because for instance the cost of reducing emissions or providing needed protection would (by some objective standard) be prohibitive, or because the needed technololgy is not yet available, then both the first and second type of policy could be justified, with certain important qualifications. Exclusionary policies could be justified in this event if the exposure is known to be hazardous to fetal health, but only actually pregnant women or women intending to become pregnant should be so excluded, not those who have no intention of bearing children. When both men and women are at risk, these exclusionary policies should apply to both, not just women. Qualified in these two respects, the twin goals of on the one hand providing for the protection of fetal health, and the other hand for equal access to job opportunities for women, could be reasonably well achieved and balanced.

Whereas such an exclusionary policy, qualified as just indicated, is justified in the most seriously hazardous conditions, the already available right to refuse hazardous work (combined with re-assignment and protected salary) should be explicitly extended (as in Quebec) to cover refusals for the sake of fetal and reproductive health. Whereas exclusionary policies should be available to employers only exceptionally and for extreme cases, this right to refuse, as an expression of employee initiative and autonomy, should be available to employees whenever it can be reasonably appealed to. Women (or men) who have reason to refuse hazardous work for the sake of their unborn children, deserve protection from severe financial sacrifice by having their wages protected.

When re-assignment and wage protection is available, it is arguable that both women and men have not only the right, but the duty, to refuse work known to be hazardous to existing or future unborn children. In such instances the sacrifice to the workers would be minimal, especially when compared to the possible defects and suffering in their offspring thereby avoided.

Chapter IV

BALANCING PRENATAL CARE AND ABORTION

It has already been noted a number of times in this study that the right of the unborn child to prenatal care and protection cannot be absolute or without qualifications and exceptions. As with all rights or interests, there will be others in competition with this right to prenatal care, and a balance must be sought. This is particularly so with regard to the pregnant woman.

Even if one succeeds in establishing that the unborn child should have juridical personality and the rights to life and inviolability, the pregnant woman has those same rights. This need to find a balance fair to both has already been examined in two specific contexts - that of court-ordered interventions on the pregnant woman for the sake of the fetus (requiring a balance between fetal health and maternal risk), and that of workplace hazards (requiring a balance between fetal health and the equal access of women to employment). We come now to a third context or issue raising that same need to balance competing rights - that of the unborn child's right to prenatal care on the one hand, and the woman's right to abortion on the other.

1. *Interpreting abortion in the Criminal Code*

It could be argued that in view of the pregnant woman's right to abortion accorded by the *Criminal Code* in s.251(4), the right to prenatal care and the fundamental rights to life and inviolability are rendered meaningless. But not so. In the first place the mother's right to abortion is itself very narrowly defined and qualified in the Criminal Code, and the Code itself betrays a clear and predominant intent to protect the unborn. Secondly, the possibility of abortion by no means renders meaningless the unborn child's rights to life, inviolability and prenatal care - it only imposes a particular condition upon them.

A careful study of the Criminal Code reveals that, although the *full* protection of the Code is available to the unborn only when it "becomes a human being" at the moment of live birth,[317] that is not to say that before birth the unborn is accorded no protection at all, or that the interests of the conceived but unborn are granted no recognition at all. Quite the contrary. In effect the Criminal Code emphasis is clearly on the side of continuing legal protection from conception to birth. Section 251 makes abortion itself a crime, and since no distinction is made as to stages of gestation, abortion is presumably equally a crime at all stages of gestation. Section 221(1) makes the killing of an unborn child in the act of birth an indictable offence (though not homicide), punishable by life imprisonment. Finally, according to s.226, a pregnant woman about to give birth who does not seek necessary assistance because she wishes her child to die, commits an indictable offence, whether her child dies immediately before or during birth.

The single and exceptional justification of abortion in the Criminal Code is that found in s.251(4), namely on condition that it is performed by a qualified medical practitioner after approval by a therapeutic abortion committee if that committee feels that, "... the continuation of the pregnancy ... would or would be likely to endanger her life or health" - s.251(4)(c).[318] Similarly, s.221(2) permits an intervention during the act of birth by one, "... who by means that, in good faith, he considers necessary to preserve the life of the mother of a child, causes the death of such child".

---

317 Criminal Code as amended s. 206 (1).

318 It should be noted that the Supreme Court decision in the *Morgantaler* case somewhat broadened the application (though not the principle) of this exception when it held that the common law defence of necessity could make an abortion legal though it had not been approved by a therapeutic abortion committee. But for this defence to apply the abortion would still have to be necessary to save the mother's life or health as specified in s. 251 (4), and it must have been impossible to follow the normal procedure of prior abortion committee approval as also specified in s.251 (4). See *Morgantaler* v. *R.*, [1976] 1 S.C.R. 616; also see [1976] C.A. 129; (1974), 42 D.L.R. (3d) 444 (Que. Q.B.)

Clearly then the woman's right to life and health has legal precedence and priority over the unborn child's right to life and health when those rights of mother and unborn directly compete and require balancing. For this reason, Weiler and Catton are essentially correct when they note that, "... the law is extending its protection to the potentiality of human life, but ... when the potentiality of life conflicts with rights of those actually living, the rights of the latter will prevail".[319] However, that comment suggests that *whenever* there is a conflict between (any of) the rights of unborn human life and born human life the rights of the latter will prevail. A more accurate phrasing would be that in a conflict between the life or health of both, then, but only then, those rights of the woman may (not necessarily will) prevail.

Having acknowledged the exceptional condition in which the law permits abortion, it becomes important to first of all recognize that the exception *is* in fact an exception, and therefore is to be restrictively interpreted. As Somerville has noted:

> Such approval constitutes an exception from the provision prohibiting the procural of a miscarriage and hence protecting the foetus. As section 251(4) is an exception it is to be restrictively interpreted. That is, section 251(4) must be interpreted in such a way that, consistently with acknowledging the lawfulness of a procedure to procure a miscarriage which falls within its terms, it *least distracts* from the provision in the general section for the protection of the foetus.[320] (Emphasis added)

Secondly, the exception allowing abortion, precisely because it is to be restrictively interpreted may well be limited only to the *evacuation of* the woman's fetus, and not as well to destruction of the fetus when the latter is avoidable. Somerville has compellingly established that:

> Such evacuation may or may not unavoidably involve the death of the foetus. But where it does not, the decriminalizing of the procural

---

[319] WEILER and CATTON, *op. cit., supra,* n. 7, at p. 647.

[320] M. SOMERVILLE, "Reflections on Canadian Abortion Law: Evacuation and Destruction - Two Separate Issues", (1981) 31 *U. Toronto L.J.,* 1, at p.15.

of the miscarriage does not in itself carry with it a right to kill the fetus unnecessarily.[321]

A third and related restriction upon the scope of the exception to the criminality of abortion, has to do with the status and rights of the fetus born alive and viable as a result of a therapeutic abortion, no matter what method was used.[322] Whether or not the intention was to abort the fetus, and whether or not the abortion was legal, once the unborn child is born alive and viable, it would appear to fall within the "definition" of "human being" in s.206(1) and thus is entitled to the full range of protections available to all (other) human beings, including the right to post-natal care and support.[323]

As a result, not only should the physician performing an abortion have a duty to choose the least harmful-to-the-unborn means possible (consistent with the mother's "higher" right to life and health). If the child is potentially viable he

---

[321] *Ibid.*

Accordingly, SOMERVILLE recommends in part that, "... the physician should have an obligation to take all reasonable measures to preserve the life of the foetus in so far as these are consistent with carrying out the abortion. To this end, when there is a reasonable possibility that a viable foetus is involved, the least mutilating means of abortion which are reasonably available should be used. This requirement would be subject to the proviso that such means need not be used if they constitute an undue added risk to the woman's life or health ... Thus section 221 could be amended or interpreted in such a way that, consistently with recognizing a woman's right to abortion under section 251 (4), it will protect the foetus against being unnecessarily and intentionally killed. Further ... two new sections, sections 203a and 204a should be added to the Code. These would legislate, respectively, the offences of negligently killing and wounding a potentially viable foetus". *Id.*, pp. 25-26.

[322] Live and viable fetuses (often unexpectedly) surviving therapeutic abortions are not rare. By roughly the twentieth week of gestation an unborn child is considered at present to be potentially viable, that is capable of living outside the womb, though usually with some degree of available "artificial" assistance. In 1974 there were apparently 174 legal abortions performed later than twenty weeks of gestation. See the *Report of the Committee on the Operation of the Abortion Law* (Known as the "Badgley Report"), Ottawa, 1977, at pp. 214, 310.

[323] See also, AMENT, "The Right to be Well Born", (*supra*, note 156), at p. 29, who correctly observes in support of the right of such newborns to postnatal care, "Would-be aborted children who survive the birth process must be accorded full human rights. The humanity of a born child cannot depend on so frail a thread as the intention of the mother, the person performing the abortion, or the medical researcher".

may also have a duty to have available for immediate use after the abortion the medical support and technology usually available to wanted but premature newborns in case of likely complications. Failing such availability, a physician might be liable to a charge of homicide, for causing, "... injury to a child before or during its birth as a result of which the child dies after becoming a human being", under section 206(2).[324]

2. *Resolving the conflicting rights*

One must therefore acknowledge that the unborn child's rights to life and inviolability, and consequently to prenatal care, must give way to what present Canadian (criminal) law considers to be a more important interest in the mother's life and health. It remains to formulate explicitly the condition thus imposed on the unborn's right to prenatal care. It is not rendered meaningless or non-existent. But neither can it be un-affected in the light of the present Criminal Code. We propose the following as a formula to balance and resolve the obviously conflicting rights:

> *The unborn child's rights to life, inviolability and prenatal care would arise at the time of conception and would continue to have effect from then to viable birth until or unless the pregnant woman decides, for the exceptional reason allowed in s.251(4) and s.221(2), to undergo a therapeutic abortion. At that point and for that reason, the pregnant woman's interest in life and health may prevail over those same rights of the unborn child.*

A somewhat different condition and formulation was initially attractive to us. It was suggested by the Report of the (B.C.) Royal Commission on Family and Children's Law, referred to several times in what precedes. In that Report, the Commission made this proposal:

---

324 See on this point DICKENS, *op. cit., supra*, n. 41, at p. 59.

> We have no jurisdiction to deal with abortion, because it is a federal matter. However, *once a woman has decided to bear the future infant*, the laws of the province should emphasize individual responsibility to provide the infant with the kind of prenatal care that will prevent unnecessary jeopardy to the child.[325] (Emphasis added)

In our view that proposal has some serious gaps. It could leave uncovered by any legal duty or liability a very long period in the unborn child's gestational life. In other words, there would be no duty to provide adequate prenatal care as long as the pregnant woman has not yet *made a decision* to bear the child. But in the first place, many very serious and often permanent injuries and disabilities may be inflicted on the unborn already in the earliest period of gestation. Assuming the pregnant mother makes a decision to bear the child, let us say in the twentieth week of gestation, by virtue of the above formulation the unborn would not have enjoyed legal protection for that entire twenty week period, nor the right of action for prenatal injuries inflicted during that same period.

Another difficulty with the British Columbia formulation is that it seems to assume that women always make a conscious and explicit decision to bear or not bear their child. It is not certain that such an assumption is justified. It is at least likely that many women make no clear decision at a particular moment in time to continue the pregnancy, and do not actively or consciously consider abortion. Should that count as a "decision", and when could it be considered to have been made with sufficient intent or consent to initiate a (legal) duty to provide adequate prenatal care? According to the formulation we proposed that problem would not seem to arise. The duty to provide adequate care would arise at the time of conception and would only cease if and when there is an abortion according to the terms of s.251 Criminal Code.

---

[325] B.C. Royal Commission on Family and Children Law, *op. cit., supra*, n. 207, at p. 65.

Another possible and initially attractive formulation would be to the effect that the unborn child's rights to life, inviolability and prenatal care would arise only at the time the parents (or pregnant woman) *know* of the pregnancy, rather than at the time of conception. It might be argued that, after all, until one actually knows of a pregnancy, one cannot yet in practice provide for specific needs and protections. But there are two flaws to such a formulation.

One is that it would leave unprotected by legal rights and duties the most vulnerable period of all, the first few weeks, the very weeks during which a pregnant woman would in most cases not yet know she is pregnant. Secondly, it would make the existence of rights such as the right to life depend upon *knowledge* of it, a quite unique and indefensible proposition. It would be equivalent to maintaining that an heir really has no right to inherit from the time of a testator's death, only because he did not know of it. A right can exist *de jure* even if all or some aspects of the right and the duties it creates cannot yet be given *de facto* effect.

Nor is it true that no specific prenatal protections (and duties to provide them) can come into play in practice until one knows of a pregnancy. The duty to provide adequate prenatal care could include the obligation for fertile sexually active women not using a reliable method of birth control to take reasonable health precautions to protect a fetus which *may* be conceived though not yet known of, since the first weeks are when the fetus is most vulnerable.[326]

---

[326] Our formulation proposed to balance and resolve conflicts between prenatal care and abortion, is consistent with and an expression of the whole line of argumentation in this study. This is so particularly in two respects. The first is with regard to the medical / biological evidence that the unborn child is vulnerable to injury and in need of care (and hence of legal protection), from the earliest period. Secondly, our formula reflects the proposal made earlier in the study that live and viable birth should constitute a "resolutory condition" of legal personality and rights, rather than a "suspensive condition." As such, the unborn child would be presumed to have the right to prenatal care from the time of conception, and would normally only lose that (and other rights) if it is *not* born alive and viable. It must be acknowledged, however, that our (or any other)

In conclusion, the unborn child's right to prenatal care, though not absolute, should not have to give way to maternal rights, interests, wishes or habits other than and lesser than the woman's life or health. For example, there should be no contest at all between a mother's desire to smoke, drink or consume drugs excessively, and the unborn child's right to be (legally) protected against the serious risk of resulting disability.

---

proposed formulation cannot resolve in advance all possible conflicts between the rights of the mother-to-be and her unborn child. For example, what if the pregnant mother wishes to commit suicide or asks that her life-saving or life-prolonging treatment be stopped ? These (and other) questions and conflicts will require careful attention on the levels of both ethical and legal principles, and with respect to the particular circumstances of each case.

Chapter V

CONCLUSION - WHETHER AND WHAT TO LEGISLATE

A first conclusion from all that precedes is that the "right to prenatal care" is potentially and ideally at home in many different contexts - the hospital, the doctor's office, the home and the workplace, to mention those contexts considered in this paper. In each of these contexts there are some constants, but also some unique considerations and conflicts to be weighed and balanced.

One of the constants in the right to prenatal care is that because the unborn child has discernible health *needs and interests*, essentially analogous to and continuous with those of the child, he or she also should have *rights* to adequate health care and health protection, and both protective and compensatory legal mechanisms analogous to those already available to children. But to provide the firm basis enabling those rights to compete with the interests and rights of other parties in the equation, the unborn child should be acknowledged to have juridical personality and the rights which flow from it, especially the rights to life and inviolability.

But another constant is that other parties not only have resulting duties to provide that adequate care and protection. They will often have competing interest and rights of their own, against which those of unborn children must be weighed and balanced.

Those constants are present no matter what the particular context at issue. But each milieu has its unique right-owers, duties owed, conflicts to be balanced, and criteria to be applied. In the home, the right-owers of prenatal care and protection are the mother and father of the unborn child, but in the workplace the employer also has duties to the fetus. For the pregnant woman the conflict to be resolved and balanced will sometimes be that between fetal health and her right to equal employment; for the employer the conflict will sometimes be between fetal health and higher profits. In the doctor's office the physician is added to the list of right-owers, and the unborn child becomes his patient along with the pregnant woman. Sometimes the needs and rights of these two patients will be in conflict and both the pregnant woman and he will be obliged to choose the health of one over the health (or life) of the other. In the hospital, when the issue is a medical intervention on the mother for the sake of the unborn child, what will require balancing is the benefit to that child in proceeding with the intervention, against the risk to the pregnant woman in so doing and the potential violation of her rights to a autonomy and inviolability.

The *general* standard of the right to prenatal care will always be the same, no matter what the context - a duty to provide adequate, reasonable care, an obligation of diligence, not a warranty of success or an obligation of result. But in some contexts there will be needed special and detailed criteria. There are a large number of factors to be weighed when the issue is fetal surgery - the benefit to the child, the intrusiveness and risk to the mother, the "wantedness" of the child, the accuracy of the diagnosis and chances of success, the gestational age of the child, and so forth. When the issue and context is the hazardous workplace, again the criteria and priorities are several and complex - single standards at a safe level for everyone, or a right to refuse hazardous work or exclusionary employment policies banning women from hazardous workplaces. When the issue is between prenatal protection or abortion, yet another criterion or standard should apply to balance the unborn child's right to prenatal care and protection with the woman's right to abortion.

In view of both the constant factors and the variety of contexts, circumstances and criteria, the policies and law reforms required to articulate and anchor the right to prenatal care, cannot be in only one form, in only one place. They should find expression in statutes, jurisprudence and (in the Civil law system) in the Civil Code. Not to incorporate that right at all these levels would be to leave the unborn child less protected by the law than are others.

This book has argued the case for a legal right to prenatal care both by defending the general principle itself that legal compensation and protection are justified, and by proposing particular legal mechanisms and reforms. As for the general principle itself, it was well expressed in the U.N. Declaration of the Rights of the Child:

> ... the Child, by reason of his physical and mental immaturity, needs special safeguards and care, including legal protection, before as well as after birth, [327]

Special emphasis was placed on the duties and liabilities of pregnant women towards their unborn children, not because they are the only parties with such duties, but in large part because present legal policy in both our systems of law does not yet generally acknowledge such legal duties on the part of pregnant women. The essential justification adopted by this paper in defence of such legal duties of pregnant women was that proposed by the B.C. Royal Commission on Family and Children's Law:

> It is recognized that the increasing capability of parents to reproduce by choice, rather than by chance, imposes upon them a responsibility to their future infant and to society for maintaining during pregnancy, and subsequently, a maternal health status that is considered not to add avoidable jeopardy to the future infant's potential for optimum development... [328]

As far as the reform of child welfare *statutes* is concerned, the most fundamental and important revision would be that of explicitly stating in such statutes that for purposes of prenatal health care and protection, the unborn child falls within the meaning of "child" or "dependant" as used in a given statute. That would establish clearly, simply and unambiguously that there is continuity and analogy between child and unborn child, and both are equally in need of and deserving of legal mechanisms to protect and promote their health. The legal

---

[327] Preamble, *Declaration of the Rights of the Child*, unanimously approved by the 14th U.N. GAOR Supp. 16, at 19, U.N. Doc. A / 4354 (1959), also reprinted as OPI / 43 and OPI / 422.

[328] B.C. Royal Commission on Family and Children's Law, *op. cit., supra*, n. 197, at p. 9.

mechanisms to be made available to the unborn child would of course have to be revised and re-formulated in most cases, to adapt them to the special prenatal circumstances. But as noted above, the thrust and framework of a number of those now available to the child, could probably be adapted as well to the unborn child.

There is also an important role for case law in articulating and defending this right. At this level what are needed are more sophisticated and sensitive criteria by which decisions to intervene prenatally or compensate postnatally, are made by courts. An example is the issue of medical interventions on the unborn child and / or pregnant woman for the sake of the child. As indicated earlier, court decisions to date in this context have been generally hasty and superficial; in the absence of existing criteria by which to guide their decision-making, they have not always been rigorous in determining the accuracy of the medical arguments for particular interventions, nor sufficiently concerned with protecting the rights and integrity of the pregnant woman. The criteria proposed in this study for the use by courts are hopefully a useful step in the direction of needed sophistication and sensitivity.

As regards the revision of the Civil Code to accommodate and highlight the right of the unborn child to prenatal care, it is not a simple matter to decide how far to go. In the body of this study several specific changes were proposed to Bill 106, (the proposed law of Persons, destined for the Civil Code), in order to bring it back into step with present law. One such change would be to omit the second phrase of a.1 of Bill 106, "He is the subject of rights from birth till death". That phrase explicitly *excludes* juridical personality and consequent rights for the conceived but unborn child. But should the Civil Code go further, and explicitly *include* (for example) an affirmation of the unborn child's juridical personality and rights, in order to provide clearly and unambiguously the Civil law foundation for the right to prenatal care?

Assuming that there was general *agreement* on the justification for extending legal personality and rights to the unborn child while still unborn, *further* justification would of course be required for including that explicit affirmation in the Code. The general criterion for inclusion of anything in the Code was expressed by Crépeau:

> Il est certes vrai que le *Code Civil* ne saurait renfermer tout le droit civil. Il est, certes, également vrai que toute législation de droit civil ne peut trouver place, ou si l'on ose dire, ne mérite pas de trouver place dans un Code Civil. Certains textes législatifs, en effet, ne répondent qu'à des besoins temporaires, éphémères, par exemple, le contrôle des prix ou la fixation des loyers en temps de guerre ou de crise économique; d'autres textes doivent passer par ce que l'on pourrait appeler le noviciat législatif afin précisément de vérifier s'ils répondent à des besoins d'un caractère permanent, s'ils peuvent, en quelque sorte, s'élever au rang des règles générales de droit commun; ainsi par exemple, la législation récente sur la protection du consommateur."329

The thrust of the analysis and argumentation in this book is clearly towards affirming that the need to clarify and underline the status and rights of the unborn child is not at all "temporary or ephemeral", and that this need has indeed passed beyond its legislative "noviciat". Such an affirmation seems to readily fit the category of general principles rather than details subject to continual change and revision.

If that is so (and obviously not everyone agrees), then the affirmation of the unborn child's legal personality and rights does indeed belong in the Civil Code.[330] But in keeping with the codification principle articulated by Crépeau, the affirmation to be included should be brief and general, not adding the sort of details and practicalities best left to statutes and case law.

---

329 P.-A. CRÉPEAU, "La révision du code civil", [1977] *Cours de perfectionnement du Notariat*, 335 at p. 344.

330 The Quebec Human Rights Commission, in its submission on Bill 106 (*op. cit., supra*, n. 28, at p. 6) is apparently in agreement with this general principle. The Commission states the following in that regard:

> La commission recommande que le législateur québécois organise, à l'intérieur du Code civil, un régime juridique propre à la condition prénatale.

For that reason, we propose that a.18 C.C. (or a.1 Bill 106) be expanded to include a further phrase affirming that "human being" or "person" is to include the conceived but unborn child, for whom juridical personality is subject to the *resolutory* condition of viable birth.

It would then follow that the unborn child, while still unborn, could have the rights and protections now generally available only once born. For example, as a "person" or "human being", the unborn child would have the right to inviolability provided by a.19 C.C. (or a.11 of Bill 106), and to the rights to life, security and physical integrity provided for by a.1 of the Quebec *Charter of Human Rights and Freedoms*.

As well, once the unborn child is affirmed to be in effect a juridical person as is the child, the various Code protections available to the child would (if applicable) be available to the unborn child as well. On the basis of a.1065 C.C. the unborn creditor, through its tutor, could demand the specific performance of the obligation of prenatal care, by having a harmful act stopped (excessive drug taking for example) or needed care provided (adequate maternal diet for example). With the clear affirmation of the unborn as a subject of rights and creditor of obligations, mechanisms such as injunctions, as provided for in a.751 C.C.P., could also be used to protect and enforce adequate prenatal care.

It has been the aim of this study to suggest that the present day awareness of the health needs of the unborn child, and the expanding commitment of law in our times to the legal protection of the most vulnerable members of society, argue strongly for the reforms suggested above. One is encouraged in this regard by the following statement in the Preface to the Draft Code:

> ... il est essentiel de suivre l'évolution de la pratique et des moeurs afin d'adapter constamment le Code civil aux besoins nouveaux et toujours changeants de la société québécoise.[331]

---

[331] P.-A. CRÉPEAU, *Rapport sur le Code civil du Québec*, Vol. 1, Projet de Code civil, Éditeur officiel, Québec, 1977, at p. XXXVIII.

BIBLIOGRAPHY

A. AMENT, "The Right to be Well Born", (Nov./Dec. 1974), *J.L. Med.* 25

H. AMIRIKIA, *et al.*, "Cesarean Section: A 15-Year Review of Changing Incidences, Indications and Risks", (1981) 140 *Am. J. Obstet. Gynec.* 81.

G. ANNAS, "Forced Cesareans: The Most Unkindest Cut of All", (1982) 12:3 *H.C.R.* 16.

"Righting the Wrong of 'Wrongful Life'", (1981) 11:1 *H.C.R.* 8.

J.-L. BAUDOUIN, *Les Obligations*, Les Éditions Yvon Blais Inc., Cowansville, 1983.

La Responsabilité civile délictuelle, Les Presses de l'Université de Montréal, 1973.

R. BAYER, "Women, Work and Reproductive Hazards", (1982) 12:5 *H.C.R.* 14.

A. BERNARDOT, R. KOURI and S. NOOTENS, Université de Sherbrooke, "Mémoire portant sur le Projet de Loi No. 106".

L. BLACK, "A Worrying Case of the VDTs", *Maclean's*, July 28, 1980, 42.

W. BLACKSTONE, Commentaries 130 (1762).

C. BOISCLAIR, *Les droits et les besoins de l'enfant en matière de garde: réalité ou apparence?* Publication de la Revue de Droit de l'Université de Sherbrooke, 1978.

BOTTOMS, *et al.*, "Maternal Passive Smoking and Fetal Serum Thiocyanate Levels", (1982) 144 *Am. J. Obstet. Gynec.* 787.

W.A. BOWES and B. SELGESTAD, "Fetal Versus Maternal Right: Medical and Legal Perspectives", (1981) 58 *Obstet. Gynec.* 209.

"Obstetrical and Infant Outcome: A Review of the Literature", in W.A. Bowes, *et al.*, *The Effects of Obstetrical Medication on Fetus and Infant*, Society for Research in Child Development, Monograph Series No. 137, 1970.

B.C. ROYAL COMMISSION ON FAMILY AND CHILDRENS' LAW, Report V, Part IV, *Special Needs of Special Children*, Vancouver, 1975.

B.C. ROYAL COMMISSION ON FAMILY AND CHILDRENS' LAW, Part V, *The Protection of Children (Child Care)*, Vancouver, 1975.

D. CALLAHAN, "The WHO Definition of Health", (1973) 1:3 *H.C.S.* 77.

CANADIAN HUMAN RIGHTS COMMISSION, *Summary of Decisions*, October/November, 1981.

A. CAPRON, "The Wrong of 'Wrongful life'", in A. Milunsky and G. Annas, (editors), *Genetics and the Law II*, Plenum Press, N.Y., 1980.

CENTRE DE DROIT PRIVÉ ET COMPARÉ DU QUÉBEC, Université McGill, "Mémoire relatif au Projet de Loi 106", March, 1983.

LA CHAMBRE DES NOTAIRES DU QUÉBEC, "Mémoire relatif au Projet de Loi 106", March, 1983.

R.F. CHASE, "Liability for Prenatal Injuries", 40 ALR 3d 1222 (1971).

N. CHENIER, *Reproductive Hazards at Work*, Canadian Advisory Council on the Status of Women, Ottawa, 1982.

CIVIL CODE REVISION OFFICE, *Report on the Québec Civil Code*, 1977, Vol. 1, Draft Civil Code, Vol. II, Commentaries, Éditeur officiel, Québec, 1977.

W.H. CLEWELL, *et al.*, "A Surgical Approach to the Treatment of Fetal Hydrocephalus", (1982) 306 *N.E.J.M.* 1320-1325.

COKE, 3 *Coke, Institutes* 58 (1648).

COMMISSION DE LA SANTÉ ET DE LA SÉCURITÉ DU TRAVAIL DU QUÉBEC, *Les conditions de travail et la santé de la travailleuse enceinte de l'enfant à naitre et de l'enfant allaité*, Québec, 1982.

COMMISSION DES DROITS DE LA PERSONNE DU QUÉBEC, "Commentaires de la Commission des droits de la personne du Québec sur le Projet de loi no. 106", April 26, 1983.

P.-A. CRÉPEAU, "Des régimes contractuel et délictuel de responsabilité civil en droit civil canadien", (1962) 22 *R. du B.* 501.

"Forword", in *Report on the Quebec Civil Code*, 1977 (2 vol.), Éditeur officiel, Québec, 1978.

"La responsabilité médicale et hospitalière dans la jurisprudence québécoise récente", (1960) 20 *R. du B.* 433.

"La révision du Code civil (1977), *Cours de perfectionnement du Notariat*, 335.

"Le consentement du mineur en matière de soins et traitements médicaux ou chirurgicaux selon le droit civil canadien", (1974) 52 *Can. Bar Rev.* 247.

"Les lendemains de la réforme du Code Civil", (1981) 59 *Can. Bar Rev*, 625.

"Liability for Damage Caused by Things", (1962) 40 *Can. Bar Rev.* 222.

The Civil Codes, A Critical Edition, Centre of Private and Comparative Law, McGill University, Montreal, 1981.

K. CROCKETT and M. HYMAN, "Live Birth: A Condition Precedent to Recognition of Rights", (1976) 4 *Hof. L. R.* 805.

E. DELEURY, "Naissance et mort de la personne humaine, ou les confrontations de la médecine et du droit", (1976) 17 *C. de D.* 265.

M. DESMOND, *et al.*, "The Relationship of Maternal Disease to Fetal and Neonatal Morbidity and Mortality", (1961) 8:2 *Pediat. Clin. N. Amer.* 421.

B. DICKENS, "Legal Responses to Child Abuse", (1979) 12 *Fam. L. Q.* 1,.

Medico-Legal Aspects of Family Law, Butterworths, Toronto, 1979.

R. DIERKENS, *Les droits sur le corps et le cadavre de l'homme*, Masson et cie., Paris, 1966.

J. FEINBERG, "The Rights of Animals and Unborn Generations", in *Social Ethics - Morality and Social Policy*, T.A. Mappes and J.S. Zembaty (editors), New York, McGraw-Hill Book Company, 1977.

J. FLEMING, *The Law of Torts*, (5th ed.), Law Book Co.Ltd., Sydney, 1977.

J. FLETCHER, "The Fetus as Patient: Ethical Issues", (1981) 246 *J.A.M.A.* 772.

V. FONTANA and D. BESHAROV, *The Maltreated Child*, (3rd ed.), Charles C. Thomas, Springfield, 1977.

T. FRAZIER, *et al.*, "Cigarette Smoking and Prematurity: A Prospective Study", (1961) 81 *Am. J. Obstet. Gynec.* 988.

G. GIERTZ, "The Rights of the Unborn Child", *Proceedings of the Sixth World Congress on Medical Law*, Ghent, Belgium, 1982.

J. GOLDSTEIN, A. FREUD and A.J. SOLNIT, *Beyond the Best Interests of the Child*, N.Y., 1973.

Before the Best Interests of the Child, N.Y., 1979.

R. GOTS and B. GOTS, *Caring for Your Unborn Child*, Bantam Books (3rd ed.) N.Y., 1981.

C. GRAY, "The Notion of Person for Medical Law", (1981) 11 *R.D.U.S.*, 341.

GREEN, "Law, Sex and the Population Explosion", (1977) 1 *L. Med. Q.* 82.

J. GUILLEMIN, "Babies by Cesarean: Who Chooses, Who Controls?", (1981) 11:3 *H.C.R.* 15.

M. HARRISON, *et al.*, "Correction of Congenital Diaphragmatic Hernia in Utero. III. Development of a Successful Surgical Technique Using Abdominoplasty to Avoid Compromise of Umbilical Blood Flow", (1981) 16 *J. Ped. Surg.* 934.

"Fetal Surgery for Congenital Hydronephrosis", (1982) 306 *N.E.J.M.* 591.

"Management of the Fetus With A Correctable Congenital Defect", (1981) 246 *J.A.M.A.* 774.

M. HARRISON and A. de LORIMIER, "Management of the Fetus with Hydronephrosis", Mimeograph, Fetal Treatment Program, Department of Surgery, University of California, San Francisco.

HEALTH AND WELFARE CANADA, *Occupational Health in Canada - Current Status*, Ottawa, 1977.

INGALLS, "Causes and Prevention of Developmental Defects", (1956) 161 *J.A.M.A.* 1047.

T. ISON, "The Dimensions of Industrial Disease", Queen's Industrial Relations Centre, Reprint No. 35, 1978.

S. KATZ, *When Parents Fail*, Beacon Press, Boton, 1971.

I. KENNEDY, "A Critique of the Law Commission Report on Injuries to Unborn Children and the proposed Congenital Disabilities (Civil Liability) Bill", (1975) 1 *J. Med. E.* 116.

E.W. KEYSERLINGK, "Devising Fairer Tests for Proving Prenatal Negligence in Court", (unpublished paper) Institute of Comparative Law, McGill University, March, 1983.

B. KNOPPERS, "Le Statut juridique du fetus: du droit comparé au droit en devenir, (1980) 2 *C. de B.* 205.

R. KOURI, "Blood transfusions, Jehovah's Witnesses and the rule of inviolability of the human body", (1974) 5 *R.D.U.S.* 156.

"Non-therapeutic Sterilization - Malpractice, and the Issues of 'Wrongful Birth' and 'Wrongful Life' in Quebec Law", (1979) 57 *Can. Bar Rev.* 89.

"Réflexions sur le statut juridique du foetus", (1980-81) 15 *R.J.T.* 193.

R. KOURI and A. BERNARDOT, *La Responsabilité Civile Médicale*, Les Éditions Revue de Droit, Université de Sherbrooke, 1980.

R.E. KRUGER, "Wrongful Death and the Unborn Child: An Examination or Recovery after *Roe v. Wade*", (1973-74) 13 *J. Fam. L.* 99.

M. LANGTON, "Double Exposure: The Fight Against Reproductive Hazards in the Workplace", (1980) 1 *Health Sharing* 14.

J.R. LIEBERMAN, et al. "The Fetal Right to Live", (1979) 53 *Obstet. Gynec.* 515.

LILIENFELD and PASAMANICK, "Association of Maternal and Fetal Factors with the Development of Mental Deficiency", (1955) 159 *J.A.M.A.* 155.

C.A. LINTGEN, "Note: The Impact of Medical knowledge on the Law Relating to Prenatal Injuries," (1962) *U. Penn. L.R.* 554.

L.O. LUBCHENCO and J.V. BRAZIE, "Neonatal Mortality Rate: Relationship to Birth Weight and Gestational Age", (1972) 81 *J. Ped.* 814.

W.J. MALEDON, "The Law and the Unborn Child: The Legal and Logical Inconsistencies", (1971) 46 *Notre Dame Law.* 349.

A. MAYRAND, *L'inviolabilité de la personne humaine*, Wilson & Lafleur, Montreal, 1975.

W.C.J. MEREDITH, *Malpractice Liability of Doctors and Hospitals*, Toronto, Carswell, 1956.

M.-T. MEULDERS-KLEIN, "Rapport sur le corps humain, personnalité juridique et famille en droit belge", (1975) 26 *Travaux de l'Association Henri Capitant* 19.

J.E. MURPHY, and R. MULCAHY, "The Effect of Age, Parity, and Cigarette Smoking on Baby Weight", (1971) 111 *Am. J. Obstet. Gynec.* 22.

M.I. NASH, *Occupational Health and Safety Law*, CCH Canadian Ltd., Don Mills, Ontario, 1983.

J. OLESKE, et al., "Immune Deficiency Syndrome in Children", (1983) 249 *J.A.M.A.* 2345.

L. PATENAUDE, *Capacité (tutelle et curatelle)*, La Librairie de l'Université de Montréal, 1975.

B. PATTEN, "Varying Developmental Mechanisms in Teratology", (1957) 19 *Pediatrics* 734.

E. POTTER, "Placental Transmission of Viruses", (1957) 74 *Am. J. Obstet. & Gynec.* 505.

J.T. QUEENAN, "Intrauterine Transfusion, A Cooperative Study", (1969) 104
　　　　Am. J. Obstet. & Gynec. 397.

REPORT OF A CONSENSUS DEVELOPMENT CONFERENCE, *Antenatal
　　　　Diagnosis*, U.S. Department of Health, Education and
　　　　Welfare, Public Health Service, National Institutes of Health,
　　　　NIH Publication No. 79-1973, April, 1979.

REPORT OF AN INTERNATIONAL WORKSHOP, *Prenatal Diagnosis -
　　　　Past, Present and Future* (Val David, Quebec, November 4-8,
　　　　1979), 1980.

REPORT OF THE COMMITTEE ON THE OPERATION OF THE
　　　　ABORTION LAW ("BADGLEY REPORT") Ottawa, 1977.

G.B. ROBERTSON, "Civil Liability Arising From 'Wrongful Birth' Following
　　　　an Unsuccessful Sterilization Operation", (1978) 4 *Am. J. L.
　　　　Med.* 131.

L.E. ROZOVSKY, *Canadian Hospital Law*, Canadian Hospital Association,
　　　　1974.

A. RUBENSTEIN, *et al.*, "Acquired Immunodeficiency ... in Infants Born to
　　　　Promiscuous and Drug-Addicted Mothers", (1983) 249
　　　　J.A.M.A. 2350.

W. RUDDICK and W. WILCOX, "Operating on the Fetus", (1982) 12:5 *H.C.R.*
　　　　10.

S.E. SEGAL, "Wrongful Death and the Stillborn Fetus - A Current Analysis",
　　　　(1970) 7 *Hous. L. R.* 449.

M.W. SHAW, "The Potential Plaintiff, Preconception and Prenatal Torts", in
　　　　A. Milunsky and G. Annas, editors, *Genetics and the Law II*,
　　　　Plenum Press, N.Y., 1980, 255.

M.W. SHAW and C. DAMME, "Legal Status of the Fetus", in A. Milunsky and
　　　　G. Annas, editors, *Genetics and the Law*, Plenum Press, N.Y.,
　　　　1975.

M. SOMERVILLE, "Reflections on Canadian Abortion Law: Evacuation and
　　　　Destruction - Two Separate Issues", (1981) 31 *U. Toronto L. J.*
　　　　1.

K. SWINTON, "Regulating Reproductive Hazards in the Workplace: Balancing Equality and Health", (1983) 33 *U. Toronto L. J.* 45.

I.B. TAGER, *et al.*, "Effect of parental cigarette smoking on the pulmonary function of children", (1979) 110:15 *Am. J. Epidemiology.*

I. TEDESCHI, "On Tort Liability for 'Wrongful Life'", (1966) 1 *Is. L. R.* 513.

W. TOMPKINS, *et al.*, "The Underweight Patient As An Increased Obstetric Hazard", (1955) 69 *Am. J. Obstet. & Gynec.* 114.

B.K. TRIMBLE and J.H. DOUGHTY, "The Amount of Hereditary Disease in Human Populations", (1974-75) 38 *Gen.* 199.

U.K. LAW COMMISSION, *Injuries to Unborn Children*, Working Paper No. 47, Her Majesty's Stationery Office, London, 1973.

U.K. LAW COMMISSION, *Report on Injuries to Unborn Children*, No. 60, Her Majesty's Stationery Office, London, 1974.

T. VERNEY, *The Secret Life of the Unborn Child*, Collins, Toronto, 1981.

J. WARKANAY, "Congenital Malformations Induced by Maternal Dietary Deficiency", (1955) 13 *Nutr. Rev.* 289.

"Etiology of Congenital Malformations", (1947) 2 *Adv. Ped.* 1.

J. WARKANAY and H. KALTER, "Congenital Malformations", (1961) 265 *N.E.J.M.* 106.

K. WEILER and K. CATTON, "The Unborn Child in Canadian Law". (1976) 14 *Osgoode Hall L.J.* 643.

J. WILSON, *Children and the Law*, Butterworths, Toronto, 1978.

TABLE OF CASES

	page
Allaire v. St. Luke's Hospital,	35
Allard v. Monette,	14, 54
Beausoleil v. Communauté des Soeurs de la Charité de la Providence,	85, 150
Becker v. Schwartz,	48
Bennet v. Hymers,	37
Bhinder v. Canadian National Railways,	164
Bliss v. A.-G. of Canada,	163
Bonbrest v. Kotz,	32, 44
Breton v. La société Canadienne des Métaux Reynolds Ltée,	164
Brown, *Re*,	81
Burdett v. Hopegood	30
Cataford, *et al.* v. Moreau,	56
Chapman v. C.N.R.,	113
Children's Aid Society for the District of Kénora and J.L., *Re*,	113-115
Curlender v. Bio-Science Laboratories,	49
Deziel v. Deziel,	95
Dietrich v. Northampton,	16, 32
Donoghue v. Stevenson,	83, 84
Duval v. Séguin,	33, 34, 87
The Earl of Bedford's case,	29
Fitzsimonds v. Royal Insurance Co. of Canada,	116
General Motors of Canada and United Automobile Workers Local 222, *Re*,	163
Gleitman v. Cosgrove,	47
G, *Re*, (unreported),	108
Hale v. Hale,	30
Harlan Nat'l Bank v. Gross,	93
Hastings v. Hastings,	93
Hoener v. Bertinato,	110, 118
Hôpital Notre-Dame v. Dame Villemure,	149
In re Brooks Estate,	118
Jefferson v. Griffin Spalding Co. Hospital Authority,	121, 122
Julien v. Roy,	54
Jorgensen v. Meade Johnson Laboratories Inc.,	51, 52
Landeros v. Flood,	90
Langlois v. Meunier,	54

	page
Laporte v. Laganière,	150
Lavoie v. Cité de Rivière-du-Loup, et autres,	54
Lorquet v. Sun Life Ass.,	152
M.E. Mone v. Greyhound Line,	44
Marsh v. Kirby,	29
Montreal Tramways Co. v. Léveillé,	13, 15-19, 29, 34, 35, 44, 58, 65, 84, 86, 87
Morgantaler v. R.,	178
Nelligan v. Clément,	85
New York Life Ins. Co. v. Desbiens,	152
Nye v. Burke,	164
Park v. Chessin,	48, 81
Parks v. Parks,	93
Paton v. Trustees of BPAS,	40
People v. Yates,	112
Pharand and Inco Metals Ltd., *Re*,	169
Puhl v. Milwaukee Auto Ins. Co.,	36, 65
Raleigh Fitkin - Paul Morgan Mem. Hospital v. Anderson,	110, 119, 120
Redwine v. Adkins,	93
Renslow v. Mennonite Hospital,	52
Roe v. Wade,	42, 120
Simms and H. *Re*,	113
Sloan Estate, *Re*,	30
Smith v. Brennan,	37, 81
Smith v. Fox,	33
Stemmer v. Kline,	35
Superintendant of Family and Child Service and McDonald, *Re*,	115
Tarasoff v. Regents of the University of California,	90
Tellier-Cohen v. Treasury Board	164
Thellusson v. Woodford	29
Toro v. Dental Co. of Canada Ltd.,	152
Verkennes v. Corniea,	44
Walker v. Great No. Ry. of Ireland,	32-33
Watt v. Rama,	33
Worrell v. Worrell,	93
X. v. Mellen,	85
Young v. Rankin,	95
Zepeda v. Zepeda,	47-48

TABLE OF STATUTES, BILLS AND OTHER INSTRUMENTS

	page
An Act Respecting Indemnities for Victims of Asbestosis and Silicosis in Mines and Quarries (Quebec), R.S.Q., c.I-7	168
An Act Respecting Occupational Health and Safety (Quebec), R.S.Q., c.S-2.1	166-168, 171
An Act to Add the Reformed Law of Persons to the Civil Code of Quebec (Bill 106) introduced December 17, 1982	22-28, 141, 148-156
An Act to Add the Reformed Law of Successions to the Civil Code of Quebec (Bill 107), introduced December 17, 1982	14, 23-24
Canada Labour Code, R.S.C. 1970, c.L-1	166
Canadian Bill of Rights, R.S.C. 1970, Appendix III	163
Charter of Human Rights and Freedoms (Quebec), R.S.Q. c.C-12	148-149, 164
Child Welfare Act (Ontario), R.S.O. 1980, c.66	88-89. 90. 104, 106-112
Children and Young Persons Act, (U.K.) Statutes, 1969, c.54	107
Children's Act (Ontario), Consultation Paper, Ministry of Community and Social Services, Toronto, 1982	105
Childrens Law Reform Act (Ontario) R.S.O. 1980 c.68 as am. by S.O. 1982 c.20, a.1, s.20	104
Civil Code of Lower Canada (1866)	13-28, 53-56, 139-144, 148-150, 188-190
Civil Code of Quebec (1981)	139, 140, 142
Code of Civil Procedure (Quebec)	152-153, 190
Congenital Disabilities (Civil Liability) Act 1976, 46 Halsbury's Statutes of England, 1837 (3rd edition) (1976)	38-41, 52, 94
Constitution of the World Health Organization done in New York, July 22, 1946, 114 UNTS 185; 4 Bevans 119; TIAS no. 1808	82
Declaration of Rights of the Child. 14 U.N.G.A.O.R. Supp. 16; UN Doc. A/4354 (1959); also reprinted as OPI/43; OPI 422.	187
Draft Civil Code (Quebec), Éditeur Officiel, Québec, 1978	22-23, 140-144
Family Law Reform Act (Ontario), R.S.O. 1980, c.152	94
Infants Act (Ontario), R.S.O., 1970, c.222	104
Mental Patients Protection Act (Quebec), R.S.Q., c.P-41	153
Minors Act (Ontario) R.S.O. 1980 c.292	104
Occupational Health and Safety Act (Ontario), R.S.O., 1980, c.321	160, 167, 171
Public Health Protection Act (Quebec), R.S.Q., c.P-35	153-155
Workmen's Compensation Act (Quebec) R.S.Q., c.A-3	153
Youth Protection Act (Quebec) R.S.Q., c.P-34.1	88, 143-147

INDEX OF SUBJECTS

Abortion
>committees: 7
>conflict with rights of unborn: 1, 6, 181-184
>defects and deformities as grounds for: 136-137
>meaning and scope of, in Criminal Code: 6-10, 177-181
>provincial law and: 6-7

Alcohol
>fetal alcohol syndrome in recent case: 113-115
>risks of to fetus: 68-70

B.C. Royal Commission on Family and Children's Law
>balancing rights of unborn and abortion and: 181-182
>rights of child and: 105-106

Bill 106 (Law of Persons)
>Bill 107 and: 25
>Draft Civil Code and: 22-23
>inviolability in: 149-151, 155-156
>juridical personality in: 22-28
>submissions on: 22-28, 151, 156

Bill 107 (Law of Successions)
>suspensive condition of inheritance and: 14, 22-25

Biological hazards
>in workplace: 76

Birth
>as suspensive condition of legal personality: 13-19
>as resolutory condition of legal personality: 101-103
>killing in act of: 8-9

Caesarean sections
>recent cases: 121-122
>rights of woman and: 122-123

Chemical hazards
>in workplace: 74-75

Children
- adequate care, not best possible: 107-109, 145
- child as "child in need of protection": 106-116
- child whose "safety and development compromised": 144-147
- reporting abuse of: 88-90
- rights and statutory protections, Common Law: 105-112
- rights and statutory protections, Civil law: 139-147

Compulsory immunizations
- Public Health Protection Act and: 153

Compulsory medical examinations
- Code of Civil procedure and: 152-153
- Public Health Protection Act and: 153

Court-ordered surgical interventions
- Bill 106 and: 149-151, 155-156
- candidates for: 126-129
- criteria for: 129-139
- medical reasons for: 135
- Public Health Protection Act and: 154-155
- types of: 118-126

Criminal law
- abortion and: 7-10, 177-181
- homicide and: 7-8
- status of unborn child and: 6-10

Curator
- extra-patrimonial rights and: 15-16
- patrimonial rights and: 14

Defects and deformities
- as grounds for abortion: 137
- causes of: 66-76
- mechanics of: 62-66
- risks of diagnostic tests for: 131, 135-137

Diagnostic tests
- risks to pregnant woman: 131, 135-137

Draft Civil Code (Quebec)
> Bill 106 and: 22-23
> duties of parents in: 141-144
> rights of child in: 140-144

Drugs
> examples of harmful: 66-68
> newborn's drug addiction, recent case: 115-116

Duty
> as ground of damages: 34

Employment policies
> exclusionary policies: 158-165
> right to refuse work: 166-171
> single exposure standards: 172-175

Environmental influences
> and genetic factors: 11-12

Extra-patrimonial rights
> defined: 13

Fetal surgery
> legal issues raised by: 126
> medical indications for: 123-124
> new possibilities of: 124-125

Foreseeability
> as ground of damages: 34

Guardians
> child welfare statutes and: 109-110
> maternal transfusions and: 118-121

Health
> definitions of: 82-83
> *see also: Alcohol*

Homemakers
> child welfare statutes and: 111

Homicide
>   and fetus: 6-8
>   defined: 7

Human
>   <u>Criminal Code</u> definition: 7-10

Infectious diseases
>   fetal health and: 70-71, 89

Injunctions
>   child welfare statutes and: 109-110
>   maternal transfusions and: 118-121

Inviolability
>   <u>Bill 106</u> and: 149-151
>   court-ordered medical interventions and: 148-156

Juridical personality of unborn child
>   <u>Bill 106</u> and: 22-28
>   <u>Bill 107</u> and: 14
>   Draft Civil Code and: 20-21
>   patrimonial rights and: 12-16
>   prenatal abuse and: 113-116
>   preconception injury to parents and: 51-53, 58-59
>   property rights and: 29-31
>   resolutory condition of: 101-103
>   suspensive condition of: 13-19
>   wrongful birth actions and: 45-46, 56-58
>   wrongful death actions and: 41-45, 53-56
>   wrongful life actions and: 47-51, 56-58
>   *see also: Right of action, prenatal injury*

Liability of pregnant woman
>   balanced with equal access to job opportunities: 157 ff., 174-175
>   balanced with inviolability: 148-156
>   balanced with right to abortion: 177-184
>   in Canada: 94-95
>   in U.K.: 93-100
>   in U.S.: 92-93
>   in workplace: 174-175
>   policy objections considered: 95-100

Manslaughter
>   of fetus: 8

Maternal diet
    and fetal health: 71

Parental duties re child
    in Civil law: 140-144
    in Common law: 103-105

Patrimonial rights
    see: Juridical personality

Parens patriae power
    and child's best interest standard: 108

Person
    potential: 10
    see also: Juridical personality

Preconception injury
    actions for: 51-53

Prenatal negligence
    proof of: 11-12, 64-66, 162
    see also: Right of action, prenatal injury

Property rights
    see: Juridical personality

Radiation
    in workplace: 75-76, 172-173

Reporting child abuse
    scope of the duty: 88-90

Resolutory condition
    see: Juridical Personality

Right of action for prenatal injury
    in Civil law: 16-19
    in Common law Canada: 33-35
    in U.K.: 32, 37-41
    in U.S.: 32, 35-37
    proof of negligence: 11-12, 64-66, 162

Right to prenatal care
> duties of employer: 90-91
> duties of father-to-be: 90
> duties of hospital: 89
> duties of physicians: 8
> duties of pregnant woman: 89
> interventions on pregnant women: 116-139
> limits to and meaning of: 80-91
> relation to prenatal negligence: 86-91
> *see also: Liability of pregnant woman*

Smoking
> fetal health and: 70-72

Supervision orders
> child welfare statutes and: 110

Suspensive condition
> *see: Juridical personality*

Teratogenic risk
> definition: 67

Transfusions for sake of fetus
> balancing the rights: 120-121
> efficacy of: 133-134
> recent cases: 118-121
> risks of: 130-131

Tutorship
> protective mechanism of: 147

U.K. Law Commission
> on liability of pregnant woman: 93-100
> on prenatal injuries: 37-41

Viability
> as criterion for court-ordered intervention: 134-135
> as restriction to right of action: 36-37
> as resolutory condition of legal personality: 101-103
> as suspensive condition of legal personality: 13-19

Wardship agreements

    in child welfare statutes: 110-112

Workplace

    biological hazards in: 76
    chemical hazards in: 74-75
    duty to avoid fetal hazards in: 174-175
    hazards to fetus in: 72-76
    male and female workers in: 172-175
    physical hazards in: 75

Wrongful birth

    actions for: 45-46, 56-58

Wrongful death

    actions for: 41-45, 53-56

Wrongful life

    actions for: 47-71, 56-58